Research and Documentation
in the Digital Age

Research and Documentation
in the Digital Age
Sixth Edition

Diana Hacker

Barbara Fister
Gustavus Adolphus College

Bedford / St. Martin's
Boston ◆ New York

For Bedford/St. Martin's

Publisher for Composition and Business and Technical Writing: Leasa Burton
Executive Editor: Michelle M. Clark
Associate Editor: Kylie Paul
Assistant Production Editor: Lidia MacDonald-Carr
Production Supervisor: Joe Ford
Marketing Manager: Emily Rowin
Project Management: Cenveo Publisher Services
Senior Art Director: Anna Palchik
Cover Design: Marine Miller
Composition: Cenveo Publisher Services
Printing and Binding: RR Donnelley and Sons

Printed in China.

1   0   9   8   7   6
f   e   d   c   b

For information, write: Bedford/St. Martin's, 75 Arlington Street, Boston, MA 02116   (617-399-4000)

ISBN 978-1-319-08350-2

At the time of publication all Internet URLs published in this text were found to accurately link to their intended Web site. If you do find a broken link, please forward the information to hackerhandbooks@macmillan.com so that it can be corrected for the next printing.

Contents

Reviewers

For their candid feedback, smart suggestions, and welcome expertise, we thank the following reviewers:

Nancy Sosna Bohm, *Lake Forest College*
Anne-Marie Deitering, *Oregon State University*
Diana Matthews, *Santa Fe College*
Ruth Mirtz, *University of Mississippi*
Maura Smale, *New York City College of Technology*
Barbara Wurtzel, *Springfield Technical Community College*

Introduction

This compact reference from Bedford/St. Martin's gives you quick access to useful tips and models you'll need as you make your way through the research process.

Parts I through III offer advice about planning and managing research projects that use information from published print and online sources. Parts IV through VII explore research tools and approaches in thirty-one academic disciplines, such as nursing, criminal justice, and anthropology, followed by documentation rules and examples for writing in the humanities, history, social sciences, and sciences. Finally, Part VIII provides a glossary of research terms used across the disciplines.

Research and Documentation in the Digital Age, Sixth Edition, is also available as a Bedford e-Book to Go. Visit **http://www.bedfordstmartins.com/resdoc/catalog** for more information.

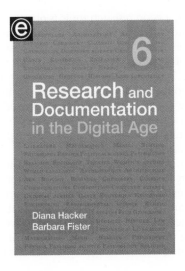

Part I. Getting Started

Research assignments in college are an invitation to join a conversation about ideas by exploring a topic in depth, weighing relevant evidence, and drawing your own conclusions. To do this, you need to explore widely to discover what issues are under debate, settle on a question to investigate, learn what others have had to say about that question, and write your own response, drawing on persuasive and well-chosen evidence. How you tackle your research will vary depending on the research question you are posing and the subject area in which conversations about the issue are being held. Historians will pose different questions about immigration than political scientists; scientists studying autism may be interested in its genetics, while education researchers may be more interested in effective teaching strategies for children with autism. Finding your way into those conversations is key to developing a focused research question and sharing your own thoughts effectively.

In general, a good research topic is one that is relevant to your course and excites your curiosity. Narrowing and defining that topic takes time. You'll need to collect background facts about your potential topics so that you have a foundation for your research. You might, for example, browse articles online and consult your textbook or other class readings. Librarians can also guide you to specialized reference works such as the *Encyclopedia of Applied Ethics* or *CQ Researcher* that cover a wide variety of controversial topics in short, thoroughly researched, even-handed articles.

With that factual foundation in place, you'll want to see how people are debating, analyzing, and interpreting the issue you are interested in. For this purpose, you might turn to the Web or search a library database to see what scholars, journalists, and members of the general public have said about it. It may also be useful to browse the Web site of a publication, organization, or government agency that covers breaking news and important issues related to your topic to get a sense of what debates exist and which ones strike you as worth exploring.

Seeing the big picture

When you get started on a research project, you need to understand the assignment, choose what direction to head in, and quickly get the big picture for the topic you choose. You then have to fit all of these tasks into a schedule that may already be a bit crowded. When you receive your assignment, set a realistic schedule of deadlines. Think about how much time you might need for each step on the way to your final draft.

At first your research will be a broad scan of the topic to see what aspect of it might be most interesting. This stage of research is like walking into a room full of people talking about a topic you're exploring. It's a babble of voices, and at first it is a bit overwhelming. As you move through the room, you overhear something interesting and pause to listen. After overhearing several bits of conversation, one discussion really grabs your attention, so you join the group, listen to various perspectives, and weigh in with your own thoughts. Throughout the process, you will be looking for information, but your search will grow more focused and purposeful over time.

As you begin the process of discovering what conversations are going on around a particular topic, a reference librarian may be able to recommend a library database that focuses on articles relevant to a particular subject such as nursing or psychology, or may help you brainstorm good search terms to use in a database that covers multiple subject areas. Most libraries also have subject guides on their Web sites that will help you find and explore resources relevant for your course. For some subjects it might be helpful to use the library's catalog to find current books relevant to your research and then browse the shelves nearby to see what approaches different writers have taken to the topic.

Thinking like a researcher 1–1

Generating ideas for research

Researchers who surveyed thousands of students at colleges and universities of all kinds found that getting started is a particularly difficult part of the research process. This exercise is intended to help you get a running start.

1. Brainstorm. Without pausing, write down whatever comes to mind in response to this prompt:

   I want to learn about . . .

2. Spend thirty minutes in preliminary exploration of your topic using the Web, a library database, or both. Then finish this sentence:

   The question I have about my topic is . . .

3. Speak with either your instructor or a reference librarian about your question to determine your options so that you can finish this sentence:

   Three good places to look for information about _____ are . . .

Developing a focused research question

By mapping out the contours of the topic, you will begin to see what kinds of debates are taking place, what questions are being raised, and what aspects of the topic are generating the most attention. Then you can begin to ask some interesting questions, such as:

- What is the cause of _____?
- What should be done about _____?
- What are the ethical implications of _____?
- What can this book, film, or other creative work tell us about _____?
- Should we be concerned about our increasing dependence on _____?

As you delve deeper into the issue, you will likely find that your initial question is too broad to tackle effectively. By sharpening your focus further, you will be able to zero in on a manageable and interesting question. You might find the following sentence templates helpful:

- Among various causes suggested for _____, why is one of them more convincing than the others?
- Why is a proposed solution to the problem of _____ especially promising (or problematic)?
- Given the ethical implications of _____, what action should we take?
- How does a particular scene or character in a book, film, or other creative work reveal something insightful about _____?
- What could we do to minimize the risks of our increasing reliance on _____?

Thinking like a researcher 1–2

Sharpening the focus of your research question

As you learn more about a topic, your research focus is likely to change so that you will be able to narrow a broad focus down to a manageable scale. When you're closing in on completing your research, reflect on where it has led you.

1. When you started, what was your research question?
2. At this point, how has your research question changed? In what ways have you narrowed or refined the scope of your research? Can you think of further ways to sharpen your focus?
3. If you had to explain your research project right now in thirty seconds, what would you say?
4. Write a single sentence about what you now plan to do as a writer. I will argue (or *explain*, *show*, *demonstrate*, *uncover the reasons for*, *recommend a solution to*) . . .

Using references to get an overview

Since its launch in 2001, Wikipedia has become a go-to source for information. Using Web-based software that allows anyone with an Internet connection to write and edit articles, it runs on volunteer labor. Among the principles that guide Wikipedia authors are a "neutral point of view" (a requirement to be as even-handed as possible), the importance of citing sources for information, and a requirement that the articles be based on previously published sources, not on original research. For these reasons, Wikipedia can help you to understand the basics of a topic and to follow leads to potentially useful sources, but its articles are not typically sources you would cite in a college paper. Wikipedia is a valuable, convenient, and up-to-date source of background information. However, the anonymity and vastness of the contributors make it hard to determine bias and accuracy.

Libraries offer vast options for research, particularly when Wikipedia falls short. Your library may have one or more reference databases—such as *Gale Virtual Reference Online*, *Credo Reference*, *JSTOR*, or *Oxford Reference Online*—that let you search the contents of thousands of journals and other publications. In contrast to Wikipedia, the books in library reference collections often focus on a single discipline, such as psychology, philosophy, or American history, and contain background articles written by experts that can give you an overview of a topic from a scholarly perspective. These specialized databases will help you narrow your focus and find the kinds of sources your instructor expects you to use.

Your library may also enable researchers to search the library catalog and multiple databases all at once with a single search box option, called discovery service. A discovery service search box is typically found on the home page of the library's Web site.

Consulting with a reference librarian or your instructor as you begin your search can help you decide how and where to devote your time.

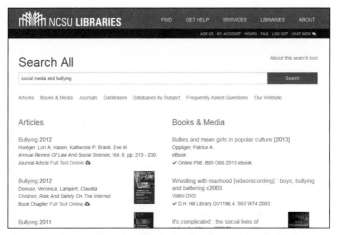

Above is a discovery layer from North Carolina State University Discovery services linking you directly to scholarly publications that you can't find online for free. (Courtesy of NCSU Libraries, reproduced with permission.)

Thinking like a researcher 1–3

Exploring your library

Spending a half hour exploring your library at the beginning of your research project will save you time in the long run. If you can't easily find answers for some of these questions, ask a reference librarian.

1. On the library's Web site, where can you find the hours the library is open and information about what is on each floor? Are there other libraries on campus or just one?

2. What guides to research are available on the library's site? Is there one that will be particularly helpful for your project?

3. How can you ask reference librarians for help? Is there a reference desk? An opportunity to make appointments? A way of getting help from a librarian online?

4. Is there a one-search option on the library's Web site that lets you find content from many databases all at once?

→

Thinking like a researcher 1–3 (*cont.*)

5. What steps should you take to locate an article found in a database that has no link to the actual article?

6. How do you borrow books or articles from other libraries? Is it free? How long does it usually take? How will you know when your requested book or article has arrived?

Developing effective search terms

Sometimes a particular word or phrase that is being used by the experts will unlock your search almost magically. As you explore, keep track of words and phrases that show up again and again in titles and descriptions of books and articles. If you're having trouble coming up with search terms that work, check with your instructor or a reference librarian.

NOTE: Many library databases, including the library's catalog, work differently than an Internet search engine. Because they don't always search the full text of books and articles, you may need to break up the words in a phrase. Rather than search for "immigration in Latino neighborhoods of Chicago" in a database, you may get better results by searching for a combination of important search terms using AND: immigration AND Latino AND Chicago for more on keyword searches. You can also expand a search term by combining synonyms with OR: Latino OR Hispanic.

Most databases offer an advanced search option that makes it easy to combine search terms. You may also be able to limit a search by article type (scholarly journal, magazine, or newspaper articles) and by publication date range. (See the box below.)

Searching: **Academic Search Premier**, Show all	Choose Databases	
gentrification	Select a Field (optional)	⯆
AND ⯆ Chicago	Select a Field (optional)	⯆
AND ⯆ Latino or Hispanic	Select a Field (optional)	⯆

Thinking like a researcher 1–4

Expanding your list of search terms

Discovering search terms that work is a critical skill for researchers, and finding a good search term can help you get useful results immediately. Try these steps as you develop familiarity with your topic.

1. Write down your topic. Think of all of the different ways to phrase your topic, and write those down, too.

2. Search for books and articles about your topic using the library's Web site. Circle the search words that worked and cross out the ones that didn't.

3. As you search, examine the details of promising sources, looking for words in the titles, abstracts, and descriptors or subject headings that relate to your research. Write those down and try searching again using those terms. Circle the ones that work best.

4. Which words and phrases are new to you? Write brief notes in which you reflect on what you have learned about your topic through this process.

At times, you may have a research question you are excited about, but you become frustrated when you can't find sources related to it. You can put insights about different parts of the topic together in an original way. For example, a book about immigration in New York City could provide ideas that you can apply to Chicago, even if the book doesn't mention Chicago. A study of Latino communities in the United States may give you general ideas that you can apply to the Latino experience in Chicago. If you can't find good sources that address your specific question, try breaking your topic up, look for related research, and make connections that no one else has made before.

Refining keyword searches in databases and search engines

Although command terms and characters vary among electronic databases and Web search engines, some of the most commonly used functions are listed here.

- Use quotation marks around words that are part of a phrase: "gateway drug".

- Use AND to connect words that must appear in a document: hyperactivity AND children. In some search engines — *Google*, for example — *and* is assumed, so typing it is unnecessary. Other search engines require a plus sign instead: hyperactivity +children.

- Use NOT in front of words that must not appear in a document: shepherd NOT dog. Some search engines require a minus sign (hyphen) instead: shepherd -dog.

- Use OR if only one of the terms must appear in a document: "mountain lion" OR cougar.

- Use an asterisk as a substitute for letters that might vary: "marine biolog*" (to find *marine biology* or *marine biologist*, for example).

- Use parentheses to group a search expression and combine it with another: (standard OR student OR test*) AND reform.

NOTE: Many search engines and databases offer an advanced search option that makes it easy to refine your search.

Identifying and filling gaps

Even after you have found useful information and have begun to draft your paper, you will likely discover gaps in your argument. To fill these gaps, you can start by brainstorming questions about your topic—questions such as: What percentage of the population is affected by this issue? Has anyone conducted an opinion poll recently that would support my claims in this section of my paper? Did that proposed legislation that

Having conversations within disciplines

Sometimes your assignment will ask you to focus on how a particular community of scholars approaches a topic. How have philosophers approached the ethics of organ donation? What questions have psychologists asked about how children develop social skills? How have nurses studied cross-cultural communication for improving health care delivery? Philosophers, psychologists, and nursing professionals ask different kinds of questions, conduct research in different ways, and develop their own lingo. In this case, using a specialized database might help you distinguish one discussion from another and give you a sense of what phrases are being used within a discipline as shortcuts for topics and approaches.

several sources mentioned ever get signed into law? A reference librarian can often help you track down those final bits of information that can make your paper stronger.

Reference librarians are trained to find information. You may find it helpful to consult with a librarian as you embark on a research project to learn what databases, Web sites, and strategies might make good starting points. As you dig deeper, a librarian can help you track down specific information you need or suggest search terms to refine your search. When meeting with a librarian, it's a good idea to have a copy of your assignment handy — and be ready to spend some time throwing ideas around. Though it may seem intimidating to ask a stranger for help, most librarians like nothing better than to dig into a research question (and it's their job to help you).

You don't actually need to be in the library to use its databases or get help from a librarian. A username and password provided by the library should allow you to use its databases remotely, and most libraries offer online chat services, e-mail help, or a telephone number for reference assistance when you're not in the library.

Accessing sources

When you are searching library databases, you will sometimes find just a reference to an article but not the article itself. Chances are, you will be able to follow a link to check if it's in another database or if the article is available at the library in print format.

If the article isn't available at your library, you may be able to find a version of it on the Web for free. In recent years, many scholars and scientists have posted a draft or a final copy of their research on their own institutional Web site. (Sometimes only an abstract or summary is online. If you plan to use the source, you'll need the full version.) If there is no free copy available, you don't need to purchase one. Your library should be able to get the books and articles that you need from another library through a service called interlibrary loan, usually at no cost to you. Ask a librarian or check the library's Web site for details.

Part II. Choosing Sources

Two problems can frustrate researchers. One is that there is simply too much information out there. Sorting through the options to find the best sources can be time consuming. The other problem is that it's hard to find "the perfect source," the one that provides the answer to your question in one handy package. Your job as a researcher is not to locate the answer, but rather to arrive at an answer by finding good information, reflecting on what others have said, adding insight, and drawing your own conclusions to become the author of your perfect source.

Finding sources

Determining what makes a source useful depends on your purpose and what your audience expects. An opinion piece from a major newspaper may be a good source to draw on for a paper on science policy but inappropriate for a review of scientific research on an invasive species. Understanding what kind of evidence will be most persuasive for your readers will help you decide which sources to pursue.

As you begin research, think about what kinds of information you need and which sources will be most effective for a particular project. You are likely to need one or more of the following types of sources.

- **Background information** (such as Wikipedia articles, information from textbooks, or brief news articles written by journalists and published in a magazine or newspaper). In some cases, you may not end up citing these sources if they simply provide you with "common knowledge" — that is, factual information that can be found in many sources — but they can be useful as a foundation that you can build on.

- **Primary sources** (such as data tables, maps, historical documents, creative works such as poems or paintings, or popular culture artifacts such as advertisements or YouTube videos). The term *primary source* is defined differently by different disciplines. In the humanities, a primary source is a historical document, such as a diary, a memoir, a work of art, or a news account published around the time the event occurred. It is a source from the historical period under examination, unfiltered by anyone else's interpretation. In the sciences, a primary source (or "primary article") is a report of original research that includes the scientist's methods and results. Using primary sources, whether in science or the humanities, helps a researcher get as close as possible to the subject under examination. Primary sources help orient your reader with the origins of your ideas and provide an opportunity for you to do your own, original analysis. You might even gather your own raw data by conducting a survey, interviews, or focus groups.

- **Secondary sources** (such as books about a historical event, articles that critique creative works, a piece of in-depth investigative reporting, an opinion essay in a newspaper or magazine, or articles by scholars that delve into an issue and discuss its meaning). Within this category, books and articles written by scholars and scientists for a specialized audience are often called "scholarly," "peer-reviewed," or "refereed" sources. Secondary sources often report useful factual information, but add a layer of interpretation or analysis. As a writer, you might draw on these sources because they offer useful perspectives on your topic, represent important schools of thought on the issue, or present information that you find useful in creating your own interpretation or analysis.

Thinking like a researcher 2–1

Speed date an article

When you are searching for information, you often have to make choices quickly between potential sources. These steps can help you decide which articles are worth your time.

1. Search a library database for your topic. Locate the full text of an article that looks good. What criteria did you use to make that choice? What might make you decide *not* to choose an article?

2. Spending *no more than 10 minutes*, use the abstract, introductory paragraphs, conclusion, and any other clues to find out enough about the article that you can answer the following questions:

   - What is the article about?

   - Who is the author (or authors)? What can you find out about the author from the article?

   - How old is the article?

   - In what journal, magazine, or newspaper was the article published?

   - Would you want to spend time with this article? Why or why not?

Evaluating sources

Once you have located several potential sources, how do you decide which to read carefully? No one has time to read them all, but you do want to select ones that will provide good information and serve as convincing, impressive evidence. The sources you choose to cite reflect on your skill as a researcher and contribute to your ability to make a point.

For most topics, one or more scholarly articles would be considered convincing evidence. Below are a few pages from an article in *College Composition and Communication*, a scholarly journal. How can you tell whether the source is scholarly? Look for these indicators in the example below:

1. The author is a scientist or scholar. Often scholarly books and articles include a note about where the author works, such as a university, a research lab, a center, or an institute.

2. The audience is other researchers, scientists, or scholars, so the language is fairly complex and assumes a level of sophistication.

3. It is more than one or two pages long.

4. It includes references to related research.

Sample Source

FIRST PAGE OF ARTICLE

Nancy Sommers and Laura Saltz

The Novice as Expert: Writing the Freshman Year

Why do some students prosper as college writers, moving forward with their writing, while others lose interest? In this essay we explore some of the paradoxes of writing development by focusing on the central role the freshman year plays in this development. We argue that students who make the greatest gains as writers throughout college (1) initially accept their status as novices and (2) see in writing a larger purpose than fulfilling an assignment. Based on the evidence of our longitudinal study, we conclude that the story of the freshman year is not one of dramatic changes on paper; it is the story of changes within the writers themselves.

> *There is a feeling of loss freshman year, the feeling of not being connected anywhere. For 18 years I lived at home. Now home is not really home anymore, and college isn't really home either.*
> —Deepak

September 7, 1997—a balmy Sunday, the kind of afternoon that New Englanders welcome after late August's gelatinous heat. From an airplane, Harvard Yard appears peaceful, even pastoral. But to the 1,650 freshmen shifting in their folding chairs, the sense of doubt about starting college is palpable.[1] Speaking straight to their opening-day anxieties, Harvard President Neil Rudenstine tries to reassure them: "Do not feel surprised if you think you are a displaced person, because that's what you are; and do not worry if all your classmates seem

AUTHOR BIOS

SOMMERS AND SALTZ / THE NOVICE AS EXPERT

Nancy Sommers
Nancy Sommers is the Sosland Director of Writing at Harvard, where she directs the Expository Writing Program, the Harvard Writing Project, and the Harvard Study of Undergraduate Writing.

Laura Saltz
Laura Saltz taught in the Expository Writing Program at Harvard for seven years and worked as a research associate for the Harvard Study of Undergraduate Writing. She is currently assistant professor of art and American studies at Colby College.

SAMPLE PAGE

hear other people's points of view rather than being surrounded by the culture and the stereotypes that I've grown up with. I'm trying to decide for myself what I agree with and what I don't.

Another student speaks of her decision freshman year to learn more about her mother's Italian heritage:

> When I arrived at college, I realized that there is no social group called "Children of Fifth-Generation British Americans," which is what I am on my father's side, but there is an Italian Cultural Club, so I joined the club and got involved. I also started taking Italian and an art history course on Michelangelo, and even wrote about Italian cooking practices in an anthropology paper.

Free to set their own intellectual agendas, many freshmen, particularly those who grew up in relatively homogeneous communities, set off to explore their identities by selecting courses that enable them, however covertly, to study themselves. It is most frequently in these courses that novices discover they can "give and get" something through writing.

When we asked students about their best freshmen writing experience, they described opportunities to write about something that matters to them, whether in Chicano literature or Italian, political science or computer science. Maura, for instance, used many of her freshman papers to think through her doubts about religion and her own social conscience. Since she does not refer to herself in her papers, her professors might not notice the connection between her writing and her religious identity, but she returns in course after course to themes of individuality, responsibility, and culpability. As a senior looking back on her freshman papers, she comments, "I spent much of my freshman year trying to figure out what I am contributing to the world through the study of religion. I was disenchanted by academia and struggled to understand what a life of action versus a life of contemplation would look like. My papers helped me think through some of these issues."

To understand the [...] look at the story of one f[...] academic writing is a me[...]

> **Free to set their own intellectual agendas, many freshmen, particularly those who grew up in relatively homogeneous communities, set off to explore their identities by selecting courses that enable them, however covertly, to study themselves. It is most frequently in these courses that novices discover they can "give and get" something through writing.**

WORKS CITED

Bartholomae, David. "Inventing the University." *When a Writer Can't Write: Studies in Writer's Block and Other Composing Problems.* Ed. Mike Rose. New York: Guilford, 1985.

Carroll, Lee Ann. *Rehearsing New Roles: How College Students Develop as Writers.* Carbondale: SIUP, 2002.

Herrington, Anne J., and Marcia Curtis. *Persons in Process: Four Stories of Writing and Personal Development in College.* Urbana: NCTE, 2000.

Light, Richard J. *Making the Most of College: Students Speak Their Minds.* Cambridge: Harvard UP, 2001.

Sternglass, Marilyn S. *Time to Know Them: A Longitudinal Study of Writing and Learning at the College Level.* Mahwah, NJ: Erlbaum, 1997.

Whether you are looking at a Web site, a book, or a scholarly article, ask yourself these questions:

- **Who** wrote it? Does the author appear to be an expert on the topic?
- **What** is it? Is it an impartial news account, an opinion piece arguing a particular point of view, or a study by a scholar? Is it the kind of source your audience will find appropriate for your purpose?
- **When** was it published? Has the information become outdated?
- **Where** was it created, or what is the geographic focus? An article about a political issue in Britain may not be relevant if your question is about American politics.
- **How** was it created? If the source is a table of numbers, how were they gathered? If it's a research study, what did the author do to conduct it? If it's a news account, did the journalist get access to a variety of sources and differing perspectives? What sources of information did the author rely on, and do they seem credible?

The first four groups of questions can help you screen possible sources quickly while scanning search results on the Web or in a database. The final group — the *How* questions — usually takes more time. To answer them, look at the introduction and conclusion and skim through information about the sources the author used. If this seems solid, you can then invest more time in reading it more closely.

Thinking like a researcher 2–2

Rating Web sites

1. Choose three Web sites that offer information about your topic and record the URL of each.

   Site A:

   Site B:

   Site C:

2. Analyze each Web site by asking yourself the following questions.

	SITE A	SITE B	SITE C
Who is responsible for creating this Web site?			
When was this Web site created?			
What are the strengths of this Web site's content in the context of my project?			
How even-handed is this Web site? Does this site advocate for a particular position?			

Thinking like a researcher 2–2 (*cont.*)

3. Compare the three sites.

	SITE A	SITE B	SITE C
Who is the intended audience? Is it an appropriate audience for my project?			
What is its primary focus? Does it match my research interest?			
What kind of evidence is provided for its claims? Is it verifiable?			

4. To cite a Web page or an entire Web site, you would need to seek out the following information. Choose the most useful of the sites and see if you can identify these elements.

   ✓ Author(s). Check bottom of page for a personal link; look for "about" links

   ✓ Title. If there is no obvious title, use the home page

   ✓ Title of entire Web site, if the page is part of a larger site

   ✓ Date the page created or updated, if available

   Write a citation for the Web page or Web site using the style required for your project.

Comparing sources

In addition to analyzing each source individually, consider how your sources contribute to the conversation as a whole. Are facts that are important to your argument validated in more than one source? How do the sources represent different approaches to the issue? You will want to acknowledge major perspectives on your topic, even those you disagree with, as you draw your own conclusions.

Checking for signs of bias

Bias is a way of thinking, a tendency to be partial, that prevents people and publications from viewing a topic objectively. Both in print and online, some sources are more objective than others. If you are exploring the rights of organizations like WikiLeaks to distribute sensitive government documents over the Internet, for example, you may not find objective, unbiased information in a US State Department report. If you are researching timber harvesting practices, you are likely to encounter bias in publications sponsored by environmental groups. As you read sources, however, you need not reject those that are biased. Publications that are known to be reputable can be editorially biased. As a researcher, you will need to consider any suspected bias as you assess the source. If you are uncertain about a source's special interests, seek the help of a reference librarian. Like publishers, some authors are more objective than others. If you have reason to believe that a writer is particularly biased, you will want to assess his or her arguments with special care. Questions such as the following can help you do this:

- Does the author or publisher endorse political or religious views that could affect objectivity?

- Is the author or publisher associated with a special-interest group, such as PETA or the National Rifle Association, that might present only one side of an issue?

- Are alternative views presented and addressed? How fairly does the author treat opposing views?

- Does the author's language show signs of bias?

Assessing an argument

As you examine an argument presented in a source, take the time to identify the main claim. You will also find it helpful to evaluate the author's reasoning and use of evidence.

For any source that makes an argument, consider asking these questions:

- What is the author's central claim or thesis?
- How does the author support this claim — with relevant and sufficient evidence or with just a few anecdotes or emotional examples?
- Are the statistics consistent with those you encounter in other sources? Have they been used fairly? Does the author explain where the statistics come from?
- Are any of the author's assumptions questionable?
- Does the author consider opposing arguments and refute them persuasively?
- Does the author use flawed logic?

Knowing what sources to avoid

When searching the Web, you may find articles that seem informative about your topic but do not list authors or are vague about the authors' credentials. These may come from "content farms" that produce unoriginal articles primarily as a platform for advertising. Since your readers will judge your work by the caliber of the sources you draw on, you should avoid relying on those that simply provide basic factual information available elsewhere or that have unclear authorship.

As you select sources, look for expert authors and try to get as close to the original source of information as you can. For example, rather than cite a local newspaper article that briefly summarizes a government report on nutrition, use the information provided in the article to seek out the actual report.

Tracing the influence of a source

When you track down books and articles using citations, you are tracing the conversation about ideas backward in time. Using Google Scholar, you can move forward in time by seeing

> **Budgeting your time with a source**
>
> Using books for research doesn't require reading them cover to cover. If you find a book that looks interesting, browse the table of contents to see if parts of it are relevant. Skim the introduction, which generally provides a quick roadmap to the book. Consult the index at the back of the book to see whether specific pages cover your topic or, if it's an e-book, use its search function to find out whether there is a section or chapter that is particularly helpful for your research.

who has cited a book or article since it was published. This is a useful strategy for finding more current research and can also help you assess the impact of a source. This "cited by" feature is also available in some library databases. The student who looked up "immigration," "Latino," and "Chicago" found an article that had been cited by seventy other researchers.

Cited
by 70

The Politics of Gentrification The Case of West Town in **Chicago**
JJ Betancur - Urban Affairs Review, 2002 - uar.sagepub.com
... have closed; public school enrollment has decreased in the most **gentrified** sections, and ... in 1989 and 1991, respectively, to explore strategies to deal with **gentrification**.18 Currently ... Our sources and observations agreed that **gentrifying** pressure on the community grows by the ...
Cited by 70 Related articles All 3 versions Cite

Courtesy of John J. Betancur, reproduced with permission.

Getting involved in scholarly conversations

Scholarly books and articles list the works the author has used in a list of works cited. These lists of sources are valuable shortcuts. The author, an expert on the topic, has selected sources that he or she found particularly relevant. As you scan through these lists of references, note authors who are cited repeatedly. They are likely to be particularly influential contributors to the conversation.

Citations give you all the information you need to access the sources you need.

- Is the reference to a book? Check the book's title in your library's catalog.
- Is the reference to a chapter or essay in a book? Check the book's title in the catalog.
- Is the reference to a journal article? Check the journal title (not the article title) in your library's list of journals. Ask a librarian if you aren't sure where to find the list.
- Is the reference to a book or article not owned by your library? Request it through interlibrary loan.

Thinking like a researcher 2–3

Who is part of your conversation?

Research involves getting to know who has interesting things to say about your topic. The key players in the conversation may be people (researchers, scientists, professionals, or activists) or organizations (nonprofits, think tanks, government agencies, professional associations) that have an interest in your topic and have helped you understand it.

Choose three of the most interesting or important voices in the conversation around your topic and introduce them.

1. Name: _____ Source: _____

   What makes this person or organization an expert worth consulting?

   What is the most valuable thing you have learned from this person or organization?

2. Name: _____ Source: _____

   What makes this person or organization an expert worth consulting?

   What is the most valuable thing you have learned from this person or organization?

3. Name: _____ Source: _____

   What makes this person or organization an expert worth consulting?

   What is the most valuable thing you have learned from this person or organization?

Some references can be hard to interpret. If you're not sure how to track down a cited work that looks interesting, ask a reference librarian for help.

Thinking like a researcher 2–4

Connecting with experts through citations

1. Choose one of your sources that was published at least four years ago. From its list of works cited (which may be labeled "References," "Works Cited", or "Bibliography") choose one text that seems important and relevant for your research. Write down the author, title, and publication information:

   CITED SOURCE

   Author(s):

   Title of book or article:

   Date of publication:

   Why did you choose this source from the Works Cited list? What makes it potentially useful?

   Can you find it in your library or online?

2. Look up the source you selected in Google Scholar <http://scholar.google.com>.

   Take note of the dates and number of times it has been cited since it was published.

   How can you tell which items that cite the source you selected are available to you through your library or online?

   See if you can find in the cited source the passage or excerpt that the author of your original source used. Why do you think the author of your original source cited this text? How does it contribute to the opinions or ideas expressed in your original source? Are there any conflicting ideas?

Part III. Managing information

Researchers develop personal preferences when it comes to keeping track of their notes and materials. What all researchers have in common is the following:

- A system for **keeping track of sources**, including all the information required for a citation. Whenever you save or print out a source from a database, make sure it includes the necessary citation information because it can be hard to track down later. Keeping a working bibliography, a record of any sources you read or view, will help you compile the list of sources that will appear at the end of your paper.

- A system for **taking notes** about those sources, such as summaries of main points or quotations that seem especially meaningful. Many writers like to mark up paper copies. Others take notes on their computer. Some prefer to write main ideas on cards that they can sort and rearrange easily. Whatever method you use, it's critical that you identify which words and thoughts are yours and which come from a source. Many writers have committed plagiarism because they mixed up their notes and thought they were using their own words when in fact they had copied material from a source.

- A strategy for **organizing ideas** as you put your project together. Some researchers find it useful to keep a log as they conduct research, making note of ideas as they occur to them. Others figure out their general approach and then make lists or outlines. Others prefer to use graphics such as flowcharts or concept maps. Some writers prefer to just start writing to see how their thoughts flow, then step back and analyze how to arrange their ideas. However you prefer to organize your work, making a plan will help you group important concepts together logically and ensure you haven't left out anything important. As you get organized, reexamine your assignment to make sure that you are covering your bases.

Staying organized anywhere

Whether you prefer to print out or keep electronic copies, you will want to find a way to access important sources as you write. If you use more than one computer to do your work, you may want to carry a flash drive to store all of your documents, e-mail PDFs of articles to yourself (an option offered in most databases), or sign up for a cloud storage account using a service such as Google Drive or Dropbox. This way, you can save and access your notes and other electronic files from any computer that connects to the Internet.

Using information from sources in your writing

Good writers make the boundaries between their ideas and their sources' ideas clear for at least three reasons:

- To demonstrate to readers that they have consulted solid, reliable sources. Having sought out experts makes a researcher more of an expert in the eyes of readers.

- To give readers enough information to look up the sources themselves.

- To give credit where it is due. Failing to acknowledge sources is unethical and carries serious academic penalties that could include losing credit for the assignment or failing the course.

In all academic disciplines, providing information about your sources is an important part of showing how your ideas fit into a broader conversation, but how sources are acknowledged varies. In the sciences, for example, writers typically summarize previous research in a "review of the literature" before reporting results of a new experiment. Being able to summarize the main point of a source clearly and briefly is an important skill for writers in the sciences. In the humanities and in interdisciplinary research, in-depth analysis of sources is more likely to be woven into an argument, using direct quotations whenever the specific wording of a source is important.

While including quotations from a source is sometimes important, it's best to quote directly from sources only if the way an idea is expressed is important. For example, if you are explaining the significance of a line of poetry or a historical document, you will likely need to provide your readers with the exact words you are analyzing. However, if you are explaining an idea or factual information that you found in a source, it's better to put it into your own words. Too much quotation from other sources makes for a choppy, unsatisfying experience for your readers and diminishes the impact of the point you are trying to make.

Avoiding unintentional plagiarism

No matter whether you are summarizing a source or doing in-depth analysis, avoiding plagiarism is critical to your academic success. In addition to providing citations to the sources of direct quotations, you need to cite the source of any *ideas* that you are writing about as well. (The exception is factual information that is available in many sources and is considered "common knowledge.") When you put a source's ideas or information in your own words, you must avoid sounding too much like the original source. Copying a sentence and changing a word or two, even if you provide a citation, is plagiarism. To prevent borrowing too much from a source, think about what it means, set the source aside, and write your understanding down without looking at the original. You can later check for accuracy, but this activity will help you avoid accidentally copying too much.

What follows is a passage about contributing factors to childhood obesity from a report published by the Henry J. Kaiser

Family Foundation. Following the passage are two unacceptable paraphrases (the student has plagiarized the source's words
in one case and the structure in the other) and an acceptable
paraphrase. The bibliographic information is recorded in APA
style.

ORIGINAL SOURCE
In an effort to seek the causes of this disturbing trend, experts have
pointed to a range of important potential contributors to the rise in
childhood obesity that are unrelated to media.

> — Henry J. Kaiser Family Foundation, "The Role of Media
> in Childhood Obesity" (2004), p. 1

UNACCEPTABLE BORROWING OF PHRASES
According to the Henry J. Kaiser Family Foundation (2004), experts
have indicated a range of significant potential contributors to the rise
in childhood obesity that are not linked to media (p. 1).

UNACCEPTABLE BORROWING OF STRUCTURE
According to the Henry J. Kaiser Family Foundation (2004), experts
have identified a variety of key factors causing a rise in childhood
obesity, factors that are not tied to media (p. 1).

ACCEPTABLE PARAPHRASE
A report by the Henry J. Kaiser Family Foundation (2004) described
causes other than media for the childhood obesity crisis.

When writing about a debatable issue, sources play an
important role in providing information about your topic
and support for your argument. However, college assignments
ask you to do more than collect quotations and glue them
together. College writers are expected to approach a topic
with an open mind, to read widely to understand multiple
perspectives on it, and in the end be able to put forth their
own argument — one that is informed by the debate happen-
ing among the sources. Rather than merely report on what
sources say, successful college researchers synthesize sources.

In other words, they create a conversation about the research topic and then add something meaningful to that conversation. Simply snatching quotes and patching them together does not do justice to your sources or to your own identity as a writer and thinker.

Using citation management tools

Many library databases and catalogs have built-in citation generators. With a click of a button, a citation for a source can be generated in MLA, APA, *Chicago*, or another format, ready to be pasted into a document. These are only rough drafts of citations. They often have errors and always need to be edited by hand.

Experienced researchers often use software programs to capture and store their references and notes, sort them into project files, and create formatted bibliographies in a variety of styles. Though there is a learning curve involved, in the long run these tools can be helpful for keeping track of a large number of sources for multiple projects. Plugins are also available for word processing programs so that your citations can be integrated into your documents as you write. As with simpler tools, bibliographies will have errors and will need to be edited. Programs available include EasyBib, EndNote, RefWorks, and Zotero. (Zotero is free and available at zotero.org to anyone with an Internet connection.) Your library may offer help getting started with one or more of these programs.

Part IV: Research and Documentation in the Humanities

Finding sources in the humanities

Research in the humanities generally involves interpreting a text or a work of art within a historical and cultural context, making connections, exploring meaning, and uncovering contradictions. Scholars in the humanities typically use library resources in at least three ways:

- to obtain primary sources to be interpreted or analyzed
- to find secondary sources to put primary sources in a critical context
- to seek answers to specific questions that arise during research

Research in the humanities is often interdisciplinary, bridging literature and history, philosophy and art, or music and religion. Because the subject areas are harder to categorize, the terminology used in humanities research may be less solid and agreed upon than in other fields. Researchers in the humanities are more likely to draw material from texts and artifacts than from original data gathering and experimentation. Successful humanities researchers are flexible, both in search terminology and in search strategy; tolerant of multiple perspectives on the same topic of study; prepared to use citations in relevant texts to locate other material and clarify connections among works; and willing to return to the library as new questions arise.

Fortunately, there are many fine research tools to help. Those listed here are not available in every library but illustrate possible options. Your library's Web site will likely have a list of resources by subject with links to locally available online and print sources. Always bear in mind that librarians are particularly user-friendly resources. Ask a librarian for recommended research tools as you begin your research, and use the librarian's expertise as your research progresses and your questions grow more specific.

General resources

Google Books. Mountain View: Google, 2004–. <http://books.google .com>. Search the full text of millions of books scanned in hundreds of libraries or selected sections of books from publishers. Books published before 1923 are generally available in full text. Newer books may have portions of text available, but typically pages are omitted. Useful for tracking down specific quotes and accessing historical publications.

HathiTrust. Ann Arbor: Hathi Trust Research Center, 2008–. <http:// www.hathitrust.org>. A collaboration of libraries that share the full text of scanned books. Older books are available in full text and can be downloaded. Some books are restricted to users at particular libraries. Particularly helpful for locating specific information in books and for historical publications. Users can create and share collections, such as books by a particular author or on a topic.

JSTOR. Ann Arbor: Ithaka, 1994–. <http://www.jstor.org>. This library database is an archive of scholarly journals and (at some libraries) books in a wide variety of subjects. Since JSTOR includes the full text of every issue of the journals included (other than the most recent years) it's helpful for finding high-quality scholarly articles in literature, history, and many other subjects. Its Google-like search makes it easy to find articles, but pay attention to publication dates as many of the articles are quite old and the most current issues are often not included.

Art and architecture

For background information

The Dictionary of Art. Ed. Jane Turner. New York: Grove's Dictionaries, 1996. An exhaustive encyclopedia of world art containing scholarly articles on artists, movements, works, and subjects, with bibliographical references and an index. In some libraries, this work is found in *Oxford Art Online.*

Databases

Art Full Text. Ipswich: EBSCO, 2011–. <http://www.ebscohost.com/academic/art-full-text>. Indexes and provides full text for many art and architecture journals. Some libraries have different versions of this database with titles such as *Art and Architecture Complete, Art-Source,* and *Art Index Retrospective.*

Bibliography of the History of Art (BHA/RILA). Los Angeles: Getty Research Institute, 1991–2007. <http://primo.getty.edu/primo_library/libweb/action/search.do?vid=BHA>. Indexes research published between 1975 and 2007 on Western art from antiquity to contemporary. Though free to all, it provides citations rather than the full text of books or articles. Some libraries may subscribe to the database that continues this free resource, the *International Bibliography of Art.*

Sources of images

ARTstor. New York: ARTstor, 2003–. <http://www.jstor.org/>. This library database contains over 1.5 million downloadable art images from hundreds of museums around the world.

National Gallery of Art Images. Washington: National Gallery. <https://images.nga.gov>. A freely available searchable collection of over 25,000 high-resolution images of art that can be used in projects.

Classics

For background information

Brill's New Pauly Encyclopedia of the Ancient World. Leiden: Brill, 2002–2010. This encyclopedia covers subjects in antiquity and the classical tradition in in-depth scholarly articles.

Oxford Encyclopedia of Ancient Greece and Rome. Oxford: Oxford University Press, 2009. Offers over 1,000 articles written by classics scholars covering topics, people, periods, and ideas that have influenced the modern world.

Database

L'Année Philologique: Bibliographie Critique et Analytique de l'Antiquité Gréco-Latine. Paris: The Société Internationale de Bibliographie Classique (SIBC), 1924/26–. <http://www.annee-philologique.com/>. A comprehensive index to research on Greek and Latin cultures, including archaeology, literature, and philosophy. It includes references to scholarship in several languages.

Primary source online

Perseus Digital Library. Boston: Tufts University, 1987–. <http://www
.perseus.tufts.edu/hopper>. This collection offers primary sources in
Greek and Latin with English translations and provides secondary
commentary on classical sources as well as images of artifacts in art
and archaeology.

Literature

For background information

American Writers. New York: Scribner, 1979–. Offers essays analyzing
the life and work of major American writers, arranged chronologically with an alphabetical index. Similar series are available in print
for British, Latin American, and European writers. Many libraries
offer this material and much more in databases called the *Literature
Resource Center* or *Gale Virtual Reference Online.*

The Oxford English Dictionary. Ed. J. A. Simpson and E. S. C. Weiner. 2nd
ed. Oxford: Clarendon, 1989–. Unlike other dictionaries, this resource
delves deeply into the various meanings of words and their changing
definitions over time. The *OED* provides chronological examples showing how a word has been used throughout history; it is unequaled in its
depth of coverage. Find online at <http://www.oed.com/>.

Database

*MLA International Bibliography of Books and Articles on the Modern
Languages and Literatures.* New York: Modern Language Association,
1921–. <http://www.mla.org/bibliography>. The most important ongoing index of scholarship in literature and linguistics, this database
provides citations to books, book chapters, articles, and dissertations
in all languages on literature, linguistics, folklore, and some film
criticism. Though it is very in-depth for literary criticism, it does not
include book reviews and articles appearing in popular magazines.

Music

For background information

New Grove Dictionary of Music and Musicians. Ed. Stanley Sadie. 2nd
ed. New York: Grove, 2001–. The definitive source on music and

music history. The articles in these volumes are carefully researched and documented and provide information on national music traditions, musical forms, composers and musicians, instruments, and more. On your library's Web site, the online version may be called *Grove Online*.

Database

RILM Abstracts of Music Literature. New York: RILM, 1967–. <http://www.rilm.org/>. An in-depth index to music journals, magazines, books, and dissertations, particularly strong in music history and musicology but also covering performance practice.

Recordings and scores

Naxos Music Library. Hong Kong: Naxos Digital Services, 2003–. <http://www.naxosmusiclibrary.com/>. This music streaming service available in some libraries offers over a million tracks of music from many labels, including classical, jazz, folk, and world music.

IMSLP Petrucci Music Library. Wilmington: Project Petrucci, 2006–. <http://imslp.org/wiki>. A free site for sharing public domain music scores, primarily classical, with over 70,000 downloadable scores.

Philosophy

For background information

Encyclopedia of Philosophy. Ed. Donald M. Borchert. 2nd ed. Detroit: Macmillan Reference, 2006. Offers articles on movements, concepts, and philosophers. A good starting place for research, offering clearly written and accessible overviews and bibliographies of key works.

Stanford Encyclopedia of Philosophy. Stanford: Stanford University Center for the Study of Language and Information, 1995–. <http://plato.stanford.edu>. A freely available resource that offers authoritative peer-reviewed articles about key concepts in the field. Entries are kept current by a team of contributing philosophers.

Database

Philosopher's Index. Bowling Green: Philosophy Documentation Center, 1967–. <http://philindex.org/>. The most in-depth index to scholarly approaches to philosophy, this database provides references and abstracts of journal articles, anthologies, and books on all aspects of the field.

Religion

For background information

Encyclopedia of Religion. Ed. Lindsay Jones. 2nd ed. New York: Macmillan, 2005. Covers religions from around the world, including information about their ideas, histories, and cultures. The articles are written by experts in their fields and include excellent bibliographies.

Database

ATLA. Evanston: American Theological Library Association, 1949–. <https://www.atla.com/>. The most thorough database for articles, books, selections in books, and reviews for the field of religion, including theology, biblical studies, church history, comparative religions, archaeology and antiquities, and pastoral work.

Data online

Pew Research Religion & Public Life Project. Washington: Pew Research Center, 2001–. <http://www.pewforum.org>. A "fact tank" that conducts research on public attitudes toward religion around the world, providing high-quality findings on contemporary topics.

Theater, dance, and film

For background information

International Encyclopedia of Dance. New York: Oxford University Press, 1998. The most extensive reference work on dance, covering the historical evolution of dance throughout the world, analysis of dance techniques, theories of aesthetics, influential individuals, important companies, and significant works.

World Encyclopedia of Contemporary Theatre. New York: Routledge, 1994–2000. Offers in-depth regional coverage of theater worldwide.

Databases

International Bibliography of Theatre & Dance. New York: Theatre Research Data Center, 1984–. Covers key journals and books in theater and dance. Some libraries have full text of some of the sources included.

Film and Television Literature Index. Albany: Film and Television Documentation Center, SUNY Albany, 1975–. Offers thorough coverage of reviews, interviews, criticism, and production information. In some libraries, full-text articles are included. Free access to references of publications 1975–2001 is available at <http://webapp1.dlib.indiana.edu/fli/index.jsp>.

World languages and linguistics

For background information

International Encyclopedia of Linguistics. Ed. William J. Frawley. 2nd ed. New York: Oxford University Press, 2003. Includes scholarly articles on all aspects of linguistics along with helpful bibliographies for further research.

Database

MLA International Bibliography of Books and Articles on the Modern Languages and Literatures. New York: Modern Language Association, 1921–. <http://www.mla.org/bibliography>. The most important ongoing index of scholarship in literature and linguistics, this database provides citations to books, book chapters, articles, and dissertations in numerous languages on literature, linguistics, folklore, and some film criticism. Though it is very in-depth for literary criticism, it does not include book reviews and articles appearing in popular magazines.

Citing sources in the humanities: MLA style

In English and other humanities classes, you may be asked to use the MLA (Modern Language Association) system for documenting sources, which is set forth in the *MLA Handbook,* eighth edition (MLA, 2016).

MLA recommends in-text citations that refer readers to a list of works cited. A typical in-text citation names the author of the source, often in a signal phrase, and gives a page number in parentheses. At the end of the paper, the list of works cited provides publication information about the source; the list is alphabetized by authors' last names (or by titles for works without authors). There is a direct connection between the in-text citation and the alphabetical listing. In the following example, that connection is highlighted in orange.

IN-TEXT CITATION

Bioethicist David Resnik emphasizes that such policies, despite their potential to make our society healthier, "open the door to excessive government control over food, which could restrict dietary choices, interfere with cultural, ethnic, and religious traditions, and exacerbate socioeconomic inequalities" (31).

ENTRY IN THE LIST OF WORKS CITED

Resnik, David. "Trans Fat Bans and Human Freedom." *American Journal of Bioethics*, vol. 10, no. 3, Mar. 2010, pp. 27-32.

For a list of works cited that includes this entry, see page 119.

MLA in-text citations

MLA in-text citations are made with a combination of signal phrases and parenthetical references. A signal phrase introduces information taken from a source (a quotation, summary, paraphrase, or fact); usually the signal phrase includes the author's name. The parenthetical reference comes after the cited material, often at the end of the sentence. It includes at least a page number (except for unpaginated sources, such as those found on the Web). In the models in this section, the elements of the in-text citation are highlighted.

IN-TEXT CITATION

Resnik acknowledges that his argument relies on "slippery slope" thinking, but he insists that "social and political pressures" regarding food regulation make his concerns valid (31).

Readers can look up the author's last name in the alphabetized list of works cited, where they will learn the work's title and other publication information. If readers decide to consult the source, the page number will take them straight to the passage that has been cited.

General guidelines for signal phrases and page numbers

Items 1–5 explain how the MLA system usually works for all sources—in print, on the Web, in other media, and with or without authors and page numbers. Items 6–27 give variations on the basic guidelines.

1. Author named in a signal phrase   Ordinarily, introduce the material being cited with a signal phrase that includes the author's name. In addition to preparing readers for the source, the signal phrase allows you to keep the parenthetical citation brief.

According to Lorine Goodwin, a food historian, nineteenth-century reformers who sought to purify the food supply were called "fanatics" and "radicals" by critics who argued that consumers should be free to buy and eat what they want (77).

The signal phrase—*According to Lorine Goodwin*—names the author; the parenthetical citation gives the page number of the book in which the quoted words may be found.

Notice that the period follows the parenthetical citation. When a quotation ends with a question mark or an exclamation

Directory to MLA in-text citation models

point, leave the end punctuation inside the quotation mark and add a period at the end of your sentence.

> Burgess asks a critical question: "How can we think differently about food labeling?" (51).

2. Author named in parentheses If you do not give the author's name in a signal phrase, put the last name in parentheses along with the page number (if the source has one). Use no punctuation between the name and the page number: (Moran 351).

> According to a nationwide poll, 75 percent of Americans are opposed to laws that restrict or put limitations on access to unhealthy foods (Neergaard and Agiesta).

3. Author unknown   If a source has no author, the works cited entry will begin with the title. In your in-text citation, either use the complete title in a signal phrase or use a short form of the title in parentheses. Titles of books and other long works are italicized; titles of articles and other short works are put in quotation marks.

> As a result, kids see about four thousand ads per year encouraging them to eat unhealthy food and drinks ("Facts").

NOTE: If the author is a corporation or a government agency, see items 8 and 17 on pp. 44 and 47, respectively.

4. Page number unknown   Do not include the page number if a work lacks page numbers, as is the case with many Web sources. Even if a printout from a Web site shows page numbers, treat the source as unpaginated in the in-text citation because not all printouts give the same page numbers. (When the pages of a Web source are stable, as in PDF files, supply a page number in your in-text citation.)

> Michael Pollan points out that "cheap food" actually has "significant costs—to the environment, to public health, to the public purse, even to the culture."

If a source has numbered paragraphs or sections, use "par." (or "pars.") or "sec." (or "secs.") in the parentheses: (Smith, par. 4). Notice that a comma follows the author's name.

5. One-page source If the source is one page long, MLA allows (but does not require) you to omit the page number. It's a good idea to include the page number because without it readers may not know where your citation ends or, worse, may not realize that you have provided a citation at all.

NO PAGE NUMBER IN CITATION

Sarah Conly uses John Stuart Mill's "harm principle" to argue that citizens need their government to intervene to prevent them from taking harmful actions—such as driving too fast or buying unhealthy foods—out of ignorance of the harm they can do. But government intervention may overstep in the case of food choices.

PAGE NUMBER IN CITATION

Sarah Conly uses John Stuart Mill's "harm principle" to argue that citizens need their government to intervene to prevent them from taking harmful actions—such as driving too fast or buying unhealthy foods—out of ignorance of the harm they can do (A23). But government intervention may overstep in the case of food choices.

Variations on the general guidelines

This section describes the MLA guidelines for handling a variety of situations not covered in items 1–5.

6. Two authors Name the authors in a signal phrase, as in the following example, or include their last names in the parenthetical reference: (Gostin and Gostin 214).

As legal scholars Gostin and Gostin explain, "[I]nterventions that do not pose a truly significant burden on individual liberty" are justified if they "go a long way towards safeguarding the health and well-being of the populace" (214).

7. Three or more authors   Give the first author's name followed by "et al." (Latin for "and others") in the signal phrase and in the parenthetical citation.

> The study was extended for two years, and only after results were reviewed by an independent panel did the researchers publish their findings (Blaine et al. 35).

8. Organization as author   When the author is a corporation or an organization, name that author either in the signal phrase or in the parentheses. (For a government agency as author, see item 17 on p. 47.)

> The American Diabetes Association estimates that the cost of diagnosed diabetes in the United States in 2012 was $245 billion.

In the list of works cited, the American Management Association is treated as the author and alphabetized under *A*. When you give the organization name in the text, spell out the name; when you use it in parentheses, abbreviate common words in the name: "Assn.," "Dept.," "Natl.," "Soc.," and so on.

> The cost of diagnosed diabetes in the United States in 2012 was estimated at $245 billion (Amer. Diabetes Assn.).

9. Authors with the same last name   If your list of works cited includes works by two or more authors with the same last name, include the author's first name in the signal phrase or first initial in the parentheses.

> One approach to the problem is to introduce nutrition literacy at the K–5 level in public schools (E. Chen 15).

10. Two or more works by the same author Mention the title of the work in the signal phrase or include a short version of the title in the parentheses.

> The American Diabetes Association tracks trends in diabetes across age groups. In 2012, more than 200,000 children and adolescents had diabetes ("Fast"). Because of an expected dramatic increase in diabetes in young people over the next forty years, the association encourages "strategies for implementing childhood obesity prevention programs and primary prevention programs for youth at risk of developing type 2 diabetes" ("Number").

Titles of articles and other short works are placed in quotation marks; titles of books and other long works are italicized. (See also p. 108.)

In the rare case when both the author's name and a short title must be given in parentheses, separate them with a comma.

> Researchers have estimated that "the number of youth with type 2 [diabetes] could quadruple and the number with type 1 could triple" by 2050, "with an increasing proportion of youth with diabetes from minority populations" (Amer. Diabetes Assn., "Number").

11. Two or more works in one citation To cite more than one source in the parentheses, list the authors (or titles) in alphabetical order and separate them with a semicolon.

> The prevalence of early-onset type 2 diabetes has been well documented (Finn 68; Sharma 2037; Whitaker 118).

It may be less distracting to use an information note for multiple citations (see p. 106).

12. Repeated citations from the same source When you are writing about a single work, you do not need to include the author's name each time you quote from or paraphrase the work. After you mention the author's name at the beginning of your paper, you may include just the page number in your parenthetical citations.

> In Susan Glaspell's short story "A Jury of Her Peers," two women accompany their husbands and a county attorney to an isolated house where a farmer named John Wright has been choked to death in his bed with a rope. The chief suspect is Wright's wife, Minnie, who is in jail awaiting trial. The sheriff's wife, Mrs. Peters, has come along to gather some personal items for Minnie, and Mrs. Hale has joined her. Early in the story, Mrs. Hale sympathizes with Minnie and objects to the way the male investigators are "snoopin' round and criticizin'" her kitchen (249). In contrast, Mrs. Peters shows respect for the law, saying that the men are doing "no more than their duty" (249).

In a paper with multiple sources, if you are citing a source more than once in a paragraph, you may omit the author's name after the first mention in the paragraph as long as it is clear that you are still referring to the same source.

13. Encyclopedia or dictionary entry When an encyclopedia or a dictionary entry does not have an author, it will be alphabetized in the list of works cited under the word or entry that you consulted (see item 28 on p. 76). Either in your text or in your parenthetical citation, mention the word or entry. No page number is required because readers can easily look up the word or entry.

> The word *crocodile* has a complex etymology ("Crocodile").

14. Multivolume work If your paper cites more than one volume of a multivolume work, indicate in the parentheses the volume you are referring to, followed by a colon and the page number.

> In his studies of gifted children, Terman describes a pattern of
> accelerated language acquisition (2: 279).

If you cite only one volume of a multivolume work, you will
include the volume number in the list of works cited and will
not need to include it in the parentheses. (See the second
example in item 38 on p. 84.)

15. Entire work   Use the author's name in a signal phrase or a
parenthetical citation. There is no need to use a page number.

> Pollan explores the issues surrounding food production and
> consumption from a political angle.

16. Selection in an anthology or a collection   Put the name of
the author of the selection (not the editor of the anthology)
in the signal phrase or the parentheses.

> In "Love Is a Fallacy," the narrator's logical teachings disintegrate
> when Polly declares that she should date Petey because "[h]e's got a
> raccoon coat" (Shulman 391).

In the list of works cited, the work is alphabetized under *Shul-
man*, the author of the story, not under the name of the editor
of the anthology. (See item 35 on p. 81.)

> Shulman, Max. "Love Is a Fallacy." *Current Issues and Enduring Questions*,
>   edited by Sylvan Barnet and Hugo Bedau, 9th ed., Bedford/St. Martin's,
>   2011, pp. 383-91.

17. Government document   When a government agency is the
author, you will alphabetize it in the list of works cited under
the name of the government, such as United States or Great
Britain (see item 70 on p. 102). For this reason, you must name
the government as well as the agency in your in-text citation.

> One government agency reports that seatbelt use saved an average
> of more than fourteen thousand lives per year in the United States

between 2000 and 2010 (United States, Dept. of Transportation, Natl. Highway Traffic Safety Administration 231).

18. Historical document   For a historical document, such as the United States Constitution or the Canadian Charter of Rights and Freedoms, provide the document title, neither italicized nor in quotation marks, along with relevant article and section numbers. In parenthetical citations, use common abbreviations such as "art." and "sec." and abbreviations of well-known titles: (US Const., art. 1, sec. 2).

> While the United States Constitution provides for the formation of new states (art. 4, sec. 3), it does not explicitly allow or prohibit the secession of states.

Cite other historical documents as you would any other work, by the first element in the works cited entry (see item 72 on p. 103).

19. Legal source   For a legislative act (law) or court case, name the act or case either in a signal phrase or in parentheses. Italicize the names of cases but not the names of acts. (See also items 73 and 74 on p. 103.)

> The Jones Act of 1917 granted US citizenship to Puerto Ricans.

> In 1857, Chief Justice Roger B. Taney declared in *Dred Scott v. Sandford* that blacks, whether enslaved or free, could not be citizens of the United States.

20. Visual such as a table, a chart, or another graphic   To cite a visual that has a figure number in the source, use the abbreviation "fig." and the number in place of a page number in your parenthetical citation: (Manning, fig. 4). If you refer to the figure in your text, spell out the word "figure."

To cite a visual that does not have a figure number in a print source, use the visual's title or a description in your text and cite the author and page number as for any other source.

For a visual not in a print source, identify the visual in your text and then in parentheses use the first element in the works cited entry: the artist's or photographer's name or the title of the work. (See items 64–69 on pp. 100–02.)

Photographs such as *Woman Aircraft Worker* (Bransby) and *Women Welders* (Parks) demonstrate the US government's attempt to document the contributions of women during World War II.

21. Personal communication and social media   Cite personal letters, personal interviews, e-mail messages, and social media posts by the name listed in the works cited entry, as you would for any other source. Identify the type of source in your text if you feel it is necessary for clarity. (See 27d on p. 75, 29c on p. 77, and 75–79 on pp. 104–05.)

22. Web source   Your in-text citation for a source from the Web should follow the same guidelines as for other sources. If the source lacks page numbers but has numbered paragraphs, sections, or divisions, use those numbers with the appropriate abbreviation in your parenthetical citation: "par.," "sec.," "ch.," and so on. Do not add such numbers if the source does not use them; simply give the author or title in your in-text citation.

Julian Hawthorne points out profound differences between his father and Ralph Waldo Emerson but concludes that, in their lives and their writing, "together they met the needs of nearly all that is worthy in human nature" (ch. 4).

23. Indirect source (source quoted in another source)   When a writer's or a speaker's quoted words appear in a source written by someone else, begin the parenthetical citation with the abbreviation "qtd. in." (See also item 12 on p. 63.) In the following example, Gostin and Gostin are the authors of the source given in the works cited list; the source contains a quotation by Dan Beauchamp.

> Public health researcher Dan Beauchamp has said that "public health practices are 'communal in nature, and concerned with the well-being of the community as a whole and not just the well-being of any particular person'" (qtd. in Gostin and Gostin 217).

Literary works and sacred texts

Literary works and sacred texts are usually available in a variety of editions. Your list of works cited will specify which edition you are using, and your in-text citation will usually consist of a page number from the edition you consulted (see item 24). When possible, give enough information—such as book parts, play divisions, or line numbers—so that readers can locate the cited passage in any edition of the work (see items 25–27).

24. Literary work without parts or line numbers   Many literary works, such as most short stories and many novels and plays, do not have parts or line numbers. In such cases, simply cite the page number.

> At the end of Kate Chopin's "The Story of an Hour," Mrs. Mallard drops dead upon learning that her husband is alive. In the final irony of the story, doctors report that she has died of a "joy that kills" (25).

25. Verse play or poem   For verse plays, give act, scene, and line numbers that can be located in any edition of the work. Use arabic numerals and separate the numbers with periods.

> In Shakespeare's *King Lear*, Gloucester, blinded for suspected treason, learns a profound lesson from his tragic experience: "A man may see how this world goes / with no eyes" (4.2.148-49).

For a poem, cite the part, stanza, and line numbers, if it has them, separated by periods.

The Green Knight claims to approach King Arthur's court "because the praise of you, prince, is puffed so high, / And your manor and your men are considered so magnificent" (1.12.258-59).

For poems that are not divided into numbered parts or stanzas, use line numbers. For a first reference, use the word "lines": (lines 5-8). Thereafter use just the numbers: (12-13).

26. Novel with numbered divisions   When a novel has numbered divisions, put the page number first, followed by a semicolon, and then the book, part, or chapter in which the passage may be found. Use abbreviations such as "bk.," "pt.," and "ch."

One of Kingsolver's narrators, teenager Rachel, pushes her vocabulary beyond its limits. For example, Rachel complains that being forced to live in the Congo with her missionary family is "a sheer tapestry of justice" because her chances of finding a boyfriend are "dull and void" (117; bk. 2, ch. 10).

27. Sacred text   When citing a sacred text such as the Bible or the Qur'an, name the edition you are using in your works cited entry (see item 39 on p. 84). In your parenthetical citation, give the book, chapter, and verse (or their equivalent), separated with periods. Common abbreviations for books of the Bible are acceptable.

Consider the words of Solomon: "If your enemy is hungry, give him bread to eat; and if he is thirsty, give him water to drink" (*Oxford Annotated Bible*, Prov. 25.21).

The title of a sacred work is italicized when it refers to a specific edition of the work, as in the preceding example. If you refer to the book in a general sense in your text, neither italicize it nor put it in quotation marks.

The Bible and the Qur'an provide allegories that help readers understand how to lead a moral life.

MLA list of works cited

The elements you will need for the works cited list at the end of your paper or project will differ slightly for some sources, but the main principles apply to all sources, whether in print or from the Web: You should identify an author, a creator, or a producer whenever possible; give a title; and provide the date on which the source was produced. Some sources will require page numbers; some will require a publisher or sponsor; and some will require other identifying information.

This section provides details for how to cite many of the sources you are likely to encounter. It also provides hints for what you can do when a source does not match one of the models exactly. When you cite sources, your goals are to show that your sources are reliable and relevant, to provide readers with enough information to find sources easily, and to provide that information consistently according to MLA conventions.

- Directory to MLA works cited models, page 54
- General guidelines for the works cited list, page 57

General guidelines for listing authors

The formatting of authors' names in items 1–12 applies to all sources—books, articles, Web sites—in print, on the Web, or in other media. For more models of specific source types, see items 13–79.

1. Single author

author: last
name first   title (book)   publisher

Bowker, Gordon. *James Joyce: A New Biography*. Farrar, Straus and Giroux,

year

2012.

2. Two authors

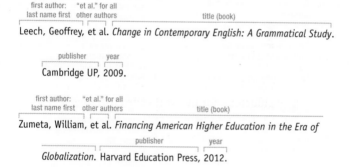

first author:
last name first

second author:
in normal order

title (book)

Gourevitch, Philip, and Errol Morris. *Standard Operating Procedure.*

publisher

year

Penguin Books, 2008.

3. Three or more authors   Name the first author followed by "et al." (Latin for "and others"). In an in-text citation, use the same form for the authors' names as you use in the works cited entry. See item 7 on page 44.

first author:
last name first

"et al." for all
other authors

title (book)

Leech, Geoffrey, et al. *Change in Contemporary English: A Grammatical Study.*

publisher

year

Cambridge UP, 2009.

first author:
last name first

"et al." for all
other authors

title (book)

Zumeta, William, et al. *Financing American Higher Education in the Era of*

publisher

year

Globalization. Harvard Education Press, 2012.

4. Organization or company as author

author: organization
name, not abbreviated

title (book)

publisher

Human Rights Watch. *World Report of 2015: Events of 2014.* Seven Stories Press,

year

2015.

Your in-text citation also should treat the organization as the author (see item 8 on p. 44).

Directory to MLA works cited models (*cont.*)

General guidelines for the works cited list

In the list of works cited, include only sources that you have quoted, summarized, or paraphrased in your paper. MLA's guidelines are applicable to a wide variety of sources. At times you may find that you have to adapt the guidelines and models in this section to source types you encounter in your research.

Organization of the list

The elements, or pieces of information, needed for a works cited entry are the following:

- The author (if a work has one)
- The title
- The title of the larger work in which the source is located (MLA calls this a "container")—a collection, a journal, a magazine, a Web site, and so on
- As much of the following information as is available about the source and the container:

  Editor, translator, director, performer

  Version

  Volume and issue numbers

  Publisher or sponsor

  Date of publication

  Location of the source: page numbers, URL, DOI, and so on

Not all sources will require every element. See specific models in this section for more details.

Authors

- Arrange the list alphabetically by authors' last names or by titles for works with no authors.
- For the first author, place the last name first, a comma, and the first name. Put a second author's name in normal order (first name followed by last name). For three or more authors, use "et al." after the first author's name.
- Spell out "editor," "translator," "edited by," and so on. →

General guidelines for the works cited list (*cont.*)

Titles

- In titles of works, capitalize all words except articles (*a, an, the*), prepositions, coordinating conjunctions, and the *to* in infinitives — unless the word is first or last in the title or subtitle.
- Use quotation marks for titles of articles and other short works.
- Italicize titles of books and other long works.

Publication information

- MLA no longer requires the place of publication for a book publisher.
- Use the complete version of publishers' names, except for terms such as "Inc." and "Co."; retain terms such as "Books" and "Press." For university publishers, use "U" and "P" for "University" and "Press."
- For a book, take the name of the publisher from the title page (or from the copyright page if it is not on the title page). For a Web site, the publisher might be at the bottom of a page or on the "About" page. If a work has two or more publishers, separate the names with slashes.
- If the title of a Web site and the publisher are the same or similar, use the title of the site but omit the publisher.

Dates

- For a book, give the most recent year on the title page or the copyright page. For a Web source, use the copyright date or the most recent update date. Use the complete date as listed in the source. (See item 13a.)
- Abbreviate all months except May, June, and July and give the date in inverted form: 13 Mar. 2016.
- If the source has no date, give your date of access at the end: Accessed 24 Feb. 2016.

Page numbers

- For most articles and other short works, give page numbers when they are available, preceded by "p." (or "pp." for more than one page).
- Do not use the page numbers from a printout of a Web source. →

General guidelines for the works cited list (cont.)

- If an article does not appear on consecutive pages, give the number of the first page followed by a plus sign: 35+.

URLs and DOIs

- Give a permalink or a DOI (digital object identifier) if a source has one. (See item 14c.)

- If a source does not have a permalink or a DOI, include a URL (omitting the protocol, such as http://).

- For a library's subscription database, such as Academic ASAP or JSTOR, include only the basic URL for the database home page. (See item 15d.)

- For open databases and archives, such as Google Books, give the complete URL for the source. (See item 30c.)

5. No author listed

a. Article or other short work

article title
newspaper title
(city in brackets)
date

"Policing Ohio's Online Courses." *Plain Dealer* [Cleveland], 9 Oct. 2012,

page(s)   label

p. A5. Editorial.

article title
title of
Web site
publisher

"Chapter 2: What Can Be Patented?" *Lemelson-MIT*, Massachusetts Institute

URL

of Technology, lemelson.mit.edu/resources/chapter-2-what-can

date of access
for undated site

-be-patented. Accessed 4 Apr. 2016.

b. Television program

episode title
title of
TV show
producer   network

"Fast Times at West Philly High." *Frontline*, produced by Debbie Morton, PBS,

date

2012.

5. No author listed (*cont.*)

c. Book, entire Web site, or other long work

title (Web site)

Women of Protest: Photographs from the Records of the National Woman's Party.

publisher/sponsor   URL

Library of Congress, www.loc.gov/collections/women-of-protest/.

date of access
for undated site

Accessed 1 May 2015.

TIP: Often the author's name is available but is not easy to find. It may appear at the end of the page, in tiny print, or on another

How to answer the basic question "Who is the author?"

PROBLEM: Sometimes when you need to cite a source, it's not clear who the author is. This is especially true for sources on the Web or other nonprint sources, which may have been created by one person and uploaded by a different person or an organization. Whom do you cite as the author in such a case? How do you determine who *is* the author?

EXAMPLE: The video "Surfing the Web on the Job" (see below) was uploaded to YouTube by CBSNewsOnline. Is the person or organization who uploads the video the author of the video? Not necessarily.

Surfing the Web on The Job

CBSNewsOnline · 42,491 videos

▶ Subscribe   85,736

Uploaded on Nov 12, 2009
As the Internet continues to emerge as a critical facet of everyday life, CBS News' Daniel Sieberg reports that companies are cracking down on employees' personal Web use.

CBS News.

page of the site, such as the home page. Also, an organization or a government may be the author (see items 4 and 70).

6. Two or more works by the same author First alphabetize the works by title (ignoring the article *A, An,* or *The* at the beginning of a title). Use the author's name for the first entry; for subsequent entries, use three hyphens and a period. The three hyphens must stand for exactly the same name as in the first entry.

García, Cristina. *Dreams of Significant Girls.* Simon and Schuster, 2011.

---. *The Lady Matador's Hotel.* Scribner, 2010.

7. Two or more works by the same group of authors Alphabetize the works by title. Use the authors' names in the proper

STRATEGY: After you view or listen to the source a few times, ask yourself whether you can tell who is chiefly responsible for creating the content in the source. It might be an organization. It might be an identifiable individual. This video consists entirely of reporting by Daniel Sieberg, so in this case the author is Sieberg.

CITATION: To cite the source, you would use the basic MLA guidelines for a video found on the Web (item 55).

author:
last name first   title of video   Web site
                                              title   update date

Sieberg, Daniel. "Surfing the Web on the Job." *YouTube,* 12 Nov. 2009,

                  URL

www.youtube.com/watch?v=1wLhNwY-enY.

If you want to include the person or organization who uploaded the video, you can add it as supplementary information.

author:
last name first   title of video   Web site   supplementary
                                              title   information

Sieberg, Daniel. "Surfing the Web on the Job." *YouTube,* uploaded by

            update date   URL

CBSNewsOnline, 12 Nov. 2009, www.youtube.com/watch?v=1wLhNwY-enY.

form for the first entry. Begin subsequent entries with three hyphens and a period. The three hyphens must stand for the same names as in the first entry.

Agha, Hussein, and Robert Malley. "The Arab Counterrevolution." *The New York Review of Books*, 29 Sept. 2011, www.nybooks.com/articles/2011/09/29/arab-counterrevolution/.

---. "This Is Not a Revolution." *The New York Review of Books*, 8 Nov. 2012, www.nybooks.com/articles/2012/11/08/not-revolution/.

8. Editor or translator   Begin with the editor's or translator's name. After the name(s), add "editor" (or "editors") or "translator" (or "translators").

first editor: last name first   other editor: in normal order   title (book)

Horner, Avril, and Anne Rowe, editors. *Living on Paper: Letters from Iris Murdoch.*

publisher   year

Princeton UP, 2016.

9. Author with editor or translator   Begin with the name of the author. Place the editor's or translator's name after the title.

author: last name first   title (book)   translator: in normal order

Ullmann, Regina. *The Country Road: Stories.* Translated by Kurt Beals,

publisher   year

New Directions Publishing, 2015.

10. Graphic narrative or other illustrated work   If a work has both an author and an illustrator, the order in your citation will depend on which of those persons you emphasize in your paper.

a. Author first   If you emphasize the author's work, begin with the author's name. After the title, add "Illustrated by" followed by the illustrator's name.

Gaiman, Neil. *The Sandman: Overture*. Illustrated by J. H. William III, DC
    Comics, 2015.

b. Illustrator first   If you emphasize the illustrator, begin your citation with the illustrator's name and the label "illustrator." After the title of the work, put the author's name, preceded by "By."

Kerascoët, illustrator. *Beautiful Darkness*. By Fabien Vehlmann, Drawn and
    Quarterly, 2014.

c. Author and illustrator the same person   If the illustrator and the author are the same person, cite the work as you would any other work with one author (not using any labels).

Ulinich, Anya. *Lena Finkle's Magic Barrel: A Graphic Novel*. Penguin Books, 2014.

11. Author using a pseudonym (pen name) or screen name   Give the author's name as it appears in the source (the pseudonym), followed by the author's real name, if available, in parentheses. (For screen names in social media, see items 78 and 79 on pp. 104 and 105.)

Grammar Girl (Mignon Fogarty). "Lewis Carroll: He Loved to Play with
    Language." *QuickandDirtyTips.com*, 21 May 2015, www.quickanddirtytips
    .com/education/grammar/lewis-carroll-he-loved-to-play-with-language.

Pauline. Comment on "Is This the End?" by James Atlas. *The New York Times*,
    25 Nov. 2012, nyti.ms/1BRUvqQ.

12. Author quoted by another author (indirect source)   If one of your sources uses a quotation from another source and you'd like to use the quotation, provide a works cited entry for the source in which you found the quotation. In your in-text citation, indicate that the quoted words appear in the source (see item 23 on p. 49). In the following examples, Belmaker is the source in the works cited list; Townson is quoted in Belmaker.

SOURCE (BELMAKER) QUOTING ANOTHER SOURCE (TOWNSON)

Peter Townson, a journalist working with the DOHA Center for Press Freedom in Qatar, says there is one obvious reason that some countries in the Middle East have embraced social media so heartily. "It's kind of the preferred way for people to get news, because they know there's no self-censorship involved," Townson said in a phone interview.

WORKS CITED ENTRY

Belmaker, Genevieve. "Five Ways Journalists Can Use Social Media for On-the-Ground Reporting in the Middle East." *Poynter*, 19 Nov. 2012, www.poynter.org/2012/5-ways-journalists-can-use-social -media-for-on-the-ground-reporting-in-the-middle-east/195899/.

IN-TEXT CITATION

Peter Townson points out that social media in the Middle East are "kind of the preferred way for people to get news, because they know there's no self-censorship involved" (qtd. in Belmaker).

Articles and other short works

- Citation at a glance: Article in a journal, page 66
- Citation at a glance: Article from a database, page 68

13. Basic format for an article or other short work

a. Print

author:
last name first   article title   journal title

Tilman, David. "Food and Health of a Full Earth." *Daedalus,*

volume,
issue   date   page(s)

vol. 144, no. 4, Fall 2015, pp. 5-7.

b. Web

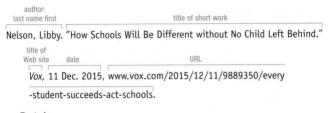

Nelson, Libby. "How Schools Will Be Different without No Child Left Behind."

Vox, 11 Dec. 2015, www.vox.com/2015/12/11/9889350/every

-student-succeeds-act-schools.

c. Database

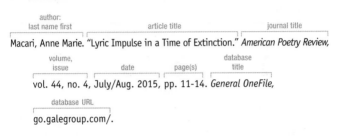

Macari, Anne Marie. "Lyric Impulse in a Time of Extinction." *American Poetry Review,*

vol. 44, no. 4, July/Aug. 2015, pp. 11-14. *General OneFile,*

go.galegroup.com/.

14. Article in a journal

a. Print

author: last
name first | article title | journal title

Matchie, Thomas. "Law versus Love in *The Round House*." *Midwest Quarterly,*

volume,
issue | date | page(s)

vol. 56, no. 4, Summer 2015, pp. 353-64.

b. Online journal

Cáceres, Sigfrido Burgos. "Towards Concert in Africa: Seeking Progress and Power

through Cohesion and Unity." *African Studies Quarterly,* vol. 12, no. 4,

Fall 2011, pp. 59-73, asq.africa.ufl.edu/files/Caceres-Vol12Is4.pdf.

Citation at a glance | Article in a journal (MLA)

To cite an article in a print journal in MLA style, include the following elements:

1 Author(s) of article
2 Title and subtitle of article
3 Title of journal
4 Volume and issue numbers

5 Date of publication (including month or season, if any)
6 Page number(s) of article

JOURNAL TABLE OF CONTENTS

RHETORIC REVIEW ❸

Volume 31, Number 4, 2012

❹ ❺

Articles

FIRST PAGE OF ARTICLE

Rhetoric Review, Vol. 31, No. 4, 371–388, 2012
Copyright © Taylor & Francis Group, LLC
ISSN: 0735-0198 print / 1532-7981 online
DOI: 10.1080/07350198.2012.711196

R Routledge
Taylor & Francis Group

1 JOSEPH TURNER

University of Delaware

2 *Sir Gawain and the Green Knight* and the History of Medieval Rhetoric

During the Middle Ages, rhetoric and literature were thoroughly intertwined, whereas current notions of disciplinarity, in which literature and rhetoric are constructed as separate traditions, muddy our understanding of medieval

WORKS CITED ENTRY FOR AN ARTICLE IN A PRINT JOURNAL

    1   **2**

Turner, Joseph. "*Sir Gawain and the Green Knight* and the History of Medieval

             3   **4**   **5**   **6**

    Rhetoric." *Rhetoric Review,* vol. 31, no. 4, 2012, pp. 371-88.

For more on citing articles in MLA style, see items 13–16.

14. Article in a journal (*cont.*)

c. Database

author:
last name first   article title   journal title

Maier, Jessica. "A 'True Likeness': The Renaissance City Portrait." *Renaissance*

               volume,   database
               issue   date   page(s)   title

    Quarterly, vol. 65, no. 3, Fall 2012, pp. 711-52. *JSTOR,*

           DOI

    doi:10.1086/668300.

Citation at a glance | Article from a database (MLA)

To cite an article from a database in MLA style, include the following elements:

1. Author(s) of article
2. Title and subtitle of article
3. Title of journal, magazine, or newspaper
4. Volume and issue numbers (for journal)
5. Date of publication (including month or season, if any)
6. Page numbers of article
7. Name of database
8. DOI or permalink, if available; otherwise, shortened URL of database

DATABASE RECORD

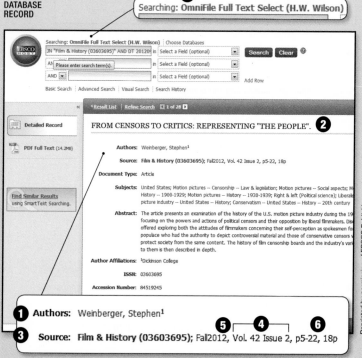

Searching: OmniFile Full Text Select (H.W. Wilson)

IN "Film & History (03603695)" AND DT 201206 in Select a Field (optional) Search Clear

AND Please enter search term(s). in Select a Field (optional)

AND in Select a Field (optional) Add Row

Basic Search | Advanced Search | Visual Search | Search History

Result List | Refine Search | 1 of 28

Detailed Record

PDF Full Text (14.2KB)

Find Similar Results using SmartText Searching.

FROM CENSORS TO CRITICS: REPRESENTING "THE PEOPLE".

Authors: Weinberger, Stephen[1]

Source: Film & History (03603695); Fall2012, Vol. 42 Issue 2, p5-22, 18p

Document Type: Article

Subjects: United States; Motion pictures -- Censorship -- Law & legislation; Motion pictures -- Social aspects; Motion pictures -- History -- 1900-1929; Motion pictures -- History -- 1930-1939; Right & left (Political science); Liberalism; Motion picture industry -- United States -- History; Conservatism -- United States -- History -- 20th century

Abstract: The article presents an examination of the history of the U.S. motion picture industry during the 19... focusing on the powers and actions of political censors and their opposition by liberal filmmakers. Dis... offered exploring both the attitudes of filmmakers concerning their self-perception as spokesmen fo... populace who had the authority to depict controversial material and those of conservative censors v... protect society from the same content. The history of film censorship boards and the industry's vari... to them is then described in depth.

Author Affiliations: [1]Dickinson College

ISSN: 03603695

Accession Number: 84519245

1. **Authors:** Weinberger, Stephen[1]

3. **Source:** Film & History (03603695); Fall2012, Vol. 42 Issue 2, p5-22, 18p

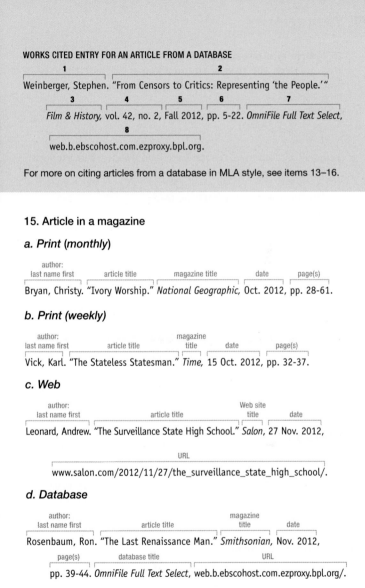

WORKS CITED ENTRY FOR AN ARTICLE FROM A DATABASE

Weinberger, Stephen. "From Censors to Critics: Representing 'the People.'"

Film & History, vol. 42, no. 2, Fall 2012, pp. 5-22. *OmniFile Full Text Select,*

web.b.ebscohost.com.ezproxy.bpl.org.

For more on citing articles from a database in MLA style, see items 13–16.

15. Article in a magazine

a. Print (monthly)

author:
last name first / article title / magazine title / date / page(s)

Bryan, Christy. "Ivory Worship." *National Geographic,* Oct. 2012, pp. 28-61.

b. Print (weekly)

author:
last name first / article title / magazine title / date / page(s)

Vick, Karl. "The Stateless Statesman." *Time,* 15 Oct. 2012, pp. 32-37.

c. Web

author:
last name first / article title / Web site title / date

Leonard, Andrew. "The Surveillance State High School." *Salon,* 27 Nov. 2012,

URL

www.salon.com/2012/11/27/the_surveillance_state_high_school/.

d. Database

author:
last name first / article title / magazine title / date

Rosenbaum, Ron. "The Last Renaissance Man." *Smithsonian,* Nov. 2012,

page(s) / database title / URL

pp. 39-44. *OmniFile Full Text Select,* web.b.ebscohost.com.ezproxy.bpl.org/.

16. Article in a newspaper If the city of publication is not obvious from the title of the newspaper, include the city in brackets after the newspaper title (see item 5a).

a. Print

author:
last name first   article title

Sherry, Allison. "Volunteers' Personal Touch Turns High-Tech Data into Votes."

newspaper
title   date   page(s)

     The Denver Post, 30 Oct. 2012, pp. 1A+.

Bray, Hiawatha. "As Toys Get Smarter, Privacy Issues Emerge." *The Boston Globe*, 10 Dec. 2015, p. C1.

b. Web

author:
last name first   article title

Crowell, Maddy. "How Computers Are Getting Better at Detecting Liars."

Web site
title   date

     The Christian Science Monitor, 12 Dec. 2015,

URL

     www.csmonitor.com/Science/Science-Notebook/2015/

     1212/How-computers-are-getting-better-at-detecting-liars.

c. Database

                    newspaper
    article title   title   date   page(s)   label

"The Road toward Peace." *The New York Times,* 15 Feb. 1945, p. 18. Editorial.

             database title   URL of database

     ProQuest Historical Newspapers: The New York Times, search.proquest

     .com/hnpnewyorktimes.

17. Abstract or executive summary Include the label "Abstract" or "Executive summary," neither italicized nor in quotation marks, at the end of the entry (and before any database information).

a. Abstract of an article

Bottomore, Stephen. "The Romance of the Cinematograph." *Film History*,
    vol. 24, no. 3, July 2012, pp. 341-44. Abstract. *JSTOR*, doi:10.2979/
    filmhistory.24.3.341.

b. Abstract of a paper

Dixon, Rosemary, et al. "The Opportunities and Challenges of Virtual
    Library Systems: A Case Study." Paper presented at the 2011 Chicago
    Colloquium on Digital Humanities and Computer Science, U of Chicago,
    20 Nov. 2011. Abstract.

c. Abstract of a dissertation

Moore, Courtney L. "Stress and Oppression: Identifying Possible Protective
    Factors for African American Men." Dissertation, Chicago School of
    Professional Psychology, 2016. Abstract. *ProQuest Dissertations and
    Theses*, search.proquest.com/docview/1707351557.

d. Executive summary

Pintak, Lawrence. *The Murrow Rural Information Initiative: Final Report*.
    Murrow College of Communication, Washington State U, 25 May 2012.
    Executive summary.

18. Article with a title in its title Use single quotation marks around a title of a short work or a quoted term that appears in an article title. Italicize a title or term normally italicized.

Silber, Nina. "From 'Great Emancipator' to 'Vampire Hunter': The Many
    Stovepipe Hats of Cinematic Lincoln." *Cognoscenti*, WBUR, 22 Nov.
    2012, cognoscenti.wbur.org/2012/11/22/abraham-lincoln-nina-silber.

19. Editorial Cite as a source with no author (see item 5) and use the label "Editorial" at the end.

"City's Blight Fight Making Difference." *The Columbus Dispatch*, 17 Nov. 2015,
www.dispatch.com/content/stories/editorials/2015/11/17/1-citys
-blight-fight-making-difference.html. Editorial.

20. Unsigned article Cite as a source with no author (see item 5).

"Drought and Health." *Centers for Disease Control and Prevention*, 30 July
2012, www.cdc.gov/nceh/drought/default.htm.

21. Letter to the editor Use the label "Letter" at the end of the
entry (and before any database information). If the letter has
no title, place the label directly after the author's name.

Fahey, John A. "Recalling the Cuban Missile Crisis." *The Washington Post,* 28
Oct. 2012, p. A16. Letter. *LexisNexis Library Express*, www.lexisnexis
.com/hottopics/Inpubliclibraryexpress/.

22. Comment on an online article If the writer of the comment uses a screen name, see item 11. After the name, include
"Comment on" followed by the title of the article and the
author of the article (preceded by "by"). Continue with publication information for the article.

author:
screen name   article title

pablosharkman. Comment on "'We Are All Implicated': Wendell Berry Laments

                    author of article

  a Disconnection from Community and the Land," by Scott Carlson.

     Web site title   date   URL

  The Chronicle of Higher Education, 23 Apr. 2012, chronicle.com/article/

  In-Jefferson-Lecture-Wendell/131648.

23. Paper or presentation at a conference If the paper or presentation is included in the proceedings of a conference, cite it as a selection in an anthology or a collection (see item 35; see also item 44 for proceedings of a conference). If you viewed the presentation live, cite it as a lecture or public address (see item 61).

first author: last name first | "et al." for other authors/ contributors | presentation title

Zuckerman, Ethan, et al. "Big Data, Big Challenges, and Big Opportunities."

conference title

Presentation at Wired for Change: The Power and the Pitfalls of Big Data,

conference information | date | URL

Ford Foundation, New York, 15 Oct. 2012, www.fordfoundation.org/

library/multimedia/wired-for-change-big-data-big-challenges-and-big

-opportunities/.

24. Book review Name the reviewer and the title of the review, if any, followed by "Review of" and the title and author of the work reviewed. Add the publication information for the publication in which the review appears. If the review has no author and no title, begin with "Review of" and alphabetize the entry by the first principal word in the title of the work reviewed.

a. Print

Flannery, Tim. "A Heroine in Defense of Nature." Review of *On a Farther Shore: The Life and Legacy of Rachel Carson*, by William Souder. *The New York Review of Books,* 22 Nov. 2012, pp. 21-23.

24. Book review (*cont.*)

b. Web

Della Subin, Anna. "It Has Burned My Heart." Review of *The Lives of Muhammad*, by Kecia Ali. *London Review of Books*, 22 Oct. 2015, www.lrb.co.uk/v37/n20/anna-della-subin/it-has-burned-my-heart.

c. Database

Spychalski, John C. Review of *American Railroads—Decline and Renaissance in the Twentieth Century*, by Robert E. Gallamore and John R. Meyer. *Transportation Journal*, vol. 54, no. 4, Fall 2015, pp. 535-38. *JSTOR*, doi:10.5325/transportationj.54.4.0535.

25. Film review or other review   Name the reviewer and the title of the review, if any, followed by "Review of" and the title and writer or director of the work reviewed. Add the publication information for the publication in which the review appears. If the review has no author and no title, begin with "Review of" and alphabetize the entry by the first principal word in the title of the work reviewed.

a. Print

Lane, Anthony. "Human Bondage." Review of *Spectre*, directed by Sam Mendes. *The New Yorker*, 16 Nov. 2015, pp. 96-97.

b. Web

Savage, Phil. "*Fallout 4* Review." Review of *Fallout 4*, by Bethesda Game Studios. *PC Gamer*, Future Publishing, 8 Nov. 2015, www.pcgamer.com/fallout-4-review/.

26. Performance review   Name the reviewer and the title of the review, if any, followed by "Review of" and the title and author of the work reviewed. Add the publication information for the publication in which the review appears. If the review has no author and no title, begin with "Review of" and alphabetize the entry by the first principal word in the title of the work reviewed.

Stout, Gene. "The Ebullient Florence + the Machine Give KeyArena a
Workout." Review of *How Big How Blue How Beautiful Odyssey*. *The
Seattle Times*, 28 Oct. 2015, www.seattletimes.com/entertainment/
music/the-ebullient-florence-the-machine-give-keyarena-a-workout/.

27. Interview   Begin with the person interviewed, followed by the title of the interview (if there is one). If the interview does not have a title, include the word "Interview" after the interviewee's name. If you wish to include the name of the interviewer, put it after the title of the interview.

a. Print

Weddington, Sarah. "Sarah Weddington: Still Arguing for *Roe*." Interview by
Michele Kort. *Ms.*, Winter 2013, pp. 32–35.

b. Web

Jaffrey, Madhur. "Madhur Jaffrey on How Indian Cuisine Won Western Taste
Buds." Interview by Shadrach Kabango. *Q*, CBC Radio, 29 Oct. 2015,
www.cbc.ca/1.3292918.

c. Television or radio

Putin, Vladimir. Interview by Charlie Rose. *Charlie Rose: The Week*, PBS, 19
June 2015.

d. Personal   To cite an interview that you conducted, begin with the name of the person interviewed. Then write "Personal interview" or "Telephone interview," followed by the date of the interview.

Akufo, Dautey. Personal interview, 11 Apr. 2016.

28. Article in a dictionary or an encyclopedia (including a wiki)
List the author of the entry (if there is one), the title of the
entry, the title of the reference work, the edition number (if
any), the publisher, and the date of the edition. Page numbers are not necessary, even for print sources, because the
entries in the source are arranged alphabetically and are
therefore easy to locate.

a. Print

Robinson, Lisa Clayton. "Harlem Writers Guild." *Africana: The Encyclopedia of
   the African and African American Experience*, 2nd ed., Oxford UP, 2005.

"Ball's in Your Court, The." *The American Heritage Dictionary of Idioms*, 2nd
   ed., Houghton Mifflin Harcourt, 2013.

b. Web

Durante, Amy M. "Finn Mac Cumhail." *Encyclopedia Mythica*, 17 Apr. 2011,
   www.pantheon.org/articles/f/finn_mac_cumhail.html.

"House Music." *Wikipedia*, 16 Nov. 2015, en.wikipedia.org/wiki/House_music.

29. Letter

a. Print   Begin with the writer of the letter, the words "Letter
to" and the recipient, and the date of the letter. Add the title
of the collection, the editor, and publication information.
Add the page range at the end.

Wharton, Edith. Letter to Henry James, 28 Feb. 1915. *Henry James and Edith
   Wharton: Letters, 1900-1915*, edited by Lyall H. Powers, Scribner, 1990,
   pp. 323-26.

b. Web   After information about the letter writer, recipient,
and date (if known), give the location of the document, neither

italicized nor in quotation marks; the name of the Web site or archive, italicized; the publisher or sponsor of the site; and the URL.

Oblinger, Maggie. Letter to Charlie Thomas, 31 Mar. 1895. *Prairie Settlement:*
 Nebraska Photographs and Family Letters, 1862-1912, Library of
 Congress / American Memory, memory.loc.gov/cgi-bin/query/r?ammem/
 ps:@field(DOCID+l306)#l3060001.

c. Personal To cite a letter that you received, begin with the writer's name and add the phrase "Letter to the author," followed by the date.

Primak, Shoshana. Letter to the author, 6 May 2016.

Books and other long works

- Citation at a glance: Book, page 78

30. Basic format for a book

a. Print or e-book If you have used an e-book, give the e-reader type at the end of the entry.

author: last
name first   book title   publisher   date

Wolfe, Tom. *Back to Blood*. Little, Brown, 2012.

Tolstoy, Leo. *War and Peace*. 1869. Translated by Richard Pevear and Larissa
 Volokhonsky, Alfred A. Knopf, 2007. Nook.

b. Web Give whatever print publication information is available for the work, followed by the title of the Web site and the URL.

Citation at a glance | Book (MLA)

To cite a print book in MLA style, include the following elements:

1 Author(s)
2 Title and subtitle
3 Publisher

4 Year of publication (latest year)

TITLE PAGE

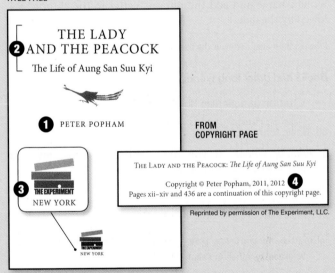

FROM COPYRIGHT PAGE

THE LADY AND THE PEACOCK: *The Life of Aung San Suu Kyi*

Copyright © Peter Popham, 2011, 2012 ❹
Pages xii–xiv and 436 are a continuation of this copyright page.

Reprinted by permission of The Experiment, LLC.

WORKS CITED ENTRY FOR A PRINT BOOK

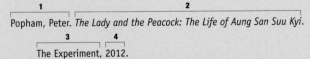

Popham, Peter. *The Lady and the Peacock: The Life of Aung San Suu Kyi.*
The Experiment, 2012.

For more on citing books in MLA style, see items 30–41.

30. Basic format for a book (*cont.*)

b. Web (*cont.*)

Piketty, Thomas. *Capital in the Twenty-First Century*. Translated by Arthur
 Goldhammer, Harvard UP, 2014. *Google Books*, books.google.com/
 books?isbn=0674369556.

Saalman, Lora, editor and translator. *The China-India Nuclear Crossroads*.
 Carnegie Endowment for International Peace, 2012. *Scribd,* www.scribd
 .com/book/142083413/The-China-India-Nuclear-Crossroads.

c. Database

author: last
name first   book title   city and date
of original

Goldsmith, Oliver. *The Vicar of Wakefield: A Tale*. Philadelphia, 1801.

       database title   URL

 America's Historical Imprints, infoweb.newsbank.com.ezproxy.bpl.org/.

31. Parts of a book

a. Foreword, introduction, preface, or afterword

author of foreword:
last name first   book part   book title

Bennett, Hal Zina. Foreword. *Shimmering Images: A Handy Little Guide to*

       author of book:
in normal order   publisher   date

 Writing Memoir, by Lisa Dale Norton, St. Martin's Griffin, 2008,

    page(s)

 pp. xiii-xvi.

Sullivan, John Jeremiah. "The Ill-Defined Plot." Introduction. *The Best
 American Essays 2014*, edited by Sullivan, Houghton Mifflin Harcourt,
 2014, pp. xvii-xxvi.

31. Parts of a book (*cont.*)

b. Chapter in a book

Rizga, Kristina. "Mr. Hsu." *Mission High: One School, How Experts Tried to Fail It, and the Students and Teachers Who Made It Triumph*, Nation Books, 2015, pp. 89-114.

32. Book with a title in its title   If the book title contains a title normally italicized, neither italicize the internal title nor place it in quotation marks. If the title within the title is normally put in quotation marks, retain the quotation marks and italicize the entire book title.

Shanahan, Timothy. *Philosophy and* Blade Runner. Palgrave Macmillan, 2014.

Lethem, Jonathan. *"Lucky Alan" and Other Stories*. Doubleday, 2015.

33. Book in a language other than English   If your readers are not familiar with the language of the book, include a translation of the title in brackets. Capitalize the title according to the conventions of the book's language.

Vargas Llosa, Mario. *El sueño del celta* [*The Dream of the Celt*]. Alfaguara Ediciones, 2010.

34. Entire anthology or collection   An anthology is a collection of works on a common theme, often with different authors for the selections and usually with an editor for the entire volume.

editor:
last name first
title of
anthology
publisher
date

Marcus, Ben, editor. *New American Stories*. Vintage Books, 2015.

35. One selection from an anthology or a collection

- Citation at a glance: Selection from an anthology or a collection, page 82

author of selection   title of selection   title of anthology

Sayrafiezadeh, Saïd. "Paranoia." *New American Stories,* edited by

editor(s) of anthology   publisher   date   page(s)

Ben Marcus, Vintage Books, 2015, pp. 3-29.

36. Two or more selections from an anthology or a collection

For two or more works from the same anthology, provide an entry for the entire anthology (see item 34) and a shortened entry for each selection. Alphabetize the entries by authors' or editors' last names.

author of selection   title of selection   editor(s) of anthology   page(s)

Eisenberg, Deborah. "Some Other, Better Otto." Marcus, pp. 94-136.

editor: last name first   title of anthology   publisher   date

Marcus, Ben, editor. *New American Stories.* Vintage Books, 2015.

author of selection   title of selection   editor(s) of anthology   page(s)

Sayrafiezadeh, Saïd. "Paranoia." Marcus, pp. 3-29.

37. Edition other than the first

Include the number of the edition (2nd, 3rd, and so on). If the book has a translator or an

(continued on p. 84)

Citation at a glance | Selection from an anthology or a collection (MLA)

To cite a selection from an anthology in MLA style, include the following elements:

1 Author(s) of selection
2 Title and subtitle of selection
3 Title and subtitle of anthology

4 Editor(s) of anthology
5 Publisher
6 Year of publication
7 Page numbers of selection

TITLE PAGE OF ANTHOLOGY

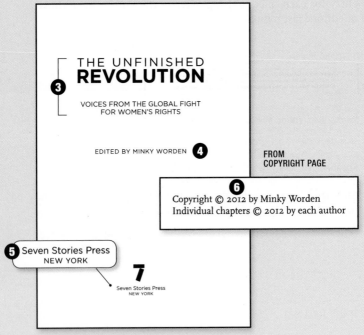

THE UNFINISHED
REVOLUTION

VOICES FROM THE GLOBAL FIGHT
FOR WOMEN'S RIGHTS

EDITED BY MINKY WORDEN **4**

FROM
COPYRIGHT PAGE

6
Copyright © 2012 by Minky Worden
Individual chapters © 2012 by each author

5 Seven Stories Press
NEW YORK

7
Seven Stories Press
NEW YORK

FIRST PAGE OF SELECTION

CHAPTER 3

② Technology's Quiet Revolution for Women

① Isobel Coleman

On the eve of Egypt's January 2011 revolution, I happened to be in Cairo, having dinner with Gamila Ismail, a longtime Egyptian political activist who had spent decades opposing the Mubarak regime. "What will happen tomorrow?" I asked her, referring to the public demonstration planned for the next day in Tahrir Square. "It will be the huge," she insisted, monitoring Twitter and Facebook feeds on her cell phone. Gamila and a young assistant had spent weeks helping to organize the demonstration through social media. "We think hundreds of thousands of people could join the protest. This could finally be our moment for real change." Indeed.

Much has been made of the role of social media in the Arab uprisings, in particular how it has given voice to youth and women in unprecedented ways. But social media is just the latest in a long line of technologies that have been driving profound changes in civil society for centuries. From the first notions of community developed

Isobel Coleman, a senior fellow at the Council on Foreign Relations, is the Director of the Council's Civil Society, Markets, and Democracy Initiative and CFR's Women and Foreign Policy Program. She is the author of Paradise Beneath Her Feet: How Women Are Transforming the Middle East (Random House, 2010) and a contributing author to Restoring the Balance: A Middle East Strategy for the Next President (Brookings Institution Press, 2008). She has also served as a track leader for the Girls and Women Action Area at the Clinton Global Initiative. In 2011, Newsweek named her as one of "150 Women Who Shake the World."

41 ●──────── ④1 **⑦**

WORKS CITED ENTRY FOR A SELECTION FROM AN ANTHOLOGY

 1 **2** **3**

Coleman, Isobel. "Technology's Quiet Revolution for Women." *The Unfinished*

 4

Revolution: Voices from the Global Fight for Women's Rights, edited by Minky

 5 **6** **7**

Worden, Seven Stories Press, 2012, pp. 41-49.

For more on citing selections from anthologies in MLA style, see items 34–36.

editor in addition to the author, give the name of the translator or editor before the edition number (see item 9 for a book with an editor or a translator).

Eagleton, Terry. *Literary Theory: An Introduction*. 3rd ed., U of Minnesota P, 2008.

38. Multivolume work   Include the total number of volumes at the end of the entry, using the abbreviation "vols." If the volumes were published over several years, give the inclusive dates of publication.

author: last name first	book title		editor(s): in normal order	publisher	inclusive dates

Stark, Freya. *Letters*. Edited by Lucy Moorehead, Compton Press, 1974-82.

total
volumes
8 vols.

If you cite only one volume in your paper, include the volume number before the publisher and give the date of publication for that volume. After the date, give the total number of volumes.

author: last name first	book title		editor(s): in normal order	volume cited	publisher	date of volume

Stark, Freya. *Letters*. Edited by Lucy Moorehead, vol. 5, Compton Press, 1978.

total
volumes
8 vols.

39. Sacred text   Give the title of the edition (taken from the title page), italicized; the editor's or translator's name (if any); and publication information. Add the name of the version, if there is one, before the publisher.

The Oxford Annotated Bible with the Apocrypha. Edited by Herbert G. May and
Bruce M. Metzger, Revised Standard Version, Oxford UP, 1965.

The Qur'an: Translation. Translated by Abdullah Yusuf Ali, Tahrike Tarsile
Qur'an, 2001.

40. Book in a series   After the publication information, give
the series name as it appears on the title page, followed by the
series number, if any.

Denham, A. E., editor. *Plato on Art and Beauty*. Palgrave Macmillan, 2012.
Philosophers in Depth.

41. Republished book   After the title of the book, give the
original year of publication, followed by the current publication information. If the republished book contains new
material, such as an introduction or an afterword, include
information about the new material after the original date.

Trilling, Lionel. *The Liberal Imagination*. 1950. Introduction by Louis Menand,
New York Review Books, 2008.

42. Pamphlet, brochure, or newsletter   Cite a pamphlet, brochure, newsletter, or other small, self-contained publication as
you would a book.

The Legendary Sleepy Hollow Cemetery. Friends of Sleepy Hollow Cemetery,
2008.

43. Dissertation

a. Published   For dissertations that have been published in
book form, italicize the title. After the title, give the label

"Dissertation," the name of the institution, and the year the dissertation was accepted.

Kidd, Celeste. *Rational Approaches to Learning and Development*. Dissertation, U of Rochester, 2013.

b. Unpublished Begin with the author's name, followed by the dissertation title in quotation marks. After the title, add the label "Dissertation," the name of the institution, and the year the dissertation was accepted.

Abbas, Megan Brankley. "Knowing Islam: The Entangled History of Western Academia and Modern Islamic Thought." Dissertation, Princeton U, 2015.

44. Proceedings of a conference Cite as you would a book, adding the name, date, and location of the conference after the title.

Sowards, Stacey K., et al., editors. *Across Borders and Environments: Communication and Environmental Justice in International Contexts*. Proceedings of Eleventh Biennial Conference on Communication and the Environment, 25-28 June 2011, U of Texas at El Paso, International Environmental Communication Association, 2012.

45. Manuscript Give the author, a title or a description of the manuscript, and the date of composition (if known), followed by the location of the manuscript, including a URL if it is found on the Web.

Arendt, Hannah. *Between Past and Future*. 1st draft, Hannah Arendt Papers, Manuscript Division, Library of Congress, pp. 108-50, memory.loc.gov/cgi-bin/ampage?collId=mharendt&fileName=05/050030/050030page.db&recNum=0.

Web sites and parts of Web sites

46. An entire Web site

a. Web site with author or editor

author or editor: title of
last name first   Web site   publisher/sponsor

Railton, Stephen. *Mark Twain in His Times*. Stephen Railton / U of Virginia Library,

date   URL

    2012, twain.lib.virginia.edu/.

Halsall, Paul, editor. *Internet Modern History Sourcebook*. Fordham U, 4 Nov.
    2011, legacy.fordham.edu/halsall/index.asp.

b. Web site with organization as author

government   title of Web site

Transparency International. *Transparency International: The Global Coalition*

date   URL

    against Corruption, 2015, www.transparency.org/.

c. Web site with no author   Begin with the title of the site. If the site has no title, begin with a label such as "Home page."

The Newton Project. U of Sussex, 2016, www.newtonproject.sussex.ac.uk/
    prism.php?id=1.

d. Web site with no title   Use the label "Home page" or another appropriate description in place of a title.

Bae, Rebecca. Home page. Iowa State U, 2015, www.engl.iastate.edu/
    rebecca-bae-directory-page/.

Citation at a glance | Short work from a Web site (MLA)

To cite a short work from a Web site in MLA style, include the following elements:

1. Author(s) of short work (if any)
2. Title and subtitle of short work
3. Title and subtitle of Web site
4. Publisher or sponsor of Web site (unless it is the same as the title of site)
5. Update date
6. URL of page (or home page of site)
7. Date of access (if no update date on site)

INTERNAL PAGE OF WEB SITE

FOOTER ON PAGE

WORKS CITED ENTRY FOR A SHORT WORK FROM A WEB SITE

2 **3** **6**

"Losing a Country, Finding a Home." *Amherst College,* www.amherst.edu/

7

academiclife/departments/russian/acrc/lcfh. Accessed 4 Jan. 2016.

For more on citing sources from Web sites in MLA style, see items 47 and 48.

47. Short work from a Web site

• Citation at a glance: Short work from a Web site, page 88

a. Short work with author

author: last name first / title of short work / title of Web site

Gallagher, Sean. "The Last Nomads of the Tibetan Plateau." *Pulitzer Center on*

date / URL

Crisis Reporting, 25 Oct. 2012, pulitzercenter.org/reporting/china

-glaciers-global-warming-climate-change-ecosystem-tibetan-plateau

-grasslands-nomads.

b. Short work with no author

title of article / title of Web site

"Social and Historical Context: Vitality." *Arapesh Grammar and Digital*

sponsor

Language Archive Project, Institute for Advanced Technology in the

URL

Humanities, www.arapesh.org/socio_historical_context_vitality.php.

date of access

Accessed 22 Mar. 2016.

48. Long work from a Web site

author: last   title of   title of
name first   long work   Web site   date

Milton, John. *Paradise Lost: Book I*. Poetry Foundation, 2014,

                                URL

www.poetryfoundation.org/poem/174987.

49. Entire blog Cite a blog as you would an entire Web site (see item 46).

Ng, Amy. *Pikaland*. Pikaland Media, 2015, www.pikaland.com/.

50. Blog post or comment Cite a blog post or comment as you would a short work from a Web site (see item 47). If the post or comment has no title, use the label "Blog post" or "Blog comment." Follow with the remaining information as for an entire blog (see item 49). (See item 11 for the use of screen names.)

author: last   title of   publisher/
name first   title of blog post   blog   sponsor   date

Eakin, Emily. "*Cloud Atlas*'s Theory of Everything." *NYR Daily*, NYREV, 2 Nov. 2012,

                                    URL

www.nybooks.com/daily/2012/11/02/ken-wilber-cloud-atlas/.

author:
screen name   label   title of blog post

mitchellfreedman. Comment on "*Cloud Atlas*'s Theory of Everything," by

        author of   title of   publisher/
        blog post   blog   sponsor   date   URL

Emily Eakin. *NYR Daily*, NYREV, 3 Nov. 2012, www.nybooks.com/

daily/2012/11/02/ken-wilber-cloud-atlas/.

51. Academic course or department home page   Cite as a short work from a Web site (see item 47). For a course home page, begin with the name of the instructor and the title of the course or title of the page (use "Course home page" if there is no other title). For a department home page, begin with the name of the department and the label "Department home page." End with the URL.

Masiello, Regina. 355:101: Expository Writing. *Rutgers School of Arts and Sciences*, 2016, wp.rutgers.edu/courses/55-355101.

Film Studies. Department home page. *Wayne State University, College of Liberal Arts and Sciences*, 2016, clas.wayne.edu/FilmStudies/.

Audio, visual, and multimedia sources

52. Podcast

author:
last name first · · · · · · · · · podcast title · · · · · · · · · Web site title · · · · · publisher/sponsor

Tanner, Laura. "Virtual Reality in 9/11 Fiction." *Literature Lab*, Department of

URL

English, Brandeis U, www.brandeis.edu/departments/english/literaturelab/

date of access

tanner.html. Accessed 14 Feb. 2016.

McDougall, Christopher. "How Did Endurance Help Early Humans Survive?" *TED Radio Hour*, National Public Radio, 20 Nov. 2015, www.npr.org/ 2015/11/20/455904655/how-did-endurance-help-early-humans-survive.

53. Film   Generally, begin the entry with the title, followed by the director and lead performers, as in the first example. If your paper emphasizes one or more people involved with the film, you may begin with those names, as in the second example.

film title

Birdman or (The Unexpected Virtue of Ignorance). Directed by

director   major performers

Alejandro González Iñárritu, performances by Michael Keaton, Emma

distributor

Stone, Zach Galifianakis, Edward Norton, and Naomi Watts, Fox Searchlight,

release
date

2014.

director:
last name first   film title   major performers

Scott, Ridley, director. *The Martian*. Performances by Matt Damon, Jessica

release
distributor   date

Chastain, Kristen Wiig, and Kate Mara, Twentieth Century Fox, 2015.

54. Supplementary material accompanying a film Begin with
the title of the supplementary material, in quotation marks,
and the names of any important contributors, as for a film.
End with information about the film, as in item 53, and about
the location of the supplementary material.

"Sweeney's London." Produced by Eric Young. *Sweeney Todd: The Demon Barber
    of Fleet Street*, directed by Tim Burton, DreamWorks, 2007, disc 2.

55. Video or audio from the Web Cite video or audio that you
accessed on the Web as you would a short work from a Web
site (see item 47), giving information about the author before
other information about the video or audio.

author: Web site
last name first   title of video   title   date   URL

Lewis, Paul. "Citizen Journalism." *YouTube*, 14 May 2011, www.youtube.com/

    watch?v=9AP09_yNbcg.

author:
last name first   title of video   Web site title

Fletcher, Antoine. "The Ancient Art of the Atlatl." *Russell Cave National*

                                narrator   publisher/sponsor

Monument, narrated by Brenton Bellomy, National Park Service,

        date   URL

12 Feb. 2014, www.nps.gov/media/video/view.htm?id=C92C0D0A

-1DD8-B71C-07CBC6 E8970CD73F.

author:
last name first   title of video   Web site
                                                 title   date   URL

Burstein, Julie. "Four Lessons in Creativity." *TED,* Feb. 2012, www.ted.com/

talks/julie_burstein_4_lessons_in_creativity.

56. Video game   List the developer or author of the game (if any); the title, italicized; the version, if there is one; and the distributor and date of publication. If the game can be played on the Web, add information as for a work from a Web site (see item 47).

Firaxis Games. *Sid Meier's Civilization Revolution*. Take-Two Interactive, 2008.

Edgeworld. Atom Entertainment, 1 May 2012, www.kabam.com/games/edgeworld.

57. Computer software or app   Cite as a video game (see item 56), giving whatever information is available about the version, distributor, and date.

Words with Friends. Version 5.84. Zynga, 2013.

58. Television or radio episode or program   If you are citing an episode or a segment of a program, begin with the title of the episode or segment, in quotation marks. Then give the title of the program, italicized; relevant information about the program, such as the writer, director, performers, or narrator; the episode number (if any); the network; and the date of broadcast.

For a program you accessed on the Web, after the information about the program give the network, the original broadcast date, and the URL. If you are citing an entire program (not an episode or a segment), begin your entry with the title of the program, italicized.

How to cite a source reposted from another source

PROBLEM: Some sources that you find online, particularly on blogs or on video-sharing sites, did not originate with the person who uploaded or published the source online. In such a case, how do you give proper credit for the source?

EXAMPLE: Say you need to cite President John F. Kennedy's inaugural address. You have found a video on YouTube that provides footage of the address (see image). The video was uploaded by PaddyIrishMan2 on October 29, 2006. But clearly, PaddyIrishMan2 is not the author of the video or of the address.

JFK Inaugural Address 1 of 2

 PaddyIrishMan2 · 12 videos

▶ Subscribe ⟨ 403

Uploaded on Oct 29, 2006
President John F. Kennedy's inaugural address, January 20th 1961.

Vice President Johnson, Mr. Speaker, Mr. Chief Justice, President Eisenhower, Vice President Nixon, President Truman, reverend clergy, fellow citizens, we observe today not a victory of party, but a celebration of freedom — symbolising an end, as well as a beginning — signifying renewal, as well as change. For I have

---

John F. Kennedy Presidential Library and Museum.

a. Broadcast

title of episode   program title
"Federal Role in Support of Autism." *Washington Journal,* narrated by

narrator / broadcast network / date
Robb Harleston, C-SPAN, 1 Dec. 2012.

The Daily Show with Trevor Noah. Comedy Central, 18 Nov. 2015.

STRATEGY: Start with what you know. The source is a video that you viewed on the Web. For this particular video, John F. Kennedy is the speaker and the author of the inaugural address. PaddyIrishMan2 is identified as the person who uploaded the source to YouTube.

CITATION: To cite the source, you can combine the basic MLA guidelines for a lecture or public address (see item 61) and for a video found on the Web (see item 55).

author/speaker: last name first / title of address / Web site title / update date
Kennedy, John F. "JFK Inaugural Address: 1 of 2." *YouTube,* 29 Oct. 2006,

URL
www.youtube.com/watch?v=xE0iPY7XGBo.

Because Kennedy's inauguration is a well-known historical event, you can be fairly certain that this is not the only version of the inauguration video. It is a good idea, therefore, to include information about the version you viewed as supplementary information.

author/speaker: last name first / title of address / Web site title / supplementary information
Kennedy, John F. "JFK Inaugural Address: 1 of 2." *YouTube,* uploaded by

update date / URL
PaddyIrishMan2, 29 Oct. 2006, www.youtube.com/watch?v=xE0iPY7XGBo.

NOTE: If your work calls for a primary source, you should try to find the original source of the video; a reference librarian can help.

58. Television or radio episode or program (*cont.*)

b. Web

```
                        program                                              publisher/
   title of episode      title                    narrator        episode    sponsor
```
"The Cathedral." *Reply All,* narrated by Sruthi Pinnamaneni, episode 50, Gimlet Media,

```
        date                        URL
```
    7 Jan. 2016, gimletmedia.com/episode/50-the-cathedral/.

"Take a Giant Step." *Prairie Home Companion*, narrated by Garrison Keillor,

    American Public Media, 27 Feb. 2016, prairiehome.publicradio.org/

    listen/full/?name=phc/2016/02/27/phc_20160227_128.

59. Transcript You might find a transcript related to an interview or a program on a radio or television Web site or in a transcript database. Cite the source as you would an interview (see item 27) or a radio or television program (see item 58). Add the label "Transcript" at the end of the entry.

"How Long Can Florida's Citrus Industry Survive?" *All Things Considered*,

    narrated by Greg Allen, National Public Radio, 27 Nov. 2015, www.npr

    .org/templates/transcript/transcript.php?storyId=457424528. Transcript.

"The Economics of Sleep, Part 1." *Freakonomics Radio*, narrated by Stephen

    J. Dubner, 9 July 2015, freakonomics.com/2015/07/09/the-economics

    -of-sleep-part-1-full-transcript/. Transcript.

60. Performance For a live performance of a concert, a play, a ballet, or an opera, begin with the title of the work performed, italicized (unless it is named by form, number, and key). Then give the author or composer of the work; relevant information such as the director, the choreographer, the conductor, or the major performers; the theater, ballet, or opera company, if any; the theater and location; and the date of the performance.

The Draft. By Peter Snoad, directed by Diego Arciniegas, Hibernian Hall, Boston, 10 Sept. 2015.

Symphony no. 4 in G. By Gustav Mahler, conducted by Mark Wigglesworth, performances by Juliane Banse and Boston Symphony Orchestra, Symphony Hall, Boston, 17 Apr. 2009.

61. Lecture or public address   Begin with the speaker's name, the title of the lecture, the sponsoring organization, location, and date. If you viewed the lecture on the Web, cite as you would a short work from a Web site (see item 47). Add the label "Address" or "Lecture" at the end if it is not clear from the title.

a. Live

Smith, Anna Deavere. "On the Road: A Search for American Character." National Endowment for the Humanities, John F. Kennedy Center for the Performing Arts, Washington, 6 Apr. 2015. Address.

b. Web

Khosla, Raj. "Precision Agriculture and Global Food Security." *US Department of State: Diplomacy in Action*, 26 Mar. 2013, www.state.gov/e/stas/series/212172.htm. Address.

62. Musical score   For both print and online versions, begin with the composer's name; the title of the work, italicized (unless it is named by form, number, and key); and the date of composition. For a print source, give the place of publication, the name of the publisher, and date of publication. For an online source, give the title of the Web site; the publisher or sponsor; the date of Web publication; and the URL.

Beethoven, Ludwig van. Symphony no. 5 in C Minor, op. 67. 1807. *Center for Computer Assisted Research in the Humanities*, Stanford U, 2000, scores .ccarh.org/beethoven/sym/beethoven-sym5-1.pdf.

How to cite course materials

PROBLEM: Sometimes you will be assigned to work with materials that an instructor has uploaded to a course Web site or has handed out in class. Complete publication information may not always be given for such sources. A PDF file or a hardcopy article, for instance, may have a title and an author's name but give no other information. Or a video may not include information about the creator or the date the video was created. When you write a paper using such sources, how should you cite them in your own work?

EXAMPLE: Perhaps your instructor has included a PDF file of an article in a collection of readings on the course Web site (see image at right). You are writing a paper in which you use a passage from the work.

THE IMAGE OF THE RAILROAD IN *ANNA KARENINA*

Gary R. Jahn, University of Minnesota

The motif of the railroad recurs so frequently in Lev Tolstoj's *Anna Karenina* that the conclusion that it is somehow integral to a full understanding of the novel is inescapable. According to a recent study the railroad is mentioned at least thirty-two times in the book,[1] and every reader will remember that Anna and Vronskij first meet at a railway station, that Levin intensely dislikes the railroad, and that Anna commits suicide by leaping under a train.[2]

M. S. Al'tman once asked why Anna, having decided to do away with herself, should have selected such a gruesome method. The question is flippant only in its formulation, and a great deal of scholarly effort has been devoted to answering it. A searching of the extensive biographical data on Tolstoj has amply attested his personal aversion for the railroad. He wrote Turgenev in 1857 that "the railroad is to travel as a whore is to love,"[3] and it is known that he was discomfited to the point of nausea by the swaying of railway carriages. These facts provide a credible physiological basis for the standard, although not unanimous,[4] Soviet view that Levin's dyspeptic attitude toward the railroad is the correlative of Tolstoj's, that the highly autobiographical Levin was expressing Tolstoj's belief that the railroad served only to pander to and further inflame the already monstrous appetite of the idle and privileged for foreign luxuries, and that this belief overlies their mutual resentment of the forces tending to displace the landholding nobility from its position of inherited privilege; forces which the railroad is said to symbolize. The railroad is present in the novel so that it can be attacked, and this is precisely what Levin does in the book which he writes about contemporary Russian life.[5] There is an indubitable measure of truth in this understanding of the railway motif. It does account for Levin's view of the railroad and it is also true that for him the railroad symbolizes forces harmful to the traditional style of life of

From The Slavic and East European Journal 25.2 (Summer 1981): 1-10. Reprinted with permission from AATSEEL of U.S., Inc.

63. Sound recording   Begin with the name of the person you want to emphasize: the composer, conductor, or performer. For a long work, give the title, italicized (unless it is named by form, number, and key); the names of pertinent artists (such as performers, readers, or musicians); and the orchestra and conductor, if relevant. End with the manufacturer and the date.

STRATEGY: Look through this section for a model that matches the type of source you're working with. Is it an article? A chapter from a book? A photograph? A video? The model or models you find will give you an idea of the information you need to gather about the source. The usual required information is (1) the author or creator, (2) the title, (3) the date the work was published or created, and (4) the URL for sources on the Web (see pp. 57–59).

CITATION: For your citation, you can give only as much of the required information as you can find in the source. In this example, you know the source is an article with an author and a title, so you can use item 13a (basic format for an article). Because you don't have much other information about the source, it is a good idea to include the description "Course materials" and supplementary information about the course (such as its title or number and the term).

author:
last name first   article title
Jahn, Gary R. "The Image of the Railroad in *Anna Karenina*."

       supplementary information
   Course materials, EN101, Fall 2013.

NOTE: When in doubt about how much information to include or where to find it, consult your instructor.

Bizet, Georges. *Carmen*. Performances by Jennifer Larmore, Thomas Moser,
　　Angela Gheorghiu, Samuel Ramey, and Bavarian State Orchestra and
　　Chorus, conducted by Giuseppe Sinopoli, Warner, 1996.

Blige, Mary J. "Don't Mind." *Life II: The Journey Continues (Act 1)*, Geffen, 2011.

64. Work of art　(a) For an original work of art, cite the artist's
name; the title of the artwork, italicized; the date of composition; and the institution and city in which the artwork is located. (b) For artworks found on the Web, include the title of
the Web site (unless it is the same as the institution) and the
URL. (c) If you viewed the artwork as a reproduction in a print
source, add publication information about the print source,
including the page number or figure number for the artwork.

a. Original

Bradford, Mark. *Let's Walk to the Middle of the Ocean*. 2015, Museum of
　　Modern Art, New York.

b. Web

Clough, Charles. *January Twenty-First*. 1988-89, Joslyn Art Museum, Omaha,
　　www.joslyn.org/collections-and-exhibitions/permanent-collections/
　　modern-and-contemporary/charles-clough-january-twenty-first/.

c. Reproduction (print)

O'Keeffe, Georgia. *Black and Purple Petunias*. 1925, private collection. *Two
　　Lives: A Conversation in Paintings and Photographs,* edited by Alexandra
　　Arrowsmith and Thomas West, HarperCollins, 1992, p. 67.

65. Photograph　(a) For an original photograph, cite the photographer's name; the title of the photograph, italicized; the
date of composition; and the institution and city in which the
photograph is located. (b) For photographs found on the Web,

include the title of the Web site (unless it is the same as the institution) and the URL. (c) If you viewed the photograph as a reproduction in a print source, add publication information about the print source, including the page number or figure number for the artwork. Add the label "Photograph" at the end if it is not clear from the rest of the entry.

a. Original

Feinstein, Harold. *Hangin' Out, Sharing a Public Bench, NYC.* 1948, Panopticon Gallery, Boston. Photograph.

Finotti, Leonardo. *Edificio Girón, Havana, Cuba.* 2014, Museum of Modern Art, New York. Photograph.

b. Web

Hura, Sohrab. *Old Man Lighting a Fire.* 2015, *Magnum Photos,* www .magnumphotos.com/C.aspx?VP3=SearchResult&ALID=2K1HRG681B_Q.

c. Reproduction (print)

Kertész, André. *Meudon.* 1928, *Street Photography: From Atget to Cartier-Bresson,* by Clive Scott, Tauris, 2011, p. 61.

Michals, Duane. *Self-Portrait Asleep in the Tomb of Mereruka at Sakkara.* 1978, *ABC Duane,* by Michals, Monacelli, 2014, p. 7.

66. Cartoon Give the cartoonist's name; the title of the cartoon, if it has one, in quotation marks; publication information; and the label "Cartoon" at the end. To cite an online cartoon, cite as a short work from a Web site (item 47).

Zyglis, Adam. "City of Light." *Buffalo News,* 8 Nov. 2015, adamzyglis .buffalonews.com/2015/11/08/city-of-light/. Cartoon.

67. Advertisement Name the product or company being advertised and publication information for the source in which the advertisement appears. Add the label "Advertisement" at the end.

AT&T. *National Geographic*, Dec. 2015, p. 14. Advertisement.

Toyota. *The Root*. Slate Group, 28 Nov. 2015, www.theroot.com.
　　Advertisement.

68. Visual such as a table, a chart, or another graphic Cite a visual as you would a short work within a longer work.

"Brazilian Waxing and Waning: The Economy." *The Economist*, 1 Dec.
　　2015, www.economist.com/blogs/graphicdetail/2015/12/
　　economic-backgrounder.

"Number of Measles Cases by Year since 2010." *Centers for Disease Control and
　　Prevention*, 2 Jan. 2016, www.cdc.gov/measles/cases-outbreaks.html.

69. Map Cite a map as you would a short work within a longer work. Or, if the map is published on its own, cite it as a book or another long work. Use the label "Map" at the end if it is not clear from the title or source information.

"Map of Sudan." *Global Citizen*, Citizens for Global Solutions, 2011,
　　globalsolutions.org/blog/bashir#.VthzNMfi_FI.

"Vote on Secession, 1861." *Perry-Castañeda Library Map Collection*, U of
　　Texas at Austin, 1976, www.lib.utexas.edu/maps/atlas_texas/texas
　　_vote_secession_1861.jpg.

Government and legal documents

70. Government document Treat the government agency as the author, giving the name of the government followed by the name of the department and the agency, if any. For sources found on the Web, follow the model for an entire Web site (see item 46) or for short or long works from a Web site (see items 47 and 48).

government   department   agency (or agencies)

United States, Department of Agriculture, Food and Nutrition Service,

                         title (long work)

Child Nutrition Programs. *Eligibility Manual for School Meals:*

                         Web site title

Determining and Verifying Eligibility. National School Lunch Program,

 date   URL

July 2015, www.fns.usda.gov/sites/default/files/cn/SP40_CACFP18_SFSP20

-2015a1.pdf.

government   department   title (long work)

Canada, Minister of Aboriginal Affairs and Northern Development. *2015-16*

                         publisher

Report on Plans and Priorities. Minister of Public Works and Government

                 date

Services Canada, 2015.

71. Testimony before a legislative body

Russel, Daniel R. "Burma's Challenge: Democracy, Human Rights, Peace, and the Plight of the Rohingya." Testimony before the US House Foreign Affairs Committee, Subcommittee on East Asian and Pacific Affairs. *US Department of State: Diplomacy in Action*, 21 Oct. 2015, www.state .gov/p/eap/rls/rm/2015/10/248420.htm.

72. Historical document   The titles of most historical documents, such as the US Constitution and the Canadian Charter of Rights and Freedoms, are neither italicized nor put in quotation marks. For a print version, cite as a selection in an anthology (see item 35) or as a book (with the title not itali-cized). For an online version, cite as a short work from a Web site (see item 47).

Jefferson, Thomas. First Inaugural Address. 1801. *The American Reader: Words That Moved a Nation*, edited by Diane Ravitch, 2nd ed., William Morrow, 2000, pp. 79-82.

Constitution of the United States. 1787. *The Charters of Freedom,* US National Archives and Records Administration, www.archives.gov/exhibits/ charters/.

Magna Carta. 1215. *Britannia History*, www.britannia.com/history/docs/ magna2.html.

73. Legislative act (law)   Begin with the name of the act, nei-ther italicized nor in quotation marks. Then provide the act's Public Law number; its Statutes at Large volume and page numbers; and its date of enactment.

Electronic Freedom of Information Act Amendments of 1996. Pub. L. 104-231. 110 Stat. 3048. 2 Oct. 1996.

74. Court case   Name the first plaintiff and the first defen-dant. Then give the volume, name, and page number of the law report; the court name; the year of the decision; and publication information. Do not italicize the name of the case. (In the text of the paper, the name of the case is itali-cized; see item 19 on p. 48.)

Utah v. Evans. 536 US 452. Supreme Court of the US. 2002. *Legal Information Institute,* Cornell U Law School, www.law.cornell.edu/supremecourt/ text/536/452.

Personal communication and social media

75. E-mail message   Begin with the writer's name and the subject line, using capitalization as for any title. Then write "Received by" followed by the name of the recipient. End with the date of the message.

Lowe, Walter. "Validity of GMAT Review Questions." Received by Rita Anderson,
20 Oct. 2015.

76. Text message

Wiley, Joanna. Message to the author, 4 Apr. 2014.

77. Posting to an online discussion list   When possible, cite archived versions of postings. If you cannot locate an archived version, keep a copy of the posting for your records. Begin with the author's name, followed by the title or subject line, in quotation marks (use the label "Online posting" if the posting has no title). Then proceed as for a short work from a Web site (see item 47).

Robin, Griffith. "Write for the Reading Teacher." *Developing Digital Literacies*,
NCTE, 23 Oct. 2015, ncte.connectedcommunity.org/communities/
community-home/digestviewer/viewthread?GroupId=1693&MID=24520
&tab=digestviewer&CommunityKey=628d2ad6-8277-4042-a376-2b370
ddceabf.

Yen, Jessica. "Quotations within Parentheses (Study Measures)."
Copyediting-L, 18 Mar. 2016, list.indiana.edu/sympa/arc/
copyediting-l/2016-03/msg00492.html.

78. Facebook post or comment   Cite as a short work from a Web site (see item 47), beginning with the writer's screen name followed by the real name in parentheses, if both are given. Otherwise use whatever name is given in the source. Follow with the title of the post, if any, in quotation marks. If there is no title, use the label "Post."

Bedford English. "Stacey Cochran explores Reflective Writing in the classroom and as a writer: http://ow.ly/YkjVB." *Facebook*, 15 Feb. 2016, www.facebook.com/BedfordEnglish/posts/10153415001259607.

79. Twitter post (tweet)   Begin with the writer's screen name followed by the real name in parentheses, if both are given. Otherwise use whatever name is given in the source. Give the text of the entire tweet in quotation marks, using the writer's capitalization and punctuation. Follow the text with the date and time noted on the tweet, and end with the URL.

Curiosity Rover. "Can you see me waving? How to spot #Mars in the night sky: https://youtu.be/hv8hVvJlcJQ." *Twitter*, 5 Nov. 2015, 11:00 a.m., twitter.com/marscuriosity/status/672859022911889408.

@grammarphobia (Patricia T. O'Conner and Steward Kellerman). "Is 'if you will,' like, a verbal tic? #English #language #grammar #etymology #usage #linguistics #WOTD." *Twitter*, 14 Mar. 2016, 9:12 a.m., twitter .com/grammarphobia.

MLA information notes (optional)

Researchers who use the MLA system of parenthetical documentation may also use information notes for one of two purposes:

1. to provide additional material that is important but might interrupt the flow of the paper
2. to refer to several sources that support a single point or to provide comments on sources

Information notes may be either footnotes or endnotes. Footnotes appear at the foot of the page; endnotes appear on a separate page at the end of the paper, just before the list of works cited. For either style, the notes are numbered consecutively throughout the paper. The text of the paper contains a raised arabic numeral that corresponds to the number of the note.

TEXT

In the past several years, employees have filed a number of lawsuits against employers because of online monitoring practices.[1]

NOTE

  1. For a discussion of federal law applicable to electronic surveillance in the workplace, see Kesan 293.

The following guidelines are consistent with advice given in the *MLA Handbook*, eighth edition (MLA, 2016), and with typical requirements for student papers. For a sample MLA research paper, see pages 112–20.

MLA manuscript format

Formatting the paper

Papers written in MLA style should be formatted as follows.

Font   If your instructor does not require a specific font, choose one that is standard and easy to read (such as Times New Roman).

Title and identification   MLA does not require a title page. On the first page of your paper, place your name, your instructor's name, the course title, and the date on separate lines against the left margin. Then center your title. (See p. 112 for a sample first page.)

If your instructor requires a title page, ask for formatting guidelines. A format similar to the one on page 156 may be acceptable.

Page numbers (running head)   Put the page number preceded by your last name in the upper right corner of each page, one-half inch below the top edge. Use arabic numerals (1, 2, 3, and so on).

Margins, line spacing, and paragraph indents   Leave margins of one inch on all sides of the page. Left-align the text.

Double-space throughout the paper. Do not add extra space above or below the title of the paper or between paragraphs.

Indent the first line of each paragraph one-half inch from the left margin.

Capitalization, italics, and quotation marks   In titles of works, capitalize all words except articles (*a, an, the*), prepositions (*to, from, between,* and so on), coordinating conjunctions (*and, but, or, nor, for, so, yet*), and the *to* in infinitives—unless the word is first or last in the title or subtitle. Follow these guidelines in your paper even if the title appears in all capital or all lowercase letters in the source.

In the text of an MLA paper, when a complete sentence follows a colon, lowercase the first word following the colon unless the sentence is a quotation or a well-known expression or principle.

Italicize the titles of books, journals, magazines, and other long works, such as Web sites. Use quotation marks around the titles of articles, short stories, poems, and other short works.

Long quotations   When a quotation is longer than four typed lines of prose or three lines of poetry, set it off from the text by indenting the entire quotation one-half inch from the left margin. Double-space the indented quotation and do not add extra space above or below it.

Do not use quotation marks when a quotation has been set off from the text by indenting. See page 117 for an example.

URLs If you need to break a URL at the end of a line in the text of a paper, break it only after a slash or a double slash or before any other mark of punctuation. Do not add a hyphen. If you will post your project online or submit it electronically and you want your readers to click on your URLs, do not insert any line breaks. For MLA guidelines on dividing URLs in your list of works cited, see page 110.

Headings MLA neither encourages nor discourages the use of headings and provides no guidelines for their use. If you would like to insert headings in a long essay or research paper, check first with your instructor.

Visuals MLA classifies visuals as tables and figures (figures include graphs, charts, maps, photographs, and drawings). Label each table with an arabic numeral ("Table 1," "Table 2," and so on) and provide a clear caption that identifies the subject. Capitalize the caption as you would a title; do not italicize the label and caption or place them in quotation marks. Place the label and caption on separate lines above the table, flush with the left margin.

For a table that you have borrowed or adapted, give the source below the table in a note like the following:

Source: Boris Groysberg and Michael Slind, "Leadership Is a Conversation," *Harvard Business Review,* June 2012, p. 83.

For each figure, place the figure number (using the abbreviation "Fig.") and a caption below the figure, flush left. Capitalize the caption as you would a sentence; include source information following the caption. (When referring to the figure in your paper, use the abbreviation "fig." in parenthetical citations; otherwise spell out the word.) See page 114 for an example of a figure in a paper.

Place visuals in the text, as close as possible to the sentences that relate to them, unless your instructor prefers that visuals appear in an appendix.

Preparing the list of works cited

Begin the list of works cited on a new page at the end of the paper. Center the title "Works Cited" about one inch from the top of the page. Double-space throughout. See page 119 for a sample list of works cited.

Alphabetizing the list   Alphabetize the list by the last names of the authors (or editors); if a work has no author or editor, alphabetize by the first word of the title other than *A*, *An*, or *The*.

If your list includes two or more works by the same author, use the author's name for the first entry only. For subsequent entries, use three hyphens followed by a period. List the titles in alphabetical order. (See items 6 and 7 on p. 61.)

Indenting   Do not indent the first line of each works cited entry, but indent any additional lines one-half inch. This technique highlights the names of the authors, making it easy for readers to scan the alphabetized list. See page 117.

URLs   If you need to include a URL in a works cited entry and it must be divided across lines, break it only after a slash or a double slash or before any other mark of punctuation. Do not add a hyphen. If you will post your project online or submit it electronically and you want your readers to click on your URLs, do not insert any line breaks.

Sample MLA research paper

On the following pages is a research paper on the topic of the role of government in legislating food choices, written by Sophie Harba, a student in a composition class. Harba's paper is documented with in-text citations and a list of works cited in MLA style. Annotations in the margins of the paper draw your attention to Harba's use of MLA style and her effective writing.

Sophie Harba

Engl 1101

Professor Baros-Moon

30 April 2013

What's for Dinner? Personal Choices vs. Public Health

Title is centered.

Should the government enact laws to regulate healthy eating choices? Many Americans would answer an emphatic "No," arguing that what and how much we eat should be left to individual choice rather than unreasonable laws. Others might argue that it would be unreasonable for the government not to enact legislation, given the rise of chronic diseases that result from harmful diets. In this debate, both the definition of reasonable regulations and the role of government to legislate food choices are at stake. In the name of public health and safety, state governments have the responsibility to shape health policies and to regulate healthy eating, especially since doing so offers a potentially large social benefit for a relatively small cost.

Debates surrounding the government's role in regulating food have a long history in the United States. According to Larine Goodwin, a food historian, nineteenth-century reformers who sought to purify the food supply were called "fanatics" and "radicals" by critics who argued that consumers should be free to buy and eat what they want (77). Thanks to regulations, though, such as the 1906 federal Pure Food and Drug Act, food, beverages, and medicine are largely free from toxins. In addition, to prevent contamination and the spread of disease, meat and dairy products are now inspected by government agents to ensure that they meet health requirements. Such regulations can be considered reasonable because they protect us from harm with little, if any, noticeable consumer cost. It is not considered an unreasonable infringement on personal

Signal phrase names the author. The parenthetical citation includes a page number.

Harba 2

choice that contaminated meat or arsenic-laced cough drops are *un*available at our local supermarket. Rather, it is an important government function to stop such harmful items from entering the marketplace.

Even though our food meets current safety standards, there is a need for further regulation. Not all food dangers, for example, arise from obvious toxins like arsenic and *E. coli*. A diet that is low in nutritional value and high in sugars, fats, and refined grains—grains that have been processed to increase shelf life but that contain little fiber, iron, and B vitamins—can be damaging over time (United States, Dept. of Agriculture and Dept. of Health and Human Services 36). A graph from the government's *Dietary Guidelines for Americans, 2010* provides a visual representation of the American diet and how far off it is from the recommended nutritional standards (see fig. 1).

Michael Pollan, who has written extensively about Americans' unhealthy eating habits, notes that "[t]he Centers for Disease Control estimates that fully three quarters of US health care spending goes to treat chronic diseases, most of which are preventable and linked to diet: heart disease, stroke, type 2 diabetes, and at least a third of all cancers." In fact, the amount of money the United States spends to treat chronic illnesses is increasing so rapidly that the Centers for Disease Control has labeled chronic disease "the public health challenge of the 21st century" (United States, Dept. of Health and Human Services 1). In fighting this epidemic, the primary challenge is not the need to find a cure; the challenge is to prevent chronic diseases from striking in the first place.

No page number is available for this Web source.

Legislation, however, is not a popular solution when it comes to most Americans and the food they eat. According to a nationwide poll, 75% of Americans are opposed to laws that restrict or put limitations on access to unhealthy foods (Neergaard and Agiesta). When New York mayor Michael Bloomberg proposed a regulation in 2012 banning the

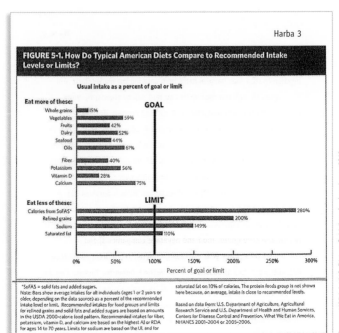

FIGURE 5-1. How Do Typical American Diets Compare to Recommended Intake Levels or Limits?

Usual intake as a percent of goal or limit

Eat more of these:
- Whole grains — 15%
- Vegetables — 59%
- Fruits — 42%
- Dairy — 52%
- Seafood — 44%
- Oils — 61%
- Fiber — 40%
- Potassium — 56%
- Vitamin D — 28%
- Calcium — 75%

GOAL

Eat less of these:
LIMIT
- Calories from SoFAS* — 280%
- Refined grains — 200%
- Sodium — 149%
- Saturated fat — 110%

Percent of goal or limit
0%   50%   100%   150%   200%   250%   300%

*SoFAS = solid fats and added sugars.
Note: Bars show average intakes for all individuals (ages 1 or 2 years or older, depending on the data source) as a percent of the recommended intake level or limit. Recommended intakes for food groups and limits for refined grains and solid fats and added sugars are based on amounts in the USDA 2000-calorie food pattern. Recommended intakes for fiber, potassium, vitamin D, and calcium are based on the highest AI or RDA for ages 14 to 70 years. Limits for sodium are based on the UL and for saturated fat on 10% of calories. The protein foods group is not shown here because, on average, intake is close to recommended levels.

Based on data from: U.S. Department of Agriculture, Agricultural Research Service and U.S. Department of Health and Human Services, Centers for Disease Control and Prevention. What We Eat in America, NHANES 2001-2004 or 2005-2006.

Source: USDA & HHS: Dietary Guidelines for Americans, 2010

Fig. 1. This graph shows that Americans consume about three times more fats and sugars and twice as many refined grains as is recommended but only half of the recommended foods (United States, Dept. of Agriculture and Dept. of Health and Human Services, fig. 5-1).

sale of soft drinks in servings greater than twelve ounces in restaurants and movie theaters, he was ridiculed as "Nanny Bloomberg." In California in 2011, legislators failed to pass a law that would impose a penny-per-ounce tax on soda, which would have funded obesity prevention programs. And in Mississippi, legislators passed "a ban on bans—a law that forbids . . . local restrictions on food or drink" (Conly A23).

Why is the public largely resistant to laws that would limit unhealthy choices or penalize those choices with so-called fat taxes? Many consumers and civil rights advocates find such laws to be an unreasonable restriction on individual freedom of choice. As health policy experts Mello et al. point out, opposition to food and beverage regulation is similar to the opposition to early tobacco legislation: the public views the issue as one of personal responsibility rather than one requiring government intervention (2602). In other words, if a person eats unhealthy food and becomes ill as a result, that is his or her choice. But those who favor legislation claim that freedom of choice is a myth because of the strong influence of food and beverage industry marketing on consumers' dietary habits. According to one nonprofit health advocacy group, food and beverage companies spend roughly two billion dollars per year marketing directly to children. As a result, kids see about four thousand ads per year encouraging them to eat unhealthy food and drinks ("Facts"). As was the case with antismoking laws passed in recent decades, taxes and legal restrictions on junk food sales could help to counter the strong marketing messages that promote unhealthy products.

The United States has a history of state and local public health laws that have successfully promoted a particular behavior by punishing an undesirable behavior. The decline in tobacco use as a result of antismoking taxes and laws is perhaps the most obvious example. Another example is legislation requiring the use of seatbelts, which have significantly reduced fatalities in car crashes. One government agency reports that seatbelt use saved an average of more than fourteen thousand lives per year in the United States between 2000 and 2010 (United States, Dept. of Transportation, Natl. Highway Traffic Safety Administration 231). Perhaps seatbelt laws have public support because the cost of wearing a seatbelt is small, especially when compared with the benefit of saving fourteen thousand lives per year.

Laws designed to prevent chronic disease by promoting healthier food and beverage consumption also have potentially enormous benefits. To give just one example, Marion Nestle, New York University professor of nutrition and public health, notes that "a 1% reduction in the intake of saturated fat across the population would prevent more than 30,000 cases of coronary heart disease annually and would save more than a billion dollars in health care costs" (7). Few would argue that saving lives and dollars is not an enormous benefit. But three-quarters of Americans say they would object to the costs needed to achieve this benefit—the regulations needed to reduce saturated fat intake.

Why do so many Americans believe there is a degree of personal choice lost when regulations such as taxes, bans, or portion limits on unhealthy foods are proposed? Some critics of anti-junk-food laws believe that even if state and local laws were successful in curbing chronic diseases, they would still be unacceptable. Bioethicist David Resnik emphasizes that such policies, despite their potential to make our society healthier, "open the door to excessive government control over food, which could restrict dietary choices, interfere with cultural, ethnic, and religious traditions, and exacerbate socioeconomic inequalities" (31). Resnik acknowledges that his argument relies on "slippery slope" thinking, but he insists that "social and political pressures" regarding food regulation make his concerns valid (31). Yet the social and political pressures that Resnik cites are really just the desire to improve public health, and limiting access to unhealthy,

Harba introduces a direct quotation with a signal phrase and follows with a comment that shows readers why she chose to use source.

artificial ingredients seems a small price to pay. As legal scholars
L. O. Gostin and K. G. Gostin explain, "[I]nterventions that do not
pose a truly significant burden on individual liberty" are justified
if they "go a long way towards safeguarding the health and well-
being of the populace" (214).

To improve public health, advocates such as Bowdoin College
philosophy professor Sarah Conly contend that it is the government's
duty to prevent people from making harmful choices whenever feasible
and whenever public benefits outweigh the costs. In response to critics
who claim that laws aimed at stopping us from eating whatever we
want are an assault on our freedom of choice, Conly offers a persuasive
counterargument:

> [L]aws aren't designed for each one of us individually. Some of
> us can drive safely at 90 miles per hour, but we're bound by the
> same laws as the people who can't, because individual speeding
> laws aren't practical. Giving up a little liberty is something we
> agree to when we agree to live in a democratic society that is
> governed by laws. (A23)

As Conly suggests, we need to change our either/or
thinking (either we have complete freedom of choice *or* we
have government regulations and lose our freedom) to instead
see health as a matter of public good, not individual liberty.
Proposals such as Mayor Bloomberg's that seek to limit portions of
unhealthy beverages aren't about giving up liberty; they are about
asking individuals to choose substantial public health benefits at
a very small cost.

Despite arguments in favor of regulating unhealthy food as a
means to improve public health, public opposition has stood in the

Including the source's credentials makes Harba more credible.

Long quotation is introduced with signal phrase naming author.

Long quotation is set off from the text. Quotation marks are omitted.

way of legislation. Americans freely eat as much unhealthy food as they want, and manufacturers and sellers of these foods have nearly unlimited freedom to promote such products and drive increased consumption, without any requirements to warn the public of potential hazards. Yet mounting scientific evidence points to unhealthy food as a significant contributing factor to chronic disease, which we know is straining our health care system, decreasing Americans' quality of life, and leading to unnecessary premature deaths. Americans must consider whether to allow the costly trend of rising chronic disease to continue in the name of personal choice or whether to support the regulatory changes and public health policies that will reverse that trend.

Harba 8

Works Cited

Conly, Sarah. "Three Cheers for the Nanny State." *The New York Times,*
25 Mar. 2013, p. A23.

"The Facts on Junk Food Marketing and Kids." *Prevention Institute,*
www.preventioninstitute.org/focus-areas/supporting-healthy
-food-a-activity/supporting-healthy-food-and-activity
-environments-advocacy/get-involved-were-not-buying-it/735
-were-not-buying-it-the-facts-on-junk-food-marketing-and-kids
.html. Accessed 21 Apr. 2013.

Goodwin, Lorine Swainston. *The Pure Food, Drink, and Drug Crusaders,*
1879-1914. McFarland, 2006.

Gostin, L. O., and K. G. Gostin, "A Broader Liberty: J. S. Mill,
Paternalism, and the Public's Health." *Public Health*, vol. 123,
no. 3, 2009, pp. 214-21, doi:10.1016/j.puhe.2008.12.024.

Mello, Michelle M., et al. "Obesity—the New Frontier of Public Health
Law." *New England Journal of Medicine,* vol. 354, no. 24, 2006,
pp. 2601-2610, www.nejm.org/doi/pdf/10.1056/NEJMhpr060227.

Neergaard, Lauran, and Jennifer Agiesta. "Obesity's a Crisis but We
Want Our Junk Food, Poll Shows." *Huffington Post*, 4 Jan.
2013, www.huffingtonpost.com/2013/01/04/obesity-junk-food
-government-intervention-poll_n_2410376.html.

Nestle, Marion. *Food Politics: How the Food Industry Influences Nutrition
and Health*. U of California P, 2013.

Pollan, Michael. "The Food Movement, Rising." *The New York Review of
Books*, 10 June 2010, www.nybooks.com/articles/2010/06/10/
food-movement-rising/.

Resnik, David. "Trans Fat Bans and Human Freedom." *American Journal
of Bioethics*, vol. 10, no. 3, Mar. 2010, pp. 27-32.

United States, Department of Agriculture and Department of Health and
Human Services. *Dietary Guidelines for Americans, 2010*, health
.gov/dietaryguidelines/dga2010/dietaryguidelines2010.pdf.

Heading is centered.

List is alphabetized by authors' last names (or by title when a work has no author).

Access date used for an online source with no update date.

First line of each entry is at the left margin; extra lines are indented ½".

Double-spacing is used throughout.

The government agency is used as the author of a government document.

United States, Department of Health and Human Services, Centers
for Disease Control and Prevention. *The Power of Prevention*,
National Center for Chronic Disease Prevention and Health
Promotion, 2009, www.cdc.gov/chronicdisease/pdf/2009-Power
-of-Prevention.pdf.

United States, Department of Transportation, National Highway Traffic
Safety Administration. *Traffic Safety Facts 2010: A Compilation
of Motor Vehicle Crash Data from the Fatality Analysis Reporting
System and the General Estimates System*. 2010, www-nrd.nhtsa
.dot.gov/Pubs/811659.pdf.

Part V: Research and Documentation in History

Finding sources in history

Research in history involves developing an understanding of the past through the examination and interpretation of evidence. Evidence may exist in the form of texts, physical remains of historic sites, recorded data, pictures, maps, artifacts, and so on. The historian's job is to find evidence, analyze its content and biases, back it up with further proof, and use that evidence to develop an interpretation of past events that holds some significance for the present. Historians use libraries to:

- locate primary sources (firsthand information such as diaries, letters, and original documents) for evidence
- find secondary sources (historians' interpretations and analyses of historical evidence)
- verify factual material as inconsistencies arise

Doing historical research is a little like excavating an archaeological site. It requires patience, insight, and imagination as well as diligence and the proper tools. As you find and examine primary sources, you need to imagine them in their original context and understand how your present-day point of view may distort your interpretation of them. You need to recognize not only your own biases but also the biases that shaped primary materials in their own period. You need to brush away the layers of interpretation that time has imposed on these materials and imaginatively re-create the complexities of the environment in which they originated. Successful historical researchers survey historians' interpretations of the past and figure out how their purposes or backgrounds might influence those interpretations; understand the context in which primary sources were generated; and identify conflicting evidence and locate factual and interpretive information that can help resolve or illuminate inconsistencies.

In addition to printed books and magazines that are primary sources (such as memoirs, letters, or advertisements in old issues of popular magazines), your library may have electronic databases focused on primary source material or have unique historical records in their archives and special collections. Secondary sources that analyze and contextualize historical events typically identify useful primary sources to track down in their notes and references. Finally, innumerable encyclopedias, dictionaries, handbooks, and chronologies can provide handy information to round out your interpretations and ground them in fact. Consult a librarian to find out what the reference shelves offer for your topic and whether the library has any special collections of microfilm, archives, manuscripts, or other primary sources especially suited to your research.

General resources

Google Books. Mountain View: Google, 2004–. <http://books .google.com>. Provides the full text of millions of books scanned in hundreds of libraries or selected sections of books from publishers. Books published before 1923 are generally available in full text. Newer books may have sections of text available, but typically pages are omitted. Useful for tracking down specific quotes and accessing historical publications.

HathiTrust. Ann Arbor: Hathi Trust Research Center, 2008–. <http://www.hathitrust.org>. A collaboration of libraries sharing the full text of scanned books. Older books can be downloaded. Some books are restricted to users at particular libraries. Particularly helpful for locating specific information in books and for historical publications. Users can create and share collections, such as books by a particular author or on a topic.

JSTOR. Ann Arbor: Ithaka, 1994–. <http://www.jstor.org/>. A library database that is an archive of scholarly journals and (at some libraries) books in a wide variety of subjects. Since JSTOR includes the full text of every issue of the journals included (other than the most recent years), it's helpful for finding high-quality scholarly articles in literature, history, and many other subjects. Its Google-like search makes it easy to find articles, but pay attention to publication dates as many of the articles are quite old and the most current issues are often not included.

Social Sciences Citation Index. Philadelphia: Thomson Reuters, 1956–. <http://thomsonreuters.com/social-sciences-citation-index/>. Part of the Web of Knowledge (sometimes called Web of Science), this multidisciplinary database of social science journals includes history, women's studies, and urban studies. Searchable by author or keyword, the index allows searches by cited source, which is an efficient way to trace the influence of a particular work. The Related Search feature also identifies works that cite one or more of the same sources and can be useful for seeking out connections.

World History Collection. Ipswich: EBSCO, 2005–. <http://www.ebscohost.com/us-high-schools/world-history-collection>. A database of journal articles covering the history of Africa, Asia, North and South America, Europe, and the Middle East.

World history

For background information

Civilizations of the Ancient Near East. New York: Scribner's, 2000. Covers Egypt, Mesopotamia, and early cultures of the Middle East, Mediterranean, and North Africa in well-documented essays.

Encyclopedia of the Enlightenment. New York: Oxford University Press, 2002. Covers topics, people, and concepts related to an influential period in European and North American history. Similar encyclopedias cover time periods such as the Middle Ages, the Renaissance, and the Reformation.

Encyclopedia of Latin American History and Culture. Ed. Jay Kinsbruner and Eric D. Langer. 2nd ed. Detroit: Gale, 2008. Presents a wide variety of topics in more than 5,000 articles that together constitute an overview of current knowledge about the region. Entries cover countries, topics (such as slavery, art, Asians in Latin America), and biographical sketches. There are similar encyclopedias for other world regional history.

Database

Historical Abstracts. Santa Barbara: EBSCO, 1955–. <http://www .ebscohost.com/academic/historical-abstracts>. Provides citations and abstracts of articles, book reviews, books, and dissertations from over 2,000 journals in world history from 1450 to the present. North American history is covered in the companion index, *America: History and Life*.

American history

For background information

American National Biography. Ed. John Arthur Garraty and Mark C. Carnes. New York: Oxford University Press, 1999. <http://www.anb.org/>. Compiled under the auspices of the American Council of Learned Societies, serves as the most important and comprehensive biographical reference work on American historical figures. Each sketch is a detailed scholarly profile followed by a critical bibliography.

Dictionary of American History. Ed. Stanley I. Kutler. 3rd ed. New York: Scribner, 2003. An encyclopedia of terms, places, and concepts in U.S. history, with maps and illustrations as well as references for further research.

Encyclopedia of African-American Culture and History. Ed. Colin A. Palmer. 2nd ed. Detroit: Gale, 2006. A wide-ranging encyclopedia covering people, places, events, concepts, and topics of all sorts. Articles are written by specialists and feature bibliographies.

Encyclopedia Latina: History, Culture, and Society in the United States. Danbury: Grolier, 2005. Covers Latinos in the United States in over 650 essays that tackle topics from baseball to Zorro, significant places, groups of people, events, and more. The fourth volume includes significant primary source documents.

Database

America: History and Life. Santa Barbara: EBSCO, 1964–. <http://www.ebscohost.com/academic/america-history-and-life>. Companion to *Historical Abstracts* that provides citations and abstracts of articles, books, dissertations, and book reviews on U.S. and Canadian history and culture. Searchable by keyword, author, subject, and source, the index offers in-depth coverage of scholarly publications in North American history and allows for interdisciplinary examinations of American culture.

Primary sources

Historical Newspapers. Ann Arbor: ProQuest, 2001–. <http://www.proquest.com/products-services/pq-hist-news.html>. Digitized newspapers offering individual articles, including images, and a view of full pages in which the articles originally appeared. Your library may offer one or more historical newspapers such as *The New York Times* or the *Chicago Tribune*.

Early English Books Online. Ann Arbor: ProQuest, 1998–. <http://www.proquest.com/products-services/eebo.html>. A digital collection of books, tracts, and pamphlets in English that were published between 1475 and 1700. Old spelling and typefaces can make interpreting these texts a challenge.

Archive of Americana. Naples: Readex, 2005–. <www.readex.com/content/archive-americana>. A digital collection of newspapers, pamphlets, books, and government documents created in collaboration with the American Antiquarian Society. Libraries may have parts of this database such as *The Civil War: Antebellum Period to Reconstruction* or other digital collections of diaries, documents, or papers related to particular historical periods.

Documents online

American Memory. Washington: Library of Congress, 1990–. <http://memory.loc.gov>. A vast site full of digitized materials from the Library of Congress and other libraries and museums. Because it is so large and some of the materials were digitized early in the history of the Web and are not in a user-friendly format, it can be daunting to navigate but it has amazing resources.

Digital Public Library of America. Boston: DPLA, 2013–. <http://dp.la>. A project that provides a platform for finding materials from American cultural institutions, including images, film, sound, and text. It also supplies the tools for Web developers to make new tools for finding and using these materials and provides leadership for the further development of a national digital public library. Many other countries have similar national digital libraries that may contain useful primary source material.

Euro-Docs: Online Sources for European History. Provo: Brigham Young University Library, 1995–. <http://eudocs.lib.byu.edu>. A large collection of links to documents, many translated into English, organized by country and period.

National Archives. Washington: National Archives and Records Administration, 2002–. <http://www.archives.gov>. Showcases a number of historical records, with information about what each archive contains and how it can be used. Countries, states, local governments, and many cultural institutions have similar digital archives that are making materials freely available online.

Citing sources in history: *Chicago* style

Chicago documentation style

In history and some other humanities courses, you may be asked to use the documentation system of *The Chicago Manual of Style*, 16th ed. (Chicago: University of Chicago Press, 2010).

Directory to *Chicago*-style notes and bibliography entries

→

In *Chicago* style, superscript numbers (like this[1]) in the text of the paper refer readers to notes with corresponding numbers either at the foot of the page (footnotes) or at the end of the paper (endnotes). A bibliography is often required as well; it appears at the end of the paper and gives publication information for all the works cited in the notes.

TEXT

A Union soldier, Jacob Thompson, claimed to have seen Forrest order the killing, but when asked to describe the six-foot-two general, he called him "a little bit of a man."[12]

FOOTNOTE OR ENDNOTE

12. Brian Steel Wills, *A Battle from the Start: The Life of Nathan Bedford Forrest* (New York: HarperCollins, 1992), 187.

BIBLIOGRAPHY ENTRY

Wills, Brian Steel. *A Battle from the Start: The Life of Nathan Bedford Forrest*. New York: HarperCollins, 1992.

First and later notes for a source

The first time you cite a source, the note should include publication information for that work as well as the page number for the passage you are citing.

1. Peter Burchard, *One Gallant Rush: Robert Gould Shaw and His Brave Black Regiment* (New York: St. Martin's, 1965), 85.

For later references to a source you have already cited, you may simply give the author's last name, a short form of the title, and the page or pages cited. A short form of the title of a book or another long work is italicized; a short form of the title of an article or another short work is put in quotation marks.

4. Burchard, *One Gallant Rush*, 31.

When you have two notes in a row from the same source, you may use "Ibid." (meaning "in the same place") and the page number for the second note. Use "Ibid." alone if the page number is the same.

5. Jack Hurst, *Nathan Bedford Forrest: A Biography* (New York: Knopf, 1993), 8.

6. Ibid., 174.

Chicago-*style bibliography*

A bibliography at the end of your paper lists the works you have cited in your notes; it may also include works you consulted but did not cite. See page 155 for how to construct the list; see page 161 for a sample bibliography.

NOTE: If you include a bibliography, *The Chicago Manual of Style* suggests that you shorten all notes, including the first reference to a source, as described at the top of this page. Check with your instructor, however, to see whether using an abbreviated note for a first reference to a source is acceptable.

Model notes and bibliography entries

The following models are consistent with guidelines in *The Chicago Manual of Style*, 16th ed. For each type of source, a model note appears first, followed by a model bibliography entry. The note shows the format you should use when citing a source for the first time. For subsequent citations of a source, use shortened notes (see pp. 128–29).

Some sources on the Web, typically periodical articles, use a permanent locator called a digital object identifier (DOI). Use the DOI, when it is available, in place of a URL in your citations of sources from the Web.

When a URL or a DOI must break across lines, do not insert a hyphen or break at a hyphen if the URL or DOI contains one. Instead, break after a colon or a double slash or before any other mark of punctuation.

General guidelines for listing authors

1. One author

1. Salman Rushdie, *Joseph Anton: A Memoir* (New York: Random House, 2012), 135.

Rushdie, Salman. *Joseph Anton: A Memoir*. New York: Random House, 2012.

2. Two or three authors   For a work with two or three authors, give all authors' names in both the note and the bibliography entry.

2. Bill O'Reilly and Martin Dugard, *Killing Lincoln: The Shocking Assassination That Changed America Forever* (New York: Holt, 2012), 33.

O'Reilly, Bill, and Martin Dugard. *Killing Lincoln: The Shocking Assassination That Changed America Forever*. New York: Holt, 2012.

3. Four or more authors   For a work with four or more authors, in the note give the first author's name followed by "et al." (for "and others"); in the bibliography entry, list all authors' names.

3. Lynn Hunt et al., *The Making of the West: Peoples and Cultures*, 4th ed. (Boston: Bedford/St. Martin's, 2012), 541.

Hunt, Lynn, Thomas R. Martin, Barbara H. Rosenwein, R. Po-chia Hsia, and Bonnie G. Smith. *The Making of the West: Peoples and Cultures*. 4th ed. Boston: Bedford/St. Martin's, 2012.

4. Organization as author

4. Johnson Historical Society, *Images of America: Johnson* (Charleston, SC: Arcadia Publishing, 2011), 24.

Johnson Historical Society. *Images of America: Johnson*. Charleston, SC: Arcadia Publishing, 2011.

5. Unknown author

5. *The Men's League Handbook on Women's Suffrage* (London, 1912), 23.

The Men's League Handbook on Women's Suffrage. London, 1912.

6. Multiple works by the same author

In the bibliography, arrange the entries alphabetically by title. Use six hyphens in place of the author's name in the second and subsequent entries.

Winchester, Simon. *The Alice behind Wonderland*. New York: Oxford University Press, 2011.

------. *Atlantic: Great Sea Battles, Heroic Discoveries, Titanic Storms, and a Vast Ocean of a Million Stories*. New York: HarperCollins, 2010.

7. Editor

7. Teresa Carpenter, ed., *New York Diaries: 1609-2009* (New York: Modern Library, 2012), 316.

Carpenter, Teresa, ed. *New York Diaries: 1609-2009*. New York: Modern Library, 2012.

8. Editor with author

8. Susan Sontag, *As Consciousness Is Harnessed to Flesh: Journals and Notebooks, 1964-1980*, ed. David Rieff (New York: Farrar, Straus and Giroux, 2012), 265.

Sontag, Susan. *As Consciousness Is Harnessed to Flesh: Journals and Notebooks, 1964-1980*. Edited by David Rieff. New York: Farrar, Straus and Giroux, 2012.

9. Translator with author

9. Richard Bidlack and Nikita Lomagin, *The Leningrad Blockade, 1941-1944: A New Documentary from the Soviet Archives*, trans. Marian Schwartz (New Haven: Yale University Press, 2012), 26.

Bidlack, Richard, and Nikita Lomagin. *The Leningrad Blockade, 1941-1944: A New Documentary from the Soviet Archives.* Translated by Marian Schwartz. New Haven: Yale University Press, 2012.

Books and other long works

- Citation at a glance: Book, page 133

10. Basic format for a book

a. Print

10. Mary N. Woods, *Beyond the Architect's Eye: Photographs and the American Built Environment* (Philadelphia: University of Pennsylvania Press, 2009), 45.

Woods, Mary N. *Beyond the Architect's Eye: Photographs and the American Built Environment.* Philadelphia: University of Pennsylvania Press, 2009.

b. E-book

10. Drew Gilpin Faust, *This Republic of Suffering: Death and the American Civil War* (New York: Knopf, 2008), Nook edition, chap. 4.

Faust, Drew Gilpin. *This Republic of Suffering: Death and the American Civil War.* New York: Knopf, 2008. Nook edition.

c. Web (or online library)

10. Charles Hursthouse, *New Zealand, or Zealandia, the Britain of the South* (1857; Hathi Trust Digital Library, n.d.), 2:356, http://babel.hathitrust.org/cgi/pt?id=nnc1.50188297;view=1up;seq=1.

Hursthouse, Charles. *New Zealand, or Zealandia, the Britain of the South.* 2 vols. 1857. Hathi Trust Digital Library, n.d. http://babel.hathitrust.org/cgi/pt?id=nnc1.50188297;view=1up;seq=1.

Citation at a glance | Book (*Chicago*)

To cite a print book in *Chicago* style, include the following elements:

1 Author(s)
2 Title and subtitle
3 City of publication

4 Publisher
5 Year of publication
6 Page number(s) cited (for notes)

TITLE PAGE

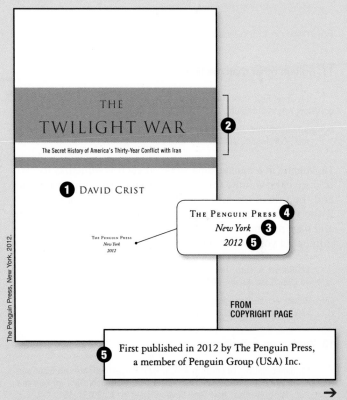

THE
TWILIGHT WAR

The Secret History of America's Thirty-Year Conflict with Iran **2**

1 DAVID CRIST

THE PENGUIN PRESS **4**
New York **3**
2012 **5**

THE PENGUIN PRESS
New York
2012

FROM
COPYRIGHT PAGE

5 First published in 2012 by The Penguin Press,
a member of Penguin Group (USA) Inc.

→

(continued)

NOTE

1. David Crist, *The Twilight War: The Secret History of America's Thirty-Year Conflict with Iran* (New York: Penguin, 2012), 354.

BIBLIOGRAPHY

Crist, David. *The Twilight War: The Secret History of America's Thirty-Year Conflict with Iran*. New York: Penguin, 2012.

For more on citing books in *Chicago* style, see items 10–18.

11. Edition other than the first

11. Josephine Donovan, *Feminist Theory: The Intellectual Traditions*, 4th ed. (New York: Continuum, 2012), 86.

Donovan, Josephine. *Feminist Theory: The Intellectual Traditions*. 4th ed. New York: Continuum, 2012.

12. Volume in a multivolume work
If each volume has its own title, give the volume title first, followed by the volume number and the title of the entire work, as in the following examples. If the volumes do not have individual titles, give the volume and page number in the note (for example, 2:356) and the total number of volumes in the bibliography entry (see item 10c).

12. Robert A. Caro, *The Passage of Power*, vol. 4 of *The Years of Lyndon Johnson* (New York: Knopf, 2012), 198.

Caro, Robert A. *The Passage of Power*. Vol. 4 of *The Years of Lyndon Johnson*. New York: Knopf, 2012.

13. Work in an anthology

13. Janet Walsh, "Unequal in Africa: How Property Rights Can Empower Women," in *The Unfinished Revolution: Voices from the Global Fight for Women's Rights,* ed. Minky Worden (New York: Seven Stories Press, 2012), 161.

Walsh, Janet. "Unequal in Africa: How Property Rights Can Empower Women." In *The Unfinished Revolution: Voices from the Global Fight for Women's Rights*, edited by Minky Worden, 159-66. New York: Seven Stories Press, 2012.

14. Introduction, preface, foreword, or afterword

14. Alice Walker, afterword to *The Indispensable Zinn: The Essential Writings of the "People's Historian,"* by Howard Zinn (New York: Free Press, 2012), 373.

Walker, Alice. Afterword to *The Indispensable Zinn: The Essential Writings of the "People's Historian,"* by Howard Zinn, 371-76. New York: Free Press, 2012.

15. Republished book

15. W. S. Blatchley, *A Nature Wooing at Ormond by the Sea* (1902; repr., Stockbridge, MA: Hard Press, 2012), 26.

Blatchley, W. S. *A Nature Wooing at Ormond by the Sea.* 1902. Reprint, Stockbridge, MA: Hard Press, 2012.

16. Book with a title in its title   Use quotation marks around any title, whether a long or a short work, within an italicized title.

16. Claudia Durst Johnson, ed., *Race in Mark Twain's "Adventures of Huckleberry Finn"* (Detroit: Greenhaven Press, 2009).

Johnson, Claudia Durst, ed. *Race in Mark Twain's "Adventures of Huckleberry Finn."* Detroit: Greenhaven Press, 2009.

17. Work in a series   The series name follows the book title.

17. Lois E. Horton, *Harriet Tubman and the Fight for Freedom: A Brief History with Documents*, Bedford Series in History and Culture (Boston: Bedford/St. Martin's, 2013), 35.

Horton, Lois E. *Harriet Tubman and the Fight for Freedom: A Brief History with Documents.* Bedford Series in History and Culture. Boston: Bedford/St. Martin's, 2013.

18. Sacred text   Sacred texts are usually not included in the bibliography.

18. Matt. 20:4-9 (Revised Standard Version).

18. Qur'an 18:1-3.

19. Government document

19. United States Senate, Committee on Foreign Relations, *Implications of the Kyoto Protocol on Climate Change: Hearing before the Committee on Foreign Relations, United States Senate*, 105th Cong., 2nd sess. (Washington, DC: GPO, 1998).

United States Senate. Committee on Foreign Relations. *Implications of the Kyoto Protocol on Climate Change: Hearing before the Committee on Foreign Relations, United States Senate*, 105th Cong., 2nd sess. Washington, DC: GPO, 1998.

20. Unpublished dissertation

20. Stephanie Lynn Budin, "The Origins of Aphrodite" (PhD diss., University of Pennsylvania, 2000), 301-2, ProQuest (AAT 9976404).

Budin, Stephanie Lynn. "The Origins of Aphrodite." PhD diss., University of Pennsylvania, 2000. ProQuest (AAT 9976404).

For a published dissertation, italicize the title and give publication information as for a book.

21. Published proceedings of a conference   Cite as a book, adding the location and dates of the conference after the title.

21. Stacey K. Sowards, Kyle Alvarado, Diana Arrieta, and Jacob Barde, eds., *Across Borders and Environments: Communication and Environmental Justice in International Contexts*, University of Texas at El Paso, June 25-28, 2011 (Cincinnati, OH: International Environmental Communication Association, 2012), 114.

Sowards, Stacey K., Kyle Alvarado, Diana Arrieta, and Jacob Barde, eds. *Across Borders and Environments: Communication and Environmental Justice in International Contexts*. University of Texas at El Paso, June 25-28, 2011. Cincinnati, OH: International Environmental Communication Association, 2012.

22. Source quoted in another source (a secondary source) Sometimes you will want to use a quotation from one source that you have found in another source. In your note and bibliography entry, cite whatever information is available about the original source of the quotation, including a page number. Then add the words "quoted in" and give publication information for the source in which you found the words. In the following examples, author John Matteson quotes the words of Thomas Wentworth Higginson. Matteson's book includes a note with information about the Higginson book.

22. Thomas Wentworth Higginson, *Margaret Fuller Ossoli* (Boston: Houghton Mifflin, 1890), 11, quoted in John Matteson, *The Lives of Margaret Fuller* (New York: Norton, 2012), 7.

Higginson, Thomas Wentworth. *Margaret Fuller Ossoli*. Boston: Houghton Mifflin, 1890, 11. Quoted in John Matteson, *The Lives of Margaret Fuller* (New York: Norton, 2012), 7.

Articles and other short works

- Citation at a glance: Article in a journal, page 139
- Citation at a glance: Article from a database, page 141

23. Article in a journal   Include the volume and issue numbers (if the journal has them) and the date; end the bibliography entry with the page range of the article. If an article in a database or on the Web shows only a beginning page, use a plus sign after the page number instead of a page range: 212+.

a. Print

23. Catherine Foisy, "Preparing the Quebec Church for Vatican II: Missionary Lessons from Asia, Africa, and Latin America, 1945-1962," *Historical Studies* 78 (2012): 8.

Foisy, Catherine. "Preparing the Quebec Church for Vatican II: Missionary Lessons from Asia, Africa, and Latin America, 1945-1962." *Historical Studies* 78 (2012): 7-26.

b. Web   Give the DOI if the article has one; if there is no DOI, give the URL for the article. For unpaginated articles on the Web, you may include in your note a locator, such as a numbered paragraph or a heading from the article.

23. Anne-Lise François, "Flower Fisting," *Postmodern Culture* 22, no. 1 (2011), doi:10.1353/pmc.2012.0004.

François, Anne-Lise. "Flower Fisting." *Postmodern Culture* 22, no. 1 (2011). doi:10.1353/pmc.2012.0004.

c. Database   Give one of the following pieces of information from the database listing, in this order of preference: a DOI for the article; or the name of the database and the article number, if any; or a "stable" or "persistent" URL for the article.

23. Patrick Zuk, "Nikolay Myaskovsky and the Events of 1948," *Music and Letters* 93, no. 1 (2012): 61, Project Muse.

Zuk, Patrick. "Nikolay Myaskovsky and the Events of 1948." *Music and Letters* 93, no. 1 (2012): 61. Project Muse.

24. Article in a magazine   Give the month and year for a monthly publication; give the month, day, and year for a weekly publication. End the bibliography entry with the page range of the article. If an article in a database or on the Web shows only a beginning page, use a plus sign after the page number instead of a page range: 212+.

a. Print

24. Alan Lightman, "Our Place in the Universe: Face to Face with the Infinite," *Harper's*, December 2012, 34.

Lightman, Alan. "Our Place in the Universe: Face to Face with the Infinite." *Harper's*, December 2012, 33-38.

b. Web   If no DOI is available, include the URL for the article.

24. James Verini, "The Tunnels of Gaza," *National Geographic*, December 2012, http://ngm.nationalgeographic.com/2012/12/gaza-tunnels /verini-text.

Verini, James. "The Tunnels of Gaza." *National Geographic*, December 2012. http://ngm.nationalgeographic.com/2012/12/gaza-tunnels /verini-text.

Citation at a glance | Article in a journal (*Chicago*)

To cite an article in a print journal in *Chicago* style, include the following elements:

1 Author(s)
2 Title and subtitle of article
3 Title of journal
4 Volume and issue numbers

5 Year of publication
6 Page number(s) cited (for notes); page range of article (for bibliography)

FIRST PAGE OF ARTICLE

2 Work, Family, and the Eighteenth-Century History of a Middle Class in the American South

By EMMA HART **1**

TITLE PAGE OF JOURNAL

 3 *The Journal of* **SOUTHERN HISTORY**

4 VOLUME LXXVIII   **5** AUGUST 2012   **4** NUMBER 3

Contents

...TA WYATT APPEARED BEFORE
...equity in Charleston District,
...unt of her married life, which
...years earlier, when she took
...The daughter of a blacksmith,
...of Charleston from childhood,
...nineteenth century, her experi-
...historical record as those of so
...Vith her husband at the head of
...he first federal census not as an
...deed, the sole records of her
...neficiary in her father's 1767
...which the documents are now
...ster. Yet, in her lengthy testi-
...rict Chancery Court, the course
...s extraordinary detail. Violetta
...ss from their marriage through
...ring the American Revolution,
...naging a household.[1]

...t the First Census of the United States
...D.C., 1908), 39; Will of James Lingard,
...pts of Charleston County Wills (South
...Charleston, S.C.). The case of *Mary
...illiam Brisbane*, September 23, 1771, is
...th Carolina under the royal government,
..., ed., *Records of the Court of Chancery
...50), 588. The case of *Executors of the
...tt, Deceased* (hereinafter *Richardsons v.
...00), is in Folder 20, Box 4, Charleston
...10090 (South Carolina Department of
...AH). The decision in the case is cited as
...m, 1807, Vol. 2, pp. 1–2, Series L10092,

(continued)

NOTE

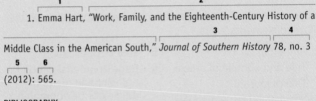

1. Emma Hart, "Work, Family, and the Eighteenth-Century History of a Middle Class in the American South," *Journal of Southern History* 78, no. 3 (2012): 565.

BIBLIOGRAPHY

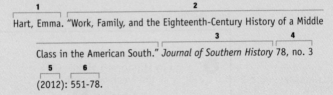

Hart, Emma. "Work, Family, and the Eighteenth-Century History of a Middle Class in the American South." *Journal of Southern History* 78, no. 3 (2012): 551-78.

For more on citing articles in *Chicago* style, see items 23–25.

24. Article in a magazine (*cont.*)

c. Database Give one of the following from the database listing, in this order of preference: a DOI for the article; or the name of the database and the article number, if any; or a "stable" or "persistent" URL for the article.

24. Ron Rosenbaum, "The Last Renaissance Man," *Smithsonian*, November 2012, 40, OmniFile Full Text Select (83097302).

Rosenbaum, Ron. "The Last Renaissance Man." *Smithsonian*, November 2012, 39-44. OmniFile Full Text Select (83097302).

Citation at a glance | Article from a database (*Chicago*)

To cite an article from a database in *Chicago* style, include the following elements:

1 Author(s)
2 Title and subtitle of article
3 Title of journal
4 Volume and issue numbers
5 Year of publication

6 Page number(s) cited (for notes); page range of article (for bibliography)
7 DOI; *or* database name and article number; *or* "stable" or "persistent" URL for article

DATABASE RECORD

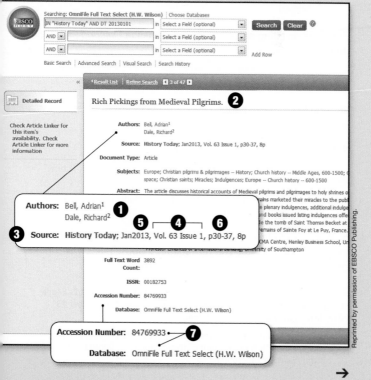

→

(continued)

NOTE

1. Adrian Bell and Richard Dale, "Rich Pickings from Medieval Pilgrims," *History Today* 63, no. 1 (2013): 33, OmniFile Full Text Select (84769933).

BIBLIOGRAPHY

Bell, Adrian, and Richard Dale. "Rich Pickings from Medieval Pilgrims." *History Today* 63, no. 1 (2013): 30-37. OmniFile Full Text Select

(84769933).

For more on citing articles from databases in *Chicago* style, see items 23–25.

25. Article in a newspaper Page numbers are not necessary; a section letter or number, if available, is sufficient.

a. Print

25. Alissa J. Rubin, "A Pristine Afghan Prison Faces a Murky Future," *New York Times*, December 18, 2012, sec. A.

Rubin, Alissa J. "A Pristine Afghan Prison Faces a Murky Future." *New York Times*, December 18, 2012, sec. A.

b. Web Include the URL for the article; if the URL is very long, use the URL for the newspaper's home page. Omit page numbers, even if the source provides them.

25. David Brown, "New Burden of Disease Study Shows World's People Living Longer but with More Disability," *Washington Post*, December 13, 2012, http://www.washingtonpost.com/.

Brown, David. "New Burden of Disease Study Shows World's People Living Longer but with More Disability." *Washington Post*, December 13, 2012. http://www.washingtonpost.com/.

c. Database   Give one of the following from the database listing, in this order of preference: a DOI for the article; or the name of the database and the number assigned by the database; or a "stable" or "persistent" URL for the article.

25. "Safe in Sioux City at Last: Union Pacific Succeeds in Securing Trackage from the St. Paul Road," *Omaha Daily Herald*, May 16, 1889, America's Historical Newspapers.

"Safe in Sioux City at Last: Union Pacific Succeeds in Securing Trackage from the St. Paul Road." *Omaha Daily Herald*, May 16, 1889. America's Historical Newspapers.

26. Unsigned newspaper article   In the note, begin with the title of the article. In the bibliography entry, begin with the title of the newspaper.

26. "Rein in Charter Schools," *Chicago Sun-Times*, December 13, 2012, http://www.suntimes.com/.

Chicago Sun-Times. "Rein in Charter Schools." December 13, 2012. http://www.suntimes.com/.

27. Article with a title in its title   Use italics for titles of long works such as books and for terms that are normally italicized. Use single quotation marks for titles of short works and terms that would otherwise be placed in double quotation marks.

27. Karen Garner, "Global Gender Policy in the 1990s: Incorporating the 'Vital Voices' of Women," *Journal of Women's History* 24, no. 4 (2012): 130.

Garner, Karen. "Global Gender Policy in the 1990s: Incorporating the 'Vital Voices' of Women." *Journal of Women's History* 24, no. 4 (2012): 121-48.

28. Review   If the review has a title, provide it immediately following the author of the review.

28. David Denby, "Dead Reckoning," review of *Zero Dark Thirty*, directed by Kathryn Bigelow, *New Yorker*, December 24/31, 2012, 130.

Denby, David. "Dead Reckoning." Review of *Zero Dark Thirty*, directed by Kathryn Bigelow. *New Yorker*, December 24/31, 2012, 130-32.

28. David Eggleton, review of *Stalking Nabokov*, by Brian Boyd, *New Zealand Listener*, December 13, 2012, http://www.listener.co.nz/culture/books/stalking-nabokov-by-brian-boyd-review/.

Eggleton, David. Review of *Stalking Nabokov*, by Brian Boyd. *New Zealand Listener*, December 13, 2012. http://www.listener.co.nz/culture/books/stalking-nabokov-by-brian-boyd-review/.

29. Letter to the editor   Do not use the letter's title, even if the publication gives one.

29. Andy Bush, letter to the editor, *Economist*, December 15, 2012, http://www.economist.com/.

Bush, Andy. Letter to the editor. *Economist*, December 15, 2012. http://www.economist.com/.

30. Article in a reference work (encyclopedia, dictionary, wiki) Reference works such as encyclopedias do not require publication information and are usually not included in the bibliography. The abbreviation "s.v." is for the Latin *sub verbo* ("under the word").

30. *Encyclopaedia Britannica*, 15th ed., s.v. "Monroe Doctrine."

30. *Wikipedia*, s.v. "James Monroe," last modified December 19, 2012, http://en.wikipedia.org/wiki/James_Monroe.

30. Bryan A. Garner, *Garner's Modern American Usage*, 3rd ed. (Oxford: Oxford University Press, 2009), s.v. "brideprice."

Garner, Bryan A. *Garner's Modern American Usage*. 3rd ed. Oxford: Oxford University Press, 2009.

31. Letter in a published collection   Use the day-month-year form for the date of the letter. If the letter writer's name is part of the book title, begin the note with only the last name but begin the bibliography entry with the full name.

- Citation at a glance: Letter in a published collection, page 145

31. Dickens to Thomas Beard, 1 June 1840, in *The Selected Letters of Charles Dickens*, ed. Jenny Hartley (New York: Oxford University Press, 2012), 65.

Dickens, Charles. *The Selected Letters of Charles Dickens*. Edited by Jenny Hartley. New York: Oxford University Press, 2012.

Citation at a glance | Letter in a published collection (*Chicago*)

To cite a letter in a published collection in *Chicago* style, include the following elements:

1. Author of letter
2. Recipient of letter
3. Date of letter
4. Title of collection
5. Editor of collection
6. City of publication
7. Publisher
8. Year of publication
9. Page number(s) cited (for notes); page range of letter (for bibliography)

TITLE PAGE

TO HIS EXCELLENCY
④ THOMAS JEFFERSON

········ *Letters to a President* ········

JACK **⑤**
McLAUGHLIN

FROM
COPYRIGHT PAGE

⑧ Copyright © 1991 by Jack McLaughlin
Cover painting by Giraudon/Art Resource, New York
Published by arrangement with W.W. Norton & Company, Inc.
Library of Congress Catalog Card Number: 90-27824
ISBN: 0-380-71964-9

AVON BOOKS ▲ NEW YORK

⑦   **⑥**
AVON BOOKS ▲ NEW YORK

→

(continued)

Washington 30th. Oct 1805 ❸

His Excellency Ths. Jefferson ❷

Sɪʀ,

I have not the honor to be personally known to your Excellency therefore you will no doubt think it strange to receive t
smallest
in as few
a young
partly ed
had beer
sequence
that unh
anything
few yea
[m]isfortu
[I] can a

Patronage   6 1 ❾

your Excellency this very prolix letter which should it please your Excellency to give me some little Office or appointment in that extensive Country of Louisiana It should be my constant endeavour to merit the same by fidelity and an indefatigable attention to whatever business I should be assigned. May I have the satisfaction in whatsoever Country or situation [I] may be in to hear of your Excellencies long continuence of your Natural powers unempaired to conduct the Helm of this Extensive Country which are the sincere wishes of your Excellencies Mo. Obt. Hum. Servt.

❶ Jᴏʜɴ O'Nᴇɪʟʟ

NOTE

    ¹   ²   ³

1. John O'Neill to Thomas Jefferson, October 30, 1805, in *To His*

       ⁴   ⁵

Excellency Thomas Jefferson: Letters to a President, ed. Jack McLaughlin

 ⁶   ⁷   ⁸   ⁹

(New York: Avon Books, 1991), 61.

BIBLIOGRAPHY

   ¹   ¹   ²   ³

O'Neill, John. John O'Neill to Thomas Jefferson, 30 October 1805. In

                 ⁴

To His Excellency Thomas Jefferson: Letters to a President, edited by

     ⁵   ⁹   ⁶   ⁷   ⁸

Jack McLaughlin, 59-61. New York: Avon Books, 1991.

For another citation of a letter in *Chicago* style, see item 31.

Web sources

For most Web sites, include an author if a site has one, the title of the site, the sponsor, the date of publication or the modified (update) date, and the site's URL. Do not italicize a Web site title unless the site is an online book or periodical. Use quotation marks for the titles of sections or pages in a Web site. If a site does not have a date of publication or a modified date, give the date you accessed the site ("accessed January 3, 2013").

32. An entire Web site

32. Chesapeake and Ohio Canal National Historical Park, National Park Service, last modified November 25, 2012, http://www.nps.gov/choh/index .htm.

Chesapeake and Ohio Canal National Historical Park. National Park Service. Last modified November 25, 2012. http://www.nps.gov/choh/index .htm.

33. Short work from a Web site

- Citation at a glance: Primary source from a Web site, page 149

33. Dan Archer, "Using Illustrated Reportage to Cover Human Trafficking in Nepal's Brick Kilns," Poynter, last modified December 18, 2012, http:// www.poynter.org/.

Archer, Dan. "Using Illustrated Reportage to Cover Human Trafficking in Nepal's Brick Kilns." Poynter, last modified December 18, 2012. http:// www.poynter.org/.

34. Blog post   Treat as a short work from a Web site (see item 33), but italicize the name of the blog. Insert "blog" in parentheses after the name if the word blog is not part of the name. If the blog is part of a larger site (such as a newspaper's or an organization's site), add the title of the site after the blog title. Do not list the blog post in the bibliography; but if you cite the blog frequently in your paper, you may give a bibliography entry for the entire blog.

34. Gregory LeFever, "Skull Fraud 'Created' the Brontosaurus," *Ancient Tides* (blog), December 16, 2012, http://ancient-tides.blogspot .com/2012/12/skull-fraud-created-brontosaurus.html.

LeFever, Gregory. *Ancient Tides* (blog). http://ancient-tides.blogspot.com/.

35. Comment on a blog post   In the bibliography entry here, the blog is given by title only because the blog has many contributors, not a single author.

35. Didomyk, comment on B.C., "A New Spokesman," *Pomegranate: The Middle East* (blog), *Economist*, December 18, 2012, http://www.economist .com/blogs/pomegranate/2012/12/christians-middle-east.

Pomegranate: The Middle East (blog). *Economist*. http://www.economist.com /blogs/pomegranate/.

Audio, visual, and multimedia sources

36. Podcast   Treat as a short work from a Web site (see item 33), including the following, if available: the name of the author, speaker, or host; the title of the podcast, in quotation marks; an identifying number, if any; the title of the site on which it appears; the sponsor of the site; and the URL. Identify the type of podcast or file format; before the URL, give the date of posting or your date of access.

36. Peter Limb, "Economic and Cultural History of the Slave Trade in Western Africa," Episode 69, Africa Past and Present, African Online Digital Library, podcast audio, December 12, 2012, http://afripod.aodl.org/.

Limb, Peter. "Economic and Cultural History of the Slave Trade in Western Africa." Episode 69. Africa Past and Present. African Online Digital Library. Podcast audio. December 12, 2012. http://afripod.aodl.org/.

37. Online audio or video   Cite as a short work from a Web site (see item 33). If the source is a downloadable file, identify the file format or medium before the URL.

37. Tom Brokaw, "Global Warming: What You Need to Know," Discovery Channel, January 23, 2012, http://www.youtube.com/watch?v=xcVwLrAavyA.

Brokaw, Tom. "Global Warming: What You Need to Know." Discovery Channel, January 23, 2012. http://www.youtube.com/watch?v=xcVwLrAavyA.

Citation at a glance | Primary source from a
Web site (*Chicago*)

To cite a primary source (or any other document) from a Web site
in *Chicago* style, include as many of the following elements as
are available:

1 Author(s)
2 Title of document
3 Title of site
4 Sponsor of site

5 Publication date or
modified date; date of
access (if no publication
date)
6 URL of document page

WEB SITE HOME PAGE

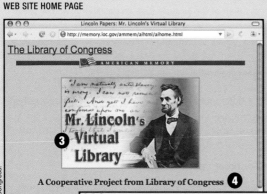

FIRST PAGE OF
DOCUMENT

(continued)

NOTE

1. Abraham Lincoln, "Draft of the Emancipation Proclamation," Mr. Lincoln's Virtual Library, Library of Congress, accessed July 24, 2013, http://memory.loc.gov/ammem/alhtml/almss/dep001.html.

BIBLIOGRAPHY

Lincoln, Abraham. "Draft of the Emancipation Proclamation." Mr. Lincoln's Virtual Library. Library of Congress. Accessed July 24, 2013. http://memory.loc.gov/ammem/alhtml/almss/dep001.html.

For more on citing documents from Web sites in *Chicago* style, see item 33.

38. Published or broadcast interview

38. Jane Goodall, interview by Suza Scalora, *Origin*, n.d., http://www.originmagazine.com/2012/12/07/dr-jane-goodall-interview-with-suza-scalora.

Goodall, Jane. Interview by Suza Scalora. *Origin*, n.d. http://www.originmagazine.com/2012/12/07/dr-jane-goodall-interview-with-suza-scalora.

38. Julian Castro and Joaquin Castro, interview by Charlie Rose, *Charlie Rose Show*, WGBH, Boston, December 17, 2012.

Castro, Julian, and Joaquin Castro. Interview by Charlie Rose. *Charlie Rose Show*. WGBH, Boston, December 17, 2012.

39. Film (DVD, BD, or other format)

39. *Argo*, directed by Ben Affleck (Burbank, CA: Warner Bros. Pictures, 2012).

Argo. Directed by Ben Affleck. Burbank, CA: Warner Bros. Pictures, 2012.

39. *The Dust Bowl,* directed by Ken Burns (Washington, DC: PBS, 2012), DVD.

The Dust Bowl. Directed by Ken Burns. Washington, DC: PBS, 2012. DVD.

40. Sound recording

40. Gustav Holst, *The Planets,* Royal Philharmonic Orchestra, conducted by André Previn, Telarc 80133, compact disc.

Holst, Gustav. *The Planets.* Royal Philharmonic Orchestra. Conducted by André Previn. Telarc 80133, compact disc.

41. Musical score or composition

41. Antonio Vivaldi, *L'Estro armonico,* op. 3, ed. Eleanor Selfridge-Field (Mineola, NY: Dover, 1999).

Vivaldi, Antonio. *L'Estro armonico,* op. 3. Edited by Eleanor Selfridge-Field. Mineola, NY: Dover, 1999.

42. Work of art

42. Aaron Siskind, *Untitled (The Most Crowded Block),* gelatin silver print, 1939, Kemper Museum of Contemporary Art, Kansas City, MO.

Siskind, Aaron. *Untitled (The Most Crowded Block).* Gelatin silver print, 1939. Kemper Museum of Contemporary Art, Kansas City, MO.

43. Performance

43. Jackie Sibblies Drury, *Social Creatures,* directed by Curt Columbus, Trinity Repertory Company, Providence, RI, March 15, 2013.

Drury, Jackie Sibblies. *Social Creatures.* Directed by Curt Columbus. Trinity Repertory Company, Providence, RI, March 15, 2013.

Personal communication and social media

44. Personal communication Personal communications are not included in the bibliography.

44. Sara Lehman, e-mail message to author, August 13, 2012.

45. Online posting or e-mail If an online posting has been archived, include a URL. E-mails that are not part of an online discussion are treated as personal communication (see item 44). Online postings and e-mails are not included in the bibliography.

45. Ruth E. Thaler-Carter to Copyediting-L discussion list, December 18, 2012, https://list.indiana.edu/sympa/arc/copyediting-l.

46. Facebook post Facebook posts are not included in the bibliography.

46. US Department of Housing and Urban Development's Facebook page, accessed October 15, 2012, http://www.facebook.com/HUD.

47. Twitter post (tweet) Tweets are not included in the bibliography.

47. National Geographic's Twitter feed, accessed December 18, 2012, https://twitter.com/NatGeo.

Chicago manuscript format

The following guidelines for formatting a *Chicago*-style paper and preparing its endnotes and bibliography are based on *The Chicago Manual of Style*, 16th ed. (Chicago: University of Chicago Press, 2010). For pages from a sample paper, see page 155.

Formatting the paper

The guidelines on pages 152–54 describe recommendations for formatting the text of your paper. For guidelines on preparing the endnotes, see pages 154–55, and for preparing the bibliography, see page 155.

Font If your instructor does not require a specific font, choose one that is standard and easy to read (such as Times New Roman).

Title page Include the full title of your paper, your name, the course title, the instructor's name, and the date. See page 156 for a sample title page.

Pagination   Using arabic numerals, number the pages in the upper right corner. Do not number the title page but count it in the manuscript numbering; that is, the first page of the text will be numbered 2. Depending on your instructor's preference, you may also use a short title or your last name before the page numbers to help identify pages.

Margins, line spacing, and paragraph indents   Leave margins of at least one inch at the top, bottom, and sides of the page. Double-space the body of the paper, including long quotations that have been set off from the text. (For line spacing in notes and the bibliography, see p. 155.) Left-align the text.

Indent the first line of each paragraph one-half inch from the left margin.

Capitalization, italics, and quotation marks   In titles of works, capitalize all words except articles (*a, an, the*), prepositions (*at, from, between,* and so on), coordinating conjunctions (*and, but, or, nor, for, so, yet*), and *to* and *as*—unless the word is first or last in the title or subtitle. Follow these guidelines in your paper even if the title is styled differently in the source.

Lowercase the first word following a colon even if the word begins a complete sentence. When the colon introduces a series of sentences or questions, capitalize the first word in all sentences in the series, including the first.

Italicize the titles of books and other long works. Use quotation marks around the titles of periodical articles, short stories, poems, and other short works.

Long quotations   You can choose to set off a long quotation of five to ten typed lines by indenting the entire quotation one-half inch from the left margin. (Always set off quotations of ten or more lines.) Double-space the quotation; do not use quotation marks and do not add extra space above or below it. (See p. 158 for a long quotation in the text of a paper.)

Visuals   *Chicago* classifies visuals as tables and figures (graphs, drawings, photographs, maps, and charts). Keep visuals as simple as possible.

Label each table with an arabic numeral (Table 1, Table 2, and so on) and provide a clear title that identifies the table's subject. The label and the title should appear on separate lines above the table, flush left. For a table that you have borrowed or adapted, give its source in a note like this one, below the table:

Source: Edna Bonacich and Richard P. Appelbaum, *Behind the Label* (Berkeley: University of California Press, 2000), 145.

For each figure, place a label and a caption below the figure, flush left. The label and caption need not appear on separate lines. The word "Figure" may be abbreviated to "Fig."

In the text of your paper, discuss the most significant features of each visual. Place visuals as close as possible to the sentences that relate to them unless your instructor prefers that visuals appear in an appendix.

URLs and DOIs   When a URL or DOI (digital object identifier) must break across lines, do not insert a hyphen or break at a hyphen. Instead, break after a colon or a double slash or before any other mark of punctuation. If your word processing program automatically turns URLs into links (by underlining them and changing the color), turn off this feature.

Headings   *Chicago* does not provide guidelines for the use of headings in student papers. If you would like to insert headings in a long essay or research paper, check first with your instructor. See pages 157 and 159 for typical placement and formatting of headings in a *Chicago*-style paper.

Preparing the endnotes

Begin the endnotes on a new page at the end of the paper. Center the title "Notes" about one inch from the top of the page, and number the pages consecutively with the rest of the paper. See page 160 for an example.

Indenting and numbering   Indent the first line of each note one-half inch from the left margin; do not indent additional lines in the note. Begin the note with the arabic numeral that corresponds to the number in the text. Put a period after the number.

Line spacing   Single-space each note and double-space between notes (unless your instructor prefers double-spacing throughout).

Preparing the bibliography

Typically, the notes in *Chicago*-style papers are followed by a bibliography, an alphabetically arranged list of all the works cited or consulted. Center the title "Bibliography" about one inch from the top of the page. Number bibliography pages consecutively with the rest of the paper. See page 161 for a sample bibliography.

Alphabetizing the list   Alphabetize the bibliography by the last names of the authors (or editors); when a work has no author or editor, alphabetize it by the first word of the title other than *A*, *An*, or *The*.

If your list includes two or more works by the same author, arrange the entries alphabetically by title. Then use six hyphens instead of the author's name in all entries after the first. (See item 6 on p. 131.)

Indenting and line spacing   Begin each entry at the left margin, and indent any additional lines one-half inch. Single-space each entry and double-space between entries (unless your instructor prefers double-spacing throughout).

Sample pages from a *Chicago* research paper

Following are pages from a research paper by Ned Bishop, a student in a history class. Bishop used *Chicago*-style endnotes, bibliography, and manuscript format.

The Massacre at Fort Pillow:

Holding Nathan Bedford Forrest Accountable

Title of paper.

Ned Bishop

Writer's name.

History 214

Professor Citro

March 22, 2012

Title of course, instructor's name, and date.

Marginal annotations indicate *Chicago*-style formatting.

Bishop 2

Although Northern newspapers of the time no doubt exaggerated some of the Confederate atrocities at Fort Pillow, most modern sources agree that a massacre of Union troops took place there on April 12, 1864. It seems clear that Union soldiers, particularly black soldiers, were killed after they had stopped fighting or had surrendered or were being held prisoner. Less clear is the role played by Major General Nathan Bedford Forrest in leading his troops. Although we will never know whether Forrest directly ordered the massacre, evidence suggests that he was responsible for it.

What happened at Fort Pillow?

Fort Pillow, Tennessee, which sat on a bluff overlooking the Mississippi River, had been held by the Union for two years. It was garrisoned by 580 men, 292 of them from United States Colored Heavy and Light Artillery regiments, 285 from the white Thirteenth Tennessee Cavalry. Nathan Bedford Forrest commanded about 1,500 troops.[1]

The Confederates attacked Fort Pillow on April 12, 1864, and had virtually surrounded the fort by the time Forrest arrived on the battlefield. At 3:30 p.m., Forrest demanded the surrender of the Union forces, sending in a message of the sort he had used before: "The conduct of the officers and men garrisoning Fort Pillow has been such as to entitle them to being treated as prisoners of war. . . . Should my demand be refused, I cannot be responsible for the fate of your command."[2] Union Major William Bradford, who had replaced Major Booth, killed earlier by sharpshooters, asked for an hour to consider the demand. Forrest, worried that vessels in the river were bringing in more troops, "shortened the time to twenty minutes."[3] Bradford refused to surrender, and Forrest quickly ordered the attack.

The Confederates charged to the fort, scaled the parapet, and fired on the forces within. Victory came quickly, with the Union forces

atistics are cited th an endnote.

uotation is cited th an endnote.

running toward the river or surrendering. Shelby Foote describes the scene like this:

> Some kept going, right on into the river, where a number drowned and the swimmers became targets for marksmen on the bluff. Others, dropping their guns in terror, ran back toward the Confederates with their hands up, and of these some were spared as prisoners, while others were shot down in the act of surrender.[4]

Long quotation is set off from text by indenting. Quotation marks are omitted.

In his own official report, Forrest makes no mention of the massacre. He does make much of the fact that the Union flag was not lowered by the Union forces, saying that if his own men had not taken down the flag, "few, if any, would have survived unhurt another volley."[5] However, as Jack Hurst points out and Forrest must have known, in this twenty-minute battle, "Federals running for their lives had little time to concern themselves with a flag."[6]

Quotation is introduced with a signal phrase.

The federal congressional report on Fort Pillow, which charged the Confederates with appalling atrocities, was strongly criticized by Southerners. Respected writer Shelby Foote, while agreeing that the report was "largely" fabrication, points out that the "casualty figures . . . indicated strongly that unnecessary killing had occurred."[7] In an important article, John Cimprich and Robert C. Mainfort Jr. argue that the most trustworthy evidence is that written within about ten days of the battle, before word of the congressional hearings circulated and Southerners realized the extent of Northern outrage. The article reprints a group of letters and newspaper sources written before April 22 and thus "untainted by the political overtones the controversy later assumed."[8] Cimprich and Mainfort conclude that these sources "support the case for the occurrence of a massacre" but that Forrest's role remains "clouded" because of inconsistencies in testimony.[9]

Did Forrest order the massacre?

We will never really know whether Forrest directly ordered the massacre, but it seems unlikely. True, Confederate soldier Achilles Clark, who had no reason to lie, wrote to his sisters that "I with several others tried to stop the butchery . . . but Gen. Forrest ordered them [Negro and white Union troops] shot down like dogs, and the carnage continued."[10] But it is not clear whether Clark heard Forrest giving the orders or was just reporting hearsay. Many Confederates had been shouting "No quarter! No quarter!" and, as Shelby Foote points out, these shouts were "thought by some to be at Forrest's command."[11] A Union soldier, Jacob Thompson, claimed to have seen Forrest order the killing, but when asked to describe the six-foot-two general, he called him "a little bit of a man."[12]

Perhaps the most convincing evidence that Forrest did not order the massacre is that he tried to stop it once it had begun. Historian Albert Castel quotes several eyewitnesses on both the Union and Confederate sides as saying that Forrest ordered his men to stop firing.[13] In a letter to his wife three days after the battle, Confederate soldier Samuel Caldwell wrote that "if General Forrest had not run between our men & the Yanks with his pistol and sabre drawn not a man would have been spared."[14]

In a respected biography of Nathan Bedford Forrest, Hurst suggests that the temperamental Forrest "may have ragingly ordered a massacre and even intended to carry it out—until he rode inside the fort and viewed the horrifying result" and ordered it stopped.[15] While this is an intriguing interpretation of events, even Hurst would probably admit that it is merely speculation.

Can Forrest be held responsible for the massacre?

Even assuming that Forrest did not order the massacre, he can still be held accountable for it. That is because he created an

Notes begin on a
new page.

Notes

1. John Cimprich and Robert C. Mainfort Jr., eds., "Fort
Pillow Revisited: New Evidence about an Old Controversy," *Civil War
History* 28, no. 4 (1982): 293-94.

First line of each
note is indented
½". Note number
is followed by a
period. Authors'
names are not
inverted.

2. Quoted in Brian Steel Wills, *A Battle from the Start: The Life of
Nathan Bedford Forrest* (New York: HarperCollins, 1992), 182.

3. Ibid., 183.

4. Shelby Foote, *The Civil War, a Narrative: Red River to
Appomattox* (New York: Vintage, 1986), 110.

Notes are
single-spaced,
with double-
spacing between
notes. (Some
instructors
may prefer
double-spacing
throughout.)

5. Nathan Bedford Forrest, "Report of Maj. Gen. Nathan B.
Forrest, C.S. Army, Commanding Cavalry, of the Capture of Fort
Pillow," Shotgun's Home of the American Civil War, accessed March 6,
2012, http://www.civilwarhome.com/forrest.htm.

6. Jack Hurst, *Nathan Bedford Forrest: A Biography* (New York:
Knopf, 1993), 174.

7. Foote, *Civil War*, 111.

8. Cimprich and Mainfort, "Fort Pillow," 295.

Last names and
title refer to
an earlier note
by the same
authors.

9. Ibid., 305.

10. Ibid., 299.

11. Foote, *Civil War*, 110.

12. Quoted in Wills, *Battle from the Start*, 187.

Writer cites an
indirect source:
words quoted in
another source.

13. Albert Castel, "The Fort Pillow Massacre: A Fresh Examination
of the Evidence," *Civil War History* 4, no. 1 (1958): 44-45.

14. Cimprich and Mainfort, "Fort Pillow," 300.

15. Hurst, *Nathan Bedford Forrest*, 177.

16. Ibid.

17. Dudley Taylor Cornish, *The Sable Arm: Black Troops in
the Union Army, 1861–1865* (Lawrence: University Press of Kansas,
1987), 175.

Bibliography

Castel, Albert. "The Fort Pillow Massacre: A Fresh Examination of the Evidence." *Civil War History* 4, no. 1 (1958): 37-50.

Cimprich, John, and Robert C. Mainfort Jr., eds. "Fort Pillow Revisited: New Evidence about an Old Controversy." *Civil War History* 28, no. 4 (1982): 293-306.

Cornish, Dudley Taylor. *The Sable Arm: Black Troops in the Union Army, 1861-1865.* Lawrence: University Press of Kansas, 1987.

Foote, Shelby. *The Civil War, a Narrative: Red River to Appomattox.* New York: Vintage, 1986.

Forrest, Nathan Bedford. "Report of Maj. Gen. Nathan B. Forrest, C.S. Army, Commanding Cavalry, of the Capture of Fort Pillow." Shotgun's Home of the American Civil War. Accessed March 6, 2012. http://www.civilwarhome.com/forrest.htm.

Hurst, Jack. *Nathan Bedford Forrest: A Biography.* New York: Knopf, 1993.

McPherson, James M. *Battle Cry of Freedom: The Civil War Era.* New York: Oxford University Press, 1988.

Wills, Brian Steel. *A Battle from the Start: The Life of Nathan Bedford Forrest.* New York: HarperCollins, 1992.

Bibliography begins on a new page.

Entries are alphabetized by authors' last names.

First line of entry is at left margin; additional lines are indented ½".

Entries are single-spaced, with double-spacing between entries. (Some instructors may prefer double-spacing throughout.)

Part VI: Research and Documentation in the Social Sciences

Finding sources in the social sciences

Social scientists interpret and analyze human behavior, generally using empirical methods of research. Though original data gathering and analysis are central to social sciences research, researchers also use library and Internet resources to:

- obtain raw data for model building or analysis
- locate information about a particular model, theory, or methodology to be used in a research project
- review the literature to place new research in context

Subjects of study in the social sciences sometimes cross disciplines and may be difficult to locate through typical subject headings in indexes and abstracts. In addition, new theories may take some time to circulate in the literature, especially in print sources. Consequently, the researcher should be prepared to identify potential search terms by scanning indexes and abstracts in relevant works, use the references in published articles and books to trace connections among theories and ideas, and work from the most recent to older sources.

A review of literature for a social sciences research project should not only identify what research has been done but also compare and contrast the available information and evaluate its significance.

Each of the social sciences has a well-developed set of research tools to help you find relevant material. The tools listed here will give you ideas for beginning your research. Consult a librarian for help in refining your search.

General resources

For background information

International Encyclopedia of the Social and Behavioral Sciences. Ed. Neil J. Smelser and Paul B. Baltes. Amsterdam: Elsevier, 2001. A vast compendium of scholarly articles on topics in the social sciences. International and interdisciplinary in perspective, this work is particularly useful for its cross-references among related topics.

Databases

Google Scholar. Mountain View: Google, 2004–. <http://scholar .google.com/>. A version of the Google search engine that focuses on scholarly sources. It searches the content of publications in many fields, including the social sciences, provides links to the publisher's site where the information is frequently behind a paywall, and links to other versions of the source. Particularly useful is the "cited by" link, giving you a quick view of how influential a source has been. Content available in your library may show up as links; if not, you can configure Google Scholar to find library links. For articles and books unavailable locally, you can request them through interlibrary loan rather than buy them; ask a librarian for details.

SAGE Premier. Thousand Oaks: Sage, 2009–. <http://www.sagepub .com/librarians/premier.sp>. Full-text content of over 600 journals published by a major social sciences publisher. Some libraries may have selected subsets of this database or may have *SAGE Knowledge*, which focuses on the content of books published by Sage.

Social Sciences Citation Index. Philadelphia: Thomson Reuters, 1956–. <http://thomsonreuters.com/social-sciences-citation-index/>. An interdisciplinary database covering journals in the social sciences. Search by author, keyword, or cited source, a way to trace the influence of a particular work. Part of the *Web of Knowledge*, sometimes called *Web of Science*, this database also offers a powerful Related Records search, which identifies articles that have sources in common.

Social Sciences Full Text. Ispwich: EBSCO, 2011–. <http://www.ebscohost .com/academic/social-sciences-full-text>. Provides access to articles and references to several hundred journals in the social sciences.

SSRN: Social Sciences Research Network. Rochester: Social Science Electronic Publishing, 1994–. <http://www.ssrn.com>. A repository of mostly free open-access scholarly research, including published articles, preprints of articles (drafts that may not include final edits), and original research reports.

Anthropology

For background information

Encyclopedia of World Cultures. Ed. David Levinson. Boston: G. K. Hall, 1991–2002. Covers more than 1,500 cultural groups, arranged alphabetically within regions. Entries summarize information on the distribution, belief systems, kinship structures, and history of the groups and provide selective bibliographies. The encyclopedia is based on information in the *Human Relations Area Files*, a vast compendium of anthropology research data.

Database

AnthroSource. Arlington: American Anthropological Association, 2005–. <http://www.aaanet.org/publications/anthrosource/>. The most important online resource for the field and contains the full text of publications of the association from the first issues to the most recent.

Business and economics

For background information

Blackwell Encyclopedia of Management. Ed. Chris Argyris, William Starbuck, and Cary L. Cooper. Hoboken: Wiley, 2005. <http://www.managementencyclopedia.com/>. Offers coverage of topics in accounting, entrepreneurship, human resources, business ethics, finance, marketing, organizational behavior, and more.

New Palgrave Dictionary of Economics. Ed. Steven N. Durlauf and Lawrence E. Blume. Rev. ed. New York: Palgrave Macmillan, 2008. <http://www.dictionaryofeconomics.com/>. A revision of the classic *Palgrave's Dictionary of Political Economy* offering scholarly analyses of economic theories and theorists.

Databases

ABI Inform. Ann Arbor: ProQuest, 1971–. <http://www.proquest.com/products-services/abi_inform_complete.html>. A database that includes many different kinds of information useful for business, including research articles, industry news, company profiles, market data, and the text of the *Wall Street Journal* and other influential publications. There are a number of similar databases that aggregate business information, including *Lexis/Nexis, Business Insights,* and *Value Line.* Check your library's Web site to see which might be available to you.

Business Source Premier. Ipswich: EBSCO, 1990–. <http://www.ebscohost.com/academic/business-source-premier>. A database of journals and magazines in business and economics, with some full-text coverage (including a few titles going as far back as the 1920s). Coverage includes management, finance, accounting, and international business.

EconLit. Nashville: American Economic Association, 1969–. <http://www.aeaweb.org/econlit/>. Provides citations (most with abstracts) to articles in scholarly journals in the field, covering all aspects of economics worldwide.

Data and documents online

Bureau of Labor Statistics. <http://www.bls.gov>. A mine of current statistical data and reports covering consumer spending, employment, wages, productivity, occupations, international trade, and industries as well as "The U.S. Economy at a Glance." The bureau is a unit of the U.S. Department of Labor.

SEC Filings and Forms. (EDGAR). <http://www.sec.gov/edgar.shtml>. Provides information about publicly held corporations, which are required by federal law to file reports on their activities with the U.S. Securities and Exchange Commission. Most reports from 1994 to the present are publicly available through the *EDGAR (Electronic Data Gathering, Analysis, and Retrieval System)* database at this site. Information in company reports includes financial status, chief officers, stock information, company history, pending litigation that might have an economic impact on the company, and more. The site provides a brief tutorial for searching *EDGAR.*

U.S. Congressional Budget Office. <http://www.cbo.gov>. Offers material compiled by a nonpartisan office for congressional decision making. The site includes federal budget analysis, the economic outlook, coverage of topics such as housing, health, education, national security, and telecommunications, and more.

Communication studies

For background information

International Encyclopedia of Communication. Ed. Wolfgang Donsbach. Malden: Blackwell, 2008. <http://www.communicationencyclopedia .com/>. A definitive global source for information about every aspect of communication, including interpersonal and group communication as well as mass media and visual communication.

Database

Communication and Mass Media Complete. Ipswich: EBSCO, 2004–. <http://www.ebscohost.com/academic/communication-mass-media-complete>. An online database that covers both scholarly articles on communication studies and trade and popular coverage of the media. A substantial portion of the contents is linked to full text, with especially rich historical material on communication theory.

Data and documents online

American Rhetoric Online Speech Bank. <http://www.americanrhetoric .com/speechbank.htm>. Offers over 5,000 speeches, many of them as audio or visual files as well as transcripts.

Journalism.org. <http://www.journalism.org>. News about the news industry, information for working journalists, background on issues of concern to journalists, and a detailed annual survey of the state of the news media, including print, broadcast, cable news, magazines, local TV, alternative media, and online news sources.

Criminal justice

For background information

Encyclopedia of Crime and Justice. Ed. Josua Dressler. 2nd ed. New York: Macmillan Reference, 2002. One of the best sources for overall coverage of the field. Includes issues in law, criminology, and sociology and references to classic studies and recent research. Though the focus is on criminal justice in the United States, international perspectives are included.

Database

Criminal Justice Abstracts. Ipswich: EBSCO, 2010–. <http://www
.ebscohost.com/academic/criminal-justice-abstracts>. A database
that provides summaries and in some cases full text of articles in
major journals in the field.

Data online

Bureau of Justice Statistics. <http://www.ojp.usdoj.gov/bjs>. Provides
information about crime and victimization, law enforcement, corrections, prosecutions, courts and sentencing, drugs, firearms, and
more. This authoritative source for data and analysis of crime in the
United States is a unit of the U.S. Department of Justice.

National Criminal Justice Reference Service. <http://www.ncjrs.gov>. A
federal information resource offering a huge amount of information on corrections, juvenile justice, the courts, law enforcement,
drug interdiction, victimization, and more. It includes a database
of criminal justice articles, some with full text. Provided by the U.S.
Department of Justice.

Education

For background information

Encyclopedia of Education. Ed. James W. Guthrie. 2nd ed. New York:
Macmillan Reference, 2003. More than 850 articles cover education
theory, history of education, education and social forces, and education reform efforts. Emphasis is on the U.S. experience, but the text
provides some international perspectives as well. Volume 8 includes
primary sources and a thematic outline.

Database

ERIC: Education Resources Information Center. Washington: Institute of Education Sciences, 1966–. Provides descriptive abstracts of
over a million journal articles and documents — research reports,
conference papers, curriculum guides, and other materials — that are
not formally published otherwise. This database service, sponsored
by the U.S. Department of Education, is available free online at

<http://www.eric.ed.gov> and may also be searchable through your library's Web site.

Data online

National Center for Education Statistics. <http://nces.ed.gov>. Provides a wealth of statistical data on schools and libraries in the United States, including academic achievement; the condition of schools; comparative information on school districts, colleges, and libraries; dropout rates; enrollment trends; school safety; and more. The center is a unit of the U.S. Department of Education.

Ethnic and area studies

For background information

Africana: The Encyclopedia of the African and African American Experience. Ed. Kwame Anthony Appiah and Henry Louis Gates Jr. 2nd ed. New York: Oxford University Press, 2005. Offers over 4,000 articles on Africa and the African diaspora, with extensive coverage of African American history and culture.

Encyclopedia Latina: History, Culture, and Society in the United States. Ed. Ilan Stavans and Harold Augenbraum. Danbury: Grolier, 2005. Covers Latino/a culture in the United States, including influential people and topics in the areas of history, family life, education, the arts, popular culture, immigration, historical periods, and places of origin.

Encyclopedia of Race, Ethnicity, and Society. Ed. Richard T. Schaefer. Thousand Oaks: Sage, 2008. <http://knowledge.sagepub.com/view/ethnicity/SAGE.xml>. Covers ethnic relations within the United States and worldwide, including information about particular groups and related topics.

Gale Encyclopedia of Multicultural America. Ed. Julie Galens et al. 2nd ed. Detroit: Gale Group, 2000. Offers more than 100 extensive essays on ethnic groups in the United States, covering origins, circumstances of arrival, family, community, culture, economy, politics, and significant contributions.

Gale Encyclopedia of Native American Tribes. Detroit: Gale Group, 1998. An authoritative guide to the history and modern status of nearly 400 tribes, with historical background, past and current location, religious beliefs, language, means of subsistence, healing practices, customs, oral literature, and current issues.

Database

Ethnic NewsWatch. Ann Arbor: ProQuest, 1985–. <http://www.proquest .com/products-services/ethnic_newswatch.html>. A full-text database specializing in publications by ethnic communities in the United States, which are often left out of general news and magazine databases. Providing valuable alternative insights, this work includes many publications in Spanish and can be searched in a Spanish-language interface.

Gender and women's studies

For background information

Encyclopedia of Sex and Gender. Ed. Fedwa Malti-Douglas. Detroit: Macmillan, 2007. Offers articles on sexuality, identity, class, ethnicity, and social institutions through the lens of gender.

Women in World History: A Biographical Encyclopedia. Ed. Anne Commire and Deborah Klezmer. Waterford: Yorkin, 1999–2002. The largest compilation of biographical material on the world's women. This work contains biographies of historically significant women from all walks of life around the world.

Databases

GenderWatch. Ann Arbor: ProQuest, 1970–. <http://www.proquest .com/products-services/genderwatch.html>. Covers over 300 periodicals, most of them in full text, focused on gender, women's studies, and LGBT issues.

Women's Studies International. Ispwich: EBSCO, 1972–. <http://www .ebscohost.com/academic/womens-studies-international>. Lists articles, books, book chapters, reports, and other materials relevant to gender and feminist research.

Geography

For background information

Columbia Gazetteer of the World. Ed. Saul B. Cohen. 2nd ed. New York: Columbia University Press, 2008. <http://www.columbiagazetteer.org>. Provides the exact location of places and geographical features around the world and gives a very brief definition or description. This is the most complete gazetteer available.

Encyclopedia of Geography. Thousand Oaks: Sage, 2010. Covers topics in human and physical geography, geographic information systems, and significant people, institutions, and methods of research in geography.

Database

GEOBASE. New York: Elsevier, 1989–. <http://www.geobase.ca/>. An index of books and articles relevant to human and physical geography, including some coverage of geology and ecology.

Data online

American FactFinder. Washington: Bureau of the Census, 1990–. <http://factfinder2.census.gov>. A site for exploring data about places in the United States down to the zip code level, drawing on the census, the American Community Survey, and other sources. For access to a vast amount of data, see the Bureau of the Census at <http://www.census.gov>.

International Human Development Indicators. Geneva: United Nations Human Development Programme, 1990–. <http://hdr.undp.org/en>. A collection of global data, much of it keyed to geographic location. Includes country profiles and tools for creating tables, visualizing, and mapping data.

Health sciences and nursing

Databases

CINAHL: Cumulative Index to Nursing and Allied Health Literature. Glendale: EBSCO, 1977–. <http://www.ebscohost.com/biomedical-libraries/the-cinahl-database>. Covers publications related to nursing research and practice, providing references to articles, books and book chapters, pamphlets and other documents, and standards of professional practice and research.

Cochrane Library. Chichester: Wiley, 1993–. <http://www.theco chranelibrary.com>. Provides well-researched systematic reviews of medical research designed to evaluate the overall efficacy of treatments to support evidence-based practice. These well-researched reviews are produced by a global nonprofit collaboration of health care professionals.

PubMed. Bethesda: National Library of Medicine, 1948–. <http://www.pubmed.gov>. The most comprehensive coverage of medical research, free to everyone in the world. Some libraries offer this database under the name *Medline*. Provides abstracts to research in medicine, nursing, dentistry, veterinary medicine, health care, and the preclinical sciences published from the 1950s to the present. *PubMed* is provided by the National Library of Medicine. Results of a search can be limited to freely available full-text articles.

Documents and data online

Centers for Disease Control and Prevention. Druid Hills: CDC, 1992–. <http://www.cdc.gov>. The CDC is the federal government's lead agency for preventing disease and promoting health. The agency's Web site provides information on health and safety topics, an index of health information, technical publications such as *The Mortality and Morbidity Weekly Report*, and current news about health risks.

National Center for Health Statistics. Hyattsville: NCHS, 1960–. <http://www.cdc.gov/nchs>. Provides a wealth of statistical data on health in the United States, including analysis of trends, health reports on specific populations, and leading causes of death. The center is part of the Centers for Disease Control.

National Institute of Nursing Research. Bethesda: NINR, 1986–. <http://www.ninr.nih.gov>. A U.S. government program devoted to clinical and basic research efforts in patient care. Included on the site are many publications and an online course for nurses who wish to conduct research.

National Institutes of Health. Bethesda: NIH, 1930–. <http://www.nih.gov>. Offers information on current medical research funded by the U.S. government in the areas of cancer, mental health, human genomes, drug and alcohol abuse, and a wide variety of other illnesses and medical specialties. Though much of the information available from the NIH is technical, every subject area contains information written for a nonspecialist audience.

Law

For background information

Gale Encyclopedia of American Law. Ed. Donna Batten. 3rd Ed. Detroit: Gale, 2005. Presents legal issues clearly in articles written for a general audience.

Database

LexisNexis Academic. Bethesda: LexisNexis, 1998–. <http://www.lexisnexis.com/us/lnacademic/>. The *LexisNexis* databases include cases, codes, legal analysis, and legal news. Of particular note is the ability to search for the full text of state and federal court decisions (also known as *case law*) by keyword, party name, or citation, and the Law Reviews section, which offers the full text of scholarly articles that analyze legal issues in depth. Also includes coverage of newspapers and business information.

Documents online

LII: Legal Information Institute. <http://www.law.cornell.edu>. A directory of legal documents on the Web, including texts of case law and statutes for state, federal, and international jurisdictions. The site, organized alphabetically by topic, also provides links to court opinions and directories to law organizations and journals. The institute is a project of the Cornell University Law School.

Political science

For background information

Encyclopedia of American Foreign Policy. 2nd ed. New York: Scribner, 2002. Offers essays on topics related to foreign-policy issues and doctrines, such as terrorism, environmental diplomacy, and refugee policies.

International Encyclopedia of Political Science. Ed. Bertrand Badie, Dirk Berg-Schlosser, and Leonardo Morlino. Thousand Oaks: Sage, 2011. <http://knowledge.sagepub.com/view/intlpoliticalscience/SAGE.xml>.

Covers theory, methodology, comparative politics, public policy, and international relations.

Database

Public Affairs Index. Ipswich: EBSCO, 2009–. <http://www.ebscohost.com/academic/public-affairs-index>. Indexes articles and documents on public policy in the United States and globally.

Data and documents online

American National Election Studies. Ann Arbor: ANES, 1948–. <http://www.electionstudies.org>. This research center, a project of Stanford University, the University of Michigan, and the National Science Foundation, conducts surveys on voting, participation in politics, and public opinion. Requires free registration.

Congress.gov. Washington: Library of Congress, 2013–. <http://www.congress.gov>. A successor to a long-running effort to make public the status of bills before the U.S. Congress, including reports and hearings, the *Congressional Record*, and information about members of Congress. State and foreign legislatures often have similar portals for legislation.

Harris Vault. Rochester: Harris Interactive, 1970–. <http://www.harrisinteractive.com/Insights/HarrisVault.aspx>. An archive of polling data on a variety of issues, with an emphasis on political issues.

Psychology

For background information

Corsini Encyclopedia of Psychology and Behavioral Science. Ed. Irving B. Weiner, and W. Edward Craighead. 4th ed. Hoboken: Wiley, 2010. Defines and discusses terms, theories, methodology, and issues in psychological practice and offers brief biographies of important psychologists.

Encyclopedia of Psychology. Ed. Alan E. Kazdin. Washington: American Psychological Association, 2000. The most thorough and scholarly encyclopedia of psychology topics, including methodology, findings, advances in research, and applications.

Database

PsycINFO. Washington: American Psychological Association, 1927–. <http://www.apa.org/pubs/databases/psycinfo/>. Provides more than 3 million references to journal articles, books, book chapters, and dissertations in psychology and related fields published from 1840 to the present. Most sources include abstracts; some also provide a complete list of cited works and links to publications that cite the source.

Sociology

For background information

Encyclopedia of Social Theory. Ed. George Ritzer. Thousand Oaks: Sage, 2005. <http://www.sage-ereference.com/view/socialtheory/SAGE.xml>. A handy place to find overviews of theories and theorists, both classical and cutting-edge. A good starting place for tracking down key ideas and foundational sources.

Encyclopedia of Sociology. Ed. Edgar G. Montgomery et al. 2nd ed. New York: Macmillan Library Reference, 2000. Provides scholarly discussions of such topics as class and race, ethnicity, economic sociology, and social structure. The articles are written by specialists and include excellent bibliographies.

Database

Sociological Abstracts. San Diego: ProQuest, 1952–. <http://www .proquest.com/products-services/socioabs-set-c.html>. The most detailed index to research in the field, covering journal articles, book chapters, dissertations, and conference presentations on cultural and social structure, demography, family and social welfare, social development, studies of violence and power, and more.

Citing sources in the social sciences: APA style

In most social science classes, you will be asked to use the APA system for documenting sources, which is set forth in the *Publication Manual of the American Psychological Association*, 6th ed. (Washington, DC: APA, 2010).

APA recommends in-text citations that refer readers to a list of references. An in-text citation gives the author of the source (often in a signal phrase), the year of publication, and often a page number in parentheses. At the end of the paper, a list of references provides publication information about the source; the list is alphabetized by authors' last names (or by titles for works with no authors). The direct link between the in-text citation and the entry in the reference list is highlighted in the following example.

IN-TEXT CITATION

Yanovski and Yanovski (2002) reported that "the current state of the treatment for obesity is similar to the state of the treatment of hypertension several decades ago" (p. 600).

ENTRY IN THE LIST OF REFERENCES

Yanovski, S. Z., & Yanovski, J. A. (2002). Drug therapy: Obesity. *The New England Journal of Medicine, 346,* 591-602.

For a reference list that includes this entry, see page 233.

APA in-text citations

APA's in-text citations provide the author's last name and the year of publication, usually before the cited material, and a page number in parentheses directly after the cited material. In the following models, the elements of the in-text citation are highlighted.

NOTE: APA style requires the use of the past tense or the present perfect tense in signal phrases introducing cited material: *Smith (2012) reported, Smith (2012) has argued.*

1. Basic format for a quotation Ordinarily, introduce the quotation with a signal phrase that includes the author's last name followed by the year of publication in parentheses. Put the page number (preceded by "p.") in parentheses after the quotation. For sources from the Web without page numbers, see item 12a on page 180.

Critser (2003) noted that despite growing numbers of overweight Americans, many health care providers still "remain either in ignorance or outright denial about the health danger to the poor and the young" (p. 5).

If the author is not named in the signal phrase, place the author's name, the year, and the page number in parentheses after the quotation: (Critser, 2003, p. 5). (See items 6 and 12 for citing sources that lack authors; item 12 also explains how to handle sources without dates or page numbers.)

NOTE: Do not include a month in an in-text citation, even if the entry in the reference list includes the month.

2. Basic format for a summary or a paraphrase   As for a quotation (see item 1), include the author's last name and the year either in a signal phrase introducing the material or in parentheses following it. Use a page number, if one is available, following the cited material. For sources from the Web without page numbers, see item 12a on page 180.

Yanovski and Yanovski (2002) explained that sibutramine suppresses appetite by blocking the reuptake of the neurotransmitters serotonin and norepinephrine in the brain (p. 594).

Sibutramine suppresses appetite by blocking the reuptake of the neurotransmitters serotonin and norepinephrine in the brain (Yanovski & Yanovski, 2002, p. 594).

3. Work with two authors   Name both authors in the signal phrase or in parentheses each time you cite the work. In the parentheses, use "&" between the authors' names; in the signal phrase, use "and."

According to Sothern and Gordon (2003), "Environmental factors may contribute as much as 80% to the causes of childhood obesity" (p. 104).

Obese children often engage in limited physical activity (Sothern & Gordon, 2003, p. 104).

4. Work with three to five authors Identify all authors in the signal phrase or in parentheses the first time you cite the source.

In 2003, Berkowitz, Wadden, Tershakovec, and Cronquist concluded, "Sibutramine . . . must be carefully monitored in adolescents, as in adults, to control increases in [blood pressure] and pulse rate" (p. 1811).

In subsequent citations, use the first author's name followed by "et al." in either the signal phrase or the parentheses.

As Berkowitz et al. (2003) advised, "Until more extensive safety and efficacy data are available, . . . weight-loss medications should be used only on an experimental basis for adolescents" (p. 1811).

5. Work with six or more authors Use the first author's name followed by "et al." in the signal phrase or in parentheses.

McDuffie et al. (2002) tested 20 adolescents, aged 12-16, over a three-month period and found that orlistat, combined with behavioral therapy, produced an average weight loss of 4.4 kg, or 9.7 pounds (p. 646).

6. Work with unknown author If the author is unknown, mention the work's title in the signal phrase or give the first word or two of the title in parentheses. Titles of short works such as articles are put in quotation marks; titles of long works such as books and reports are italicized.

Children struggling to control their weight must also struggle with the pressures of television advertising that, on the one hand, encourages the consumption of junk food and, on the other, celebrates thin celebrities ("Television," 2002).

NOTE: In the rare case when "Anonymous" is specified as the author, treat it as if it were a real name: (Anonymous, 2001). In the list of references, also use the name Anonymous as author.

7. Organization as author   If the author is an organization or a government agency, name the organization in the signal phrase or in the parentheses the first time you cite the source.

> Obesity puts children at risk for a number of medical complications, including Type 2 diabetes, hypertension, sleep apnea, and orthopedic problems (Henry J. Kaiser Family Foundation, 2004, p. 1).

If the organization has a familiar abbreviation, you may include it in brackets the first time you cite the source and use the abbreviation alone in later citations.

> FIRST CITATION   (Centers for Disease Control and Prevention [CDC], 2012)
>
> LATER CITATIONS   (CDC, 2012)

8. Authors with the same last name   To avoid confusion if your reference list includes two or more authors with the same last name, use initials with the last names in your in-text citations.

> Research by E. Smith (1989) revealed that. . . .

> One 2012 study contradicted . . . (R. Smith, p. 234).

9. Two or more works by the same author in the same year   When your list of references includes more than one work by the same author in the same year, you will use lowercase letters ("a," "b," and so on) with the year to order the entries in the reference list. (See item 8 on p. 190.) Use those same letters with the year in the in-text citation.

> Research by Durgin (2003b) has yielded new findings about the role of counseling in treating childhood obesity.

10. Two or more works in the same parentheses   Put the works in the same order that they appear in the reference list, separated with semicolons.

Researchers have indicated that studies of pharmacological treatments for childhood obesity are inconclusive (Berkowitz et al., 2003; McDuffie et al., 2002).

11. Multiple citations to the same work in one paragraph If you give the author's name in the text of your paper (not in parentheses) and you mention that source again in the text of the same paragraph, give only the author's name, not the date, in the later citation. If any subsequent reference in the same paragraph is in parentheses, include both the author and the date in the parentheses.

Principal Jean Patrice said, "You have to be able to reach students where they are instead of making them come to you. If you don't, you'll lose them" (personal communication, April 10, 2006). Patrice expressed her desire to see all students get something out of their educational experience. This feeling is common among members of Waverly's faculty. With such a positive view of student potential, it is no wonder that 97% of Waverly High School graduates go on to a four-year university (Patrice, 2006).

12. Web source Cite sources from the Web as you would cite any other source, giving the author and the year when they are available.

Atkinson (2001) found that children who spent at least four hours a day watching TV were less likely to engage in adequate physical activity during the week.

Usually a page number is not available; occasionally a Web source will lack an author or a date (see 12a, 12b, and 12c).

a. No page numbers When a Web source lacks stable numbered pages, you may include paragraph numbers or headings to help readers locate the passage being cited.

If the source has numbered paragraphs, use the paragraph number preceded by the abbreviation "para.": (Hall, 2012, para. 5). If the source has no numbered paragraphs but contains headings, cite the appropriate heading in parentheses;

you may also indicate which paragraph under the heading you are referring to, even if the paragraphs are not numbered.

> Hoppin and Taveras (2004) pointed out that several other medications were classified by the Drug Enforcement Administration as having the "potential for abuse" ("Weight-Loss Drugs," para. 6).

NOTE: For PDF documents that have stable page numbers, give the page number in the parenthetical citation.

b. Unknown author   If no author is named in the source, mention the title of the source in a signal phrase or give the first word or two of the title in parentheses (see also item 6). (If an organization serves as the author, see item 7.)

> The body's basal metabolic rate, or BMR, is a measure of its at-rest energy requirement ("Exercise," 2003).

c. Unknown date   When the source does not give a date, use the abbreviation "n.d." (for "no date").

> Attempts to establish a definitive link between television programming and children's eating habits have been problematic (Magnus, n.d.).

13. An entire Web site   If you are citing an entire Web site, not an internal page or a section, give the URL in the text of your paper but do not include it in the reference list.

> The U.S. Center for Nutrition Policy and Promotion website (http://www.cnpp.usda.gov/) provides useful information about diet and nutrition for children and adults.

14. Multivolume work   If you have used more than one volume from a multivolume work, add the volume number in parentheses with the page number.

> Banford (2009) has demonstrated stable weight loss over time from a combination of psychological counseling, exercise, and nutritional planning (Volume 2, p. 135).

15. Personal communication   Interviews that you conduct, memos, letters, e-mail messages, social media posts, and similar communications that would be difficult for your readers to retrieve should be cited in the text only, not in the reference list. (Use the first initial with the last name in parentheses.)

> One of Atkinson's colleagues, who has studied the effect of the media on children's eating habits, has contended that advertisers for snack foods will need to design ads responsibly for their younger viewers (F. Johnson, personal communication, October 20, 2013).

16. Course materials   Cite lecture notes from your instructor or your own class notes as personal communication (see item 15). If your instructor distributes or posts materials that contain publication information, cite as you would the appropriate source (for instance, an article, a section in a Web document, or a video). See also item 65 on page 216.

17. Part of a source (chapter, figure)   To cite a specific part of a source, such as a whole chapter or a figure or table, identify the element in parentheses. Don't abbreviate terms such as "Figure," "Chapter," and "Section"; "page" is always abbreviated "p." (or "pp." for more than one page).

> The data support the finding that weight loss stabilizes with consistent therapy and ongoing monitoring (Hanniman, 2010, Figure 8-3, p. 345).

18. Indirect source (source quoted in another source)   When a writer's or a speaker's quoted words appear in a source written by someone else, begin the parenthetical citation with the words "as cited in." In the following example, Critser is the author of the source given in the reference list; that source contains a quotation by Satcher.

> Former surgeon general Dr. David Satcher described "a nation of young people seriously at risk of starting out obese and dooming themselves to the difficult task of overcoming a tough illness" (as cited in Critser, 2003, p. 4).

19. Sacred or classical text Identify the text, the version or edition you used, and the relevant part (chapter, verse, line). It is not necessary to include the source in the reference list.

> Peace activists have long cited the biblical prophet's vision of a world without war: "And they shall beat their swords into plowshares, and their spears into pruning hooks; nation shall not lift up sword against nation, neither shall they learn war any more" (Isaiah 2:4, Revised Standard Version).

APA list of references

As you gather sources for an assignment, you will likely find sources in print, on the Web, and in other places. The information you will need for the reference list at the end of your paper will differ slightly for some sources, but the main principles apply to all sources: You should identify an author, a creator, or a producer whenever possible; give a title; and provide the date on which the source was produced. Some sources will require page numbers; some will require a publisher; and some will require retrieval information. For general guidelines on the reference list, see the box that begins on page 187.

Directory to APA reference list models

General guidelines for listing authors

1. Single author, 186
2. Two to seven authors, 186
3. Eight or more authors, 186
4. Organization as author, 189
5. Unknown author, 189
6. Author using a pseudonym (pen name) or screen name, 189

7. Two or more works by the same author, 190
8. Two or more works by the same author in the same year, 190
9. Editor, 190
10. Author and editor, 191
11. Translator, 191
12. Editor and translator, 191

Directory to APA reference list models (*cont.*)

Section 61b provides specific requirements for and examples of many of the sources you are likely to encounter. When you cite sources, your goals are to show that the sources you've used are reliable and relevant to your work, to provide your readers with enough information so that they can find your sources easily, and to provide that information in a consistent way according to APA conventions.

In the list of references, include only sources that you have quoted, summarized, or paraphrased in your paper.

General guidelines for listing authors

The formatting of authors' names in items 1–12 applies to all sources in print and on the Web — books, articles, Web sites, and so on. For more models of specific source types, see items 13–69.

1. Single author

author: last name + initial(s) | year (book) | title (book)

Rosenberg, T. (2011). *Join the club: How peer pressure can transform the world.*

place of publication | publisher

New York, NY: Norton.

2. Two to seven authors
List up to seven authors by last names followed by initials. Use an ampersand (&) before the name of the last author. (See items 3–5 on pp. 177–78 for citing works with multiple authors in the text of your paper.)

all authors: last name + initial(s) | year (book) | title (book)

Stanford, D. J., & Bradley, B. A. (2012). *Across the Atlantic ice: The origins of*

place of publication | publisher

America's Clovis culture. Berkeley: University of California Press.

all authors: last name + initial(s)

Ludwig, J., Duncan, G. J., Gennetian, L. A., Katz, L. F., Kessler, R. C., Kling,

year (journal) | title (article)

J. R., & Sanbonmatsu, L. (2012). Neighborhood effects on the long-

journal title | volume | page(s)

term well-being of low-income adults. *Science, 337,* 1505-1510.

DOI

doi:10.1126/science.1224648

3. Eight or more authors
List the first six authors followed by three ellipsis dots and the last author's name.

Tøttrup, A. P., Klaassen, R. H. G., Kristensen, M. W., Strandberg, R., Vardanis, Y., Lindström, Å., . . . Thorup, K. (2012). Drought in Africa caused delayed arrival of European songbirds. *Science, 338,* 1307. doi:10.1126 /science.1227548

General guidelines for the reference list

In APA style, the alphabetical list of works cited, which appears at the end of the paper, is titled "References."

Authors and dates

- Alphabetize entries in the list of references by authors' last names; if a work has no author, alphabetize it by its title.

- For all authors' names, put the last name first, followed by a comma; use initials for the first and middle names.

- With two or more authors, use an ampersand (&) before the last author's name. Separate the names with commas. Include names for the first seven authors; if there are eight or more authors, give the first six authors, three ellipsis dots, and the last author.

- If the author is a company or an organization, give the name in normal order.

- Put the date of publication immediately after the first element of the citation. Enclose the date in parentheses, followed by a period (outside the parentheses).

- For books, give the year of publication. For magazines, newspapers, and newsletters, give the exact date as in the publication (the year plus the month or the year plus the month and the day). For sources on the Web, give the date of posting, if it is available. Use the season if the publication gives only a season and not a month.

Titles

- Italicize the titles and subtitles of books, journals, and other long works.

- Use no italics or quotation marks for the titles of articles.

- For books and articles, capitalize only the first word of the title and subtitle and all proper nouns.

- For the titles of journals, magazines, and newspapers, capitalize all words of four letters or more (and all nouns, pronouns, verbs, adjectives, and adverbs of any length). →

General guidelines for the reference list (*cont.*)

Place of publication and publisher

- Take the information about a book from its title page and copyright page. If more than one place of publication is listed, use only the first.

- Give the city and state for all US cities. Use postal abbreviations for all states.

- Give the city and country for all non-US cities; include the province for Canadian cities. Do not abbreviate the country and province.

- Do not give a state if the publisher's name includes it (Ann Arbor: University of Michigan Press, for example).

- In publishers' names, omit terms such as "Company" (or "Co.") and "Inc." but keep "Books" and "Press." Omit first names or initials (Norton, not W. W. Norton, for example).

- If the publisher is the same as the author, use the word "Author" in the publisher position.

Volume, issue, and page numbers

- For a journal or a magazine, give only the volume number if the publication is paginated continuously through each volume; give the volume and issue numbers if each issue begins on page 1.

- Italicize the volume number and put the issue number, not italicized, in parentheses.

- For monthly magazines, give the year and the month; for weekly magazines, add the day.

- For daily and weekly newspapers, give the month, day, and year; use "p." or "pp." before page numbers (if any). For journals and magazines, do not add "p." or "pp."

- When an article appears on consecutive pages, provide the range of pages. When an article does not appear on consecutive pages, give all page numbers: A1, A17. →

General guidelines for the reference list (*cont.*)

URLs, DOIs, and other retrieval information

- For articles and books from the Web, use the DOI (digital object identifier) if the source has one, and do not give a URL. If a source does not have a DOI, give the URL.

- Use a retrieval date for a Web source only if the content is likely to change. Most of the examples in this section do not show a retrieval date because the content of the sources is stable. If you are unsure about whether to use a retrieval date, include the date or consult your instructor.

4. Organization as author

author:
organization name   year   title (book)

American Psychiatric Association. (2013). *Diagnostic and statistical manual of*

                                         organization
                      place   as author
        edition   of publication and publisher

    mental disorders (5th ed.). Washington, DC: Author.

5. Unknown author   Begin the entry with the work's title.

                      year + month + day
    title (article)   (weekly publication) journal title

The rise of the sharing economy. (2013, March 9). *The Economist,*

    volume,
    issue page(s)

    406(8826), 14.

                       place of
    title (book)   year   publication   publisher

New concise world atlas. (2010). New York, NY: Oxford University Press.

6. Author using a pseudonym (pen name) or screen name   Use the author's real name, if known, and give the pseudonym or screen name in brackets exactly as it appears in the source. If only the screen name is known, begin with that name and do

not use brackets. (See also items 47 and 68 on citing screen names in social media.)

screen name   year + month + day (daily publication)   title of original article

littlebigman. (2012, December 13). Re: Who's watching? Privacy concerns

                  label   title of publication

     persist as smart meters roll out [Comment]. *National Geographic Daily News.*

                URL for Web publication

     Retrieved from http://news.nationalgeographic.com/

7. Two or more works by the same author   Use the author's name for all entries. List the entries by year, the earliest first.

Heinrich, B. (2009). *Summer world: A season of bounty.* New York, NY: Ecco.

Heinrich, B. (2012). *Life everlasting: The animal way of death.* New York, NY:
     Houghton Mifflin Harcourt.

8. Two or more works by the same author in the same year   List the works alphabetically by title. In the parentheses, following the year add "a," "b," and so on. Use these same letters when giving the year in the in-text citation. (See also p. 222 and item 9 on p. 179.)

Bower, B. (2012a, December 15). Families in flux. *Science News, 182*(12), 16.

Bower, B. (2012b, November 3). Human-Neandertal mating gets a new date.
     Science News, 182(9), 8.

9. Editor   Begin with the name of the editor or editors; place the abbreviation "Ed." (or "Eds." for more than one editor) in parentheses following the name. (See item 10 for a work with both an author and an editor.)

           all editors:
         last name + initial(s)   year   title (book)

Carr, S. C., MacLachlan, M., & Furnham, A. (Eds.). (2012). *Humanitarian work*

         place of
         publication   publisher

     psychology. New York, NY: Palgrave.

10. Author and editor   Begin with the name of the author, followed by the name of the editor and the abbreviation "Ed." For an author with two or more editors, use the abbreviation "Ed." after each editor's name: Gray, W., & Jones, P. (Ed.), & Smith, A. (Ed.).

author	editor	year	title (book)

James, W., & Pelikan, J. (Ed.). (2009). *The varieties of religious experience.*

place of publication	publisher	original publication information

New York, NY: Library of America. (Original work published 1902)

11. Translator   Begin with the name of the author. After the title, in parentheses place the name of the translator (in normal order) and the abbreviation "Trans." (for "Translator"). Add the original date of publication at the end of the entry.

author	year	title (book)	translator	place of publication

Scheffer, P. (2011). *Immigrant nations* (L. Waters, Trans.). Cambridge, England:

publisher	original publication information

Polity Press. (Original work published 2007)

12. Editor and translator   If the editor and translator are the same person, the same name appears in both the editor position and the translator position.

Girard, R., & Williams, J. G. (Ed.). (2012). *Resurrection from the underground*
(J. G. Williams, Trans.). East Lansing: Michigan State University Press.
(Original work published 1996)

Articles and other short works

13. Article in a journal   If an article from the Web or a database has no DOI, include the URL for the journal's home page.

a. Print

all authors: last name + initial(s) — year — article title

Bippus, A. M., Dunbar, N. E., & Liu, S.-J. (2012). Humorous responses to

interpersonal complaints: Effects of humor style and nonverbal expression.

journal title — volume — page(s)

The Journal of Psychology, 146, 437-453.

b. Web

all authors: last name + initial(s) — year — article title

Vargas, N., & Schafer, M. H. (2013). Diversity in action: Interpersonal networks

journal title — volume, issue — page(s)

and the distribution of advice. *Social Science Research, 42*(1), 46-58.

DOI

doi:10.1016/j.ssresearch.2012.08.013

author — year — article title

Brenton, S. (2011). When the personal becomes political: Mitigating damage

journal title (no volume available)

following scandals. *Current Research in Social Psychology.* Retrieved from

URL for journal home page

http://www.uiowa.edu/~grpproc/crisp/crisp.html

Citation at a glance | Article in a journal or magazine (APA)

To cite an article in a print journal or magazine in APA style, include the following elements:

1 Author(s)
2 Year of publication for journal; complete date for magazine
3 Title and subtitle of article

4 Name of journal or magazine
5 Volume number; issue number, if required (see p. 188)
6 Page number(s) of article

JOURNAL TABLE OF CONTENTS

→

(continued)

TITLE PAGE OF ARTICLE

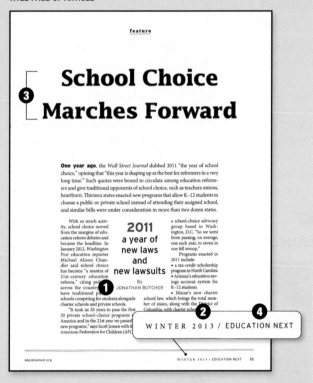

REFERENCE LIST ENTRY FOR AN ARTICLE IN A PRINT JOURNAL OR MAGAZINE

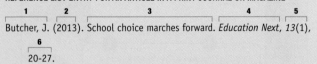

Butcher, J. (2013). School choice marches forward. *Education Next, 13*(1), 20-27.

For more on citing articles in APA style, see items 13–15.

Citation at a glance | Article from a database (APA)

To cite an article from a database in APA style, include the following elements:

1 Author(s)
2 Year of publication for journal; complete date for magazine or newspaper
3 Title and subtitle of article
4 Name of periodical
5 Volume number; issue number, if required (see p. 188)
6 Page number(s)
7 DOI (digital object identifier)
8 URL for periodical's home page (if there is no DOI)

DATABASE RECORD

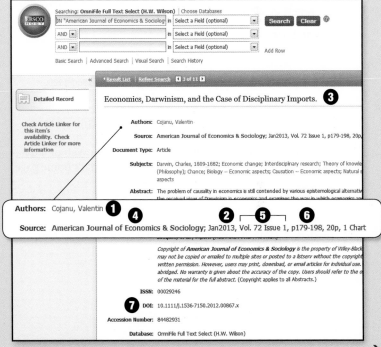

(continued)

REFERENCE LIST ENTRY FOR AN ARTICLE FROM A DATABASE

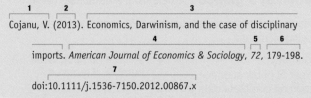

Cojanu, V. (2013). Economics, Darwinism, and the case of disciplinary imports. *American Journal of Economics & Sociology, 72*, 179-198. doi:10.1111/j.1536-7150.2012.00867.x

For more on citing articles from a database in APA style, see items 13–15.

13. Article in a journal (*cont.*)

c. Database

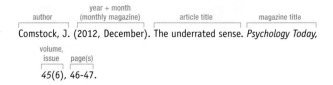

Sohn, K. (2012). The social class origins of U.S. teachers, 1860-1920. *Journal of Social History, 45*(4), 908-935. doi:10.1093/jsh/shr121

14. Article in a magazine   If an article from the Web or a database has no DOI, include the URL for the journal's home page.

a. Print

author | year + month (monthly magazine) | article title | magazine title

Comstock, J. (2012, December). The underrated sense. *Psychology Today,*

volume, issue   page(s)

45(6), 46-47.

14. Article in a magazine (*cont.*)

b. Web

author   date of posting (when available)   article title   magazine title

Burns, J. (2012, December 3). The measure of all things. *The American Prospect.*

URL for home page

Retrieved from http://prospect.org/

c. Database

author   year + month (monthly magazine)   article title   magazine title   volume, issue   page(s)

Tucker, A. (2012, November). Primal instinct. *Smithsonian, 43*(7), 54-63.

URL for magazine home page

Retrieved from http://www.smithsonianmag.com/

15. Article in a newspaper

a. Print

author   year + month + day   article title

Swarns, R. L. (2012, December 9). A family, for a few days a year. *The*

newspaper title   page(s)

New York Times, pp. 1, 20.

b. Web

author: last name + initial(s)   year + month + day   article title

Villanueva-Whitman, E. (2012, November 27). Working to stimulate

newspaper title

memory function. *Des Moines Register.* Retrieved from http://www

URL for home page

.desmoinesregister.com/

16. Abstract   Add the label "Abstract," in brackets, after the title.

a. Abstract of a journal article

Morales, J., Calvo, A., & Bialystok, E. (2013). Working memory development
in monolingual and bilingual children [Abstract]. *Journal of
Experimental Child Psychology, 114*, 187-202. Retrieved from http://
www.sciencedirect.com/

b. Abstract of a paper

Denham, B. (2012). Diffusing deviant behavior: A communication perspective
on the construction of moral panics [Abstract]. Paper presented at the
AEJMC 2012 Conference, Chicago, IL. Retrieved from http://www.aejmc
.org/home/2012/04/ctm-2012-abstracts/

17. Supplemental material   If an article on the Web contains
supplemental material that is, not part of the main article cite
the material as you would an article and add the label "Supplemental material" in brackets following the title.

Reis, S., Grennfelt, P., Klimont, Z., Amann, M., ApSimon, H., Hettelingh,
J.-P., . . . Williams, M. (2012). From acid rain to climate change
[Supplemental material]. *Science 338*(6111), 1153-1154. doi:10.1126
/science.1226514

18. Article with a title in its title   If an article title contains
another article title or a term usually placed in quotation
marks, use quotation marks around the internal title or the
term.

Easterling, D., & Millesen, J. L. (2012, Summer). Diversifying civic
leadership: What it takes to move from "new faces" to adaptive
problem solving. *National Civic Review*, 20-27. doi:10.1002/ncr.21073

19. Letter to the editor   Insert the words "Letter to the editor" in brackets after the title of the letter. If the letter has no title, use the bracketed words as the title (as in the following example).

Lim, C. (2012, November-December). [Letter to the editor]. *Sierra*. Retrieved from http://www.sierraclub.org/sierra/

20. Editorial or other unsigned article

The business case for transit dollars [Editorial]. (2012, December 9). *Star Tribune*. Retrieved from http://www.startribune.com/

21. Newsletter article   Cite as you would an article in a magazine, giving whatever publication information is available (volume, issue, page numbers, and so on).

Scrivener, L. (n.d.). Why is the minimum wage issue important for food justice advocates? *Food Workers — Food Justice, 15*. Retrieved from http://www.thedatabank.com/dpg/199 /pm.asp?nav=1&ID=41429

22. Review   Give the author and title of the review (if any) and, in brackets, the type of work, the title, and the author for a book or the year for a film. If the review has no author or title, use the material in brackets as the title.

author of review / year (journal)

Aviram, R. B. (2012). [Review of the book *What do I say? The therapist's guide*   book title

book author(s)

to answering client questions, by L. N. Edelstein & C. A. Waehler].

journal title / volume, issue / page(s) / DOI

Psychotherapy, 49(4), 570-571. doi:10.1037/a0029815

Bradley, A., & Olufs, E. (2012). Family dynamics and school violence [Review of

the motion picture *We need to talk about Kevin*, 2011]. *PsycCRITIQUES*,

57(49). doi:10.1037/a0030982

Annotations above the reference, left to right: author(s); year (journal); review title; film title; year (film); journal title; volume, issue; DOI

23. Published interview Begin with the person interviewed, and put the interviewer in brackets following the title (if any).

Githongo, J. (2012, November 20). A conversation with John Githongo
    [Interview by Baobab]. *The Economist*. Retrieved from http://
    www.economist.com/

24. Article in a reference work (encyclopedia, dictionary, wiki)

a. Print See also item 32 on citing a volume in a multivolume work.

Konijn, E. A. (2008). Affects and media exposure. In W. Donsbach (Ed.), *The
    international encyclopedia of communication* (Vol. 1, pp. 123-129).
    Malden, MA: Blackwell.

b. Web

Ethnomethodology. (2006). In *STS wiki*. Retrieved December 15, 2012, from
    http://www.stswiki.org/index.php?title=Ethnomethodology

25. Comment on an online article Begin with the writer's real name or screen name. If both are given, put the real name first, followed by the screen name in brackets. Before the title, use "Re" and a colon. Add "Comment" in brackets following the title.

Danboy125. (2012, November 9). Re: No flowers on the psych ward
    [Comment]. *The Atlantic*. Retrieved from http://www.theatlantic.com/

26. Testimony before a legislative body

Carmona, R. H. (2004, March 2). *The growing epidemic of childhood obesity.* Testimony before the Subcommittee on Competition, Foreign Commerce, and Infrastructure of the U.S. Senate Committee on Commerce, Science, and Transportation. Retrieved from http://www.hhs.gov/asl/testify /t040302.html

27. Paper presented at a meeting or symposium (unpublished)

Karimi, S., Key, G., & Tat, D. (2011, April 22). *Complex predicates in focus.* Paper presented at the West Coast Conference on Formal Linguistics, Tucson, AZ.

28. Poster session at a conference

Lacara, N. (2011, April 24). *Predicate which appositives.* Poster session presented at the West Coast Conference on Formal Linguistics, Tucson, AZ.

Books and other long works

- Citation at a glance: Book, page 202

29. Basic format for a book

a. Print

author(s):
last name
+ initial(s)   year   book title

Child, B. J. (2012). *Holding our world together: Ojibwe women and the survival*

place of
publication   publisher

of community. New York, NY: Viking.

Citation at a glance | Book (APA)

To cite a print book in APA style, include the following elements:

1 Author(s)
2 Year of publication
3 Title and subtitle
4 Place of publication
5 Publisher

TITLE PAGE

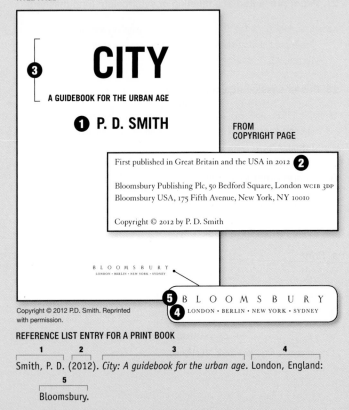

FROM COPYRIGHT PAGE

First published in Great Britain and the USA in 2012 **2**

Bloomsbury Publishing Plc, 50 Bedford Square, London WC1B 3DP
Bloomsbury USA, 175 Fifth Avenue, New York, NY 10010

Copyright © 2012 by P. D. Smith

5 **4** B L O O M S B U R Y
LONDON · BERLIN · NEW YORK · SYDNEY

REFERENCE LIST ENTRY FOR A PRINT BOOK

| 1 | 2 | 3 | 4 |

Smith, P. D. (2012). *City: A guidebook for the urban age.* London, England:

5

Bloomsbury.

For more on citing books in APA style, see items 29–37.

29. Basic format for a book (*cont.*)

b. Web (or online library)   Give the URL for the home page of the Web site or the online library after the book title.

Amponsah, N. A., & Falola, T. (2012). *Women's roles in sub-Saharan Africa.*

Retrieved from http://books.google.com/

c. E-book   Give the version in brackets after the title ("Kindle version," "Nook version," and so on). Include the DOI, or if a DOI is not available, the URL for the home page of the site from which you downloaded the book.

Wolf, D. A., & Folbre, N. (Eds.). (2012). *Universal coverage of long-term care in the United States* [Adobe Digital Editions version]. Retrieved from https://www.russellsage.org/

d. Database   Give the URL for the database after the book title.

Beasley, M. H. (2012). *Women of the Washington press: Politics, prejudice, and persistence.* Retrieved from http://muse.jhu.edu/

30. Edition other than the first   Include the edition number (abbreviated) in parentheses after the title.

Harvey, P. (2013). *An introduction to Buddhism: Teachings, history, and practices* (2nd ed.). Cambridge, England: Cambridge University Press.

31. Selection in an anthology or a collection   An anthology is a collection of works on a common theme, often with different authors for the selections and usually with an editor for the entire volume.

a. Entire anthology

editor(s)   year

Warren, A. E. A., Lerner, R. M., & Phelps, E. (Eds.). (2011). *Thriving and*

title of anthology

spirituality among youth: Research perspectives and future possibilities.

place of
publication   publisher

Hoboken, NJ: Wiley.

b. Selection in an anthology

author of
selection   year   title of selection

Lazar, S. W. (2012). Neural correlates of positive youth development.

editors of anthology

In A. E. A. Warren, R. M. Lerner, & E. Phelps (Eds.), *Thriving and spirituality*

page numbers
of selection

title of anthology

among youth: Research perspectives and future possibilities (pp. 77-90).

place of
publication   publisher

Hoboken, NJ: Wiley.

32. Multivolume work If the volumes have been published over several years, give the span of years in parentheses. If you have used only one volume of a multivolume work, indicate the volume number after the title of the complete work; if the volume has its own title, add that title after the volume number.

a. All volumes

Khalakdina, M. (2008-2011). *Human development in the Indian context: A socio-cultural focus* (Vols. 1-2). New Delhi, India: Sage.

32. Multivolume work (*cont.*)

b. One volume, with title

Jensen, R. E. (Ed.). (2012). *Voices of the American West: Vol. 1. The Indian interviews of Eli S. Ricker, 1903-1919*. Lincoln: University of Nebraska Press.

33. Introduction, preface, foreword, or afterword

Zachary, L. J. (2012). Foreword. In L. A. Daloz, *Mentor: Guiding the journey of adult learners* (pp. v-vii). San Francisco, CA: Jossey-Bass.

34. Dictionary or other reference work

Leong, F. T. L. (Ed.). (2008). *Encyclopedia of counseling* (Vols. 1-4). Thousand Oaks, CA: Sage.

Nichols, J. D., & Nyholm, E. (2012). *A concise dictionary of Minnesota Ojibwe*. Minneapolis: University of Minnesota Press.

35. Republished book

Mailer, N. (2008). *Miami and the siege of Chicago: An informal history of the Republican and Democratic conventions of 1968*. New York, NY: New York Review Books. (Original work published 1968)

36. Book with a title in its title   If the book title contains another book title or an article title, do not italicize the internal title and do not put quotation marks around it.

Marcus, L. (Ed.). (1999). *Sigmund Freud's* The interpretation of dreams*: New interdisciplinary essays*. Manchester, England: Manchester University Press.

37. Book in a language other than English   Place the English translation, not italicized, in brackets.

Carminati, G. G., & Méndez, A. (2012). *Étapes de vie, étapes de soins* [Stages of life, stages of care]. Chêne-Bourg, Switzerland: Médecine & Hygiène.

38. Dissertation

a. Published

Hymel, K. M. (2009). *Essays in urban economics* (Doctoral dissertation). Available from ProQuest Dissertations and Theses database. (AAT 3355930)

b. Unpublished

Mitchell, R. D. (2007). *The Wesleyan Quadrilateral: Relocating the conversation* (Unpublished doctoral dissertation). Claremont School of Theology, Claremont, CA.

39. Conference proceedings

Yu, F.-Y., Hirashima, T., Supnithi, T., & Biswas, G. (2011). *Proceedings of the 19th International Conference on Computers in Education: ICCE 2011.* Retrieved from http://www.apsce.net:8080/icce2011/program /proceedings/

40. Government document   If the document has a number, place the number in parentheses after the title.

U.S. Transportation Department, Pipeline and Hazardous Materials Safety Administration. (2012). *Emergency response guidebook 2012.* Washington, DC: Author.

U.S. Census Bureau, Bureau of Economic Analysis. (2012, December). *U.S. international trade in goods and services, October 2012* (Report No. CB12-232, BEA12-55, FT-900 [12-10]). Retrieved from http://www .census.gov/foreign-trade/Press-Release/2012pr/10/

41. Report from a private organization If the publisher and the author are the same, begin with the publisher. For a print source, use "Author" as the publisher at the end of the entry (see item 4 on p. 189); for an online source, give the URL. If the report has a number, put it in parentheses following the title.

Ford Foundation. (2012, November). *Eastern Africa*. Retrieved from http://
www.fordfoundation.org/pdfs/library/Eastern-Africa-brochure-2012.pdf

Atwood, B., Beam, M., Hindman, D. B., Hindman, E. B., Pintak, L., & Shors,
B. (2012, May 25). *The Murrow Rural Information Initiative: Final
report*. Pullman: Murrow College of Communication, Washington State
University.

42. Legal source The title of a court case is italicized in an in-text citation, but it is not italicized in the reference list.

Sweatt v. Painter, 339 U.S. 629 (1950). Retrieved from Cornell University Law
School, Legal Information Institute website: http://www.law.cornell
.edu/supct/html/historics/USSC_CR_0339_0629_ZS.html

43. Sacred or classical text It is not necessary to list sacred works such as the Bible or the Qur'an or classical Greek and Roman works (such as the *Odyssey*) in your reference list. See item 19 on page 183 for how to cite these sources in the text of your paper.

Web sites and parts of Web sites

- Citation at a glance: Section in a Web document, page 209

NOTE: In an APA paper or an APA reference list entry, the word "website" is spelled all lowercase, as one word.

44. Entire Web site Do not include an entire Web site in the reference list. Give the URL in parentheses when you mention it in the text of your paper. (See item 13 on p. 181.)

45. Document from a Web site List as many of the following elements as are available: author's name, publication date (or "n.d." if there is no date), title (in italics), publisher (if any), and URL. If the publisher is known and is not named as the author, include the publisher in your retrieval statement.

Wagner, D. A., Murphy, K. M., & De Korne, H. (2012, December). *Learning first: A research agenda for improving learning in low-income countries*. Retrieved from Brookings Institution website: http://www.brookings .edu/research/papers/2012/12/learning-first-wagner-murphy-de-korne

Gerber, A. S., & Green, D. P. (2012). *Field experiments: Design, analysis, and interpretation*. Retrieved from Yale Institution for Social and Policy Studies website: http://isps.yale.edu/research/data/d081#.UUy2HFdPL5w

Centers for Disease Control and Prevention. (2012, December 10). *Concussion in winter sports*. Retrieved from http://www.cdc.gov/Features /HockeyConcussions/index.html

46. Section in a Web document Cite as you would a chapter in a book or a selection in an anthology (see item 31b).

Pew Research Center. (2012, December 12). About the 2012 Pew global attitudes survey. In *Social networking popular across globe*. Retrieved from http://www.pewglobal.org/2012/12/12 /social-networking-popular-across-globe

Chang, W.-Y., & Milan, L. M. (2012, October). Relationship between degree field and emigration. In *International mobility and employment characteristics among recent recipients of U.S. doctorates*. Retrieved from National Science Foundation website: http://www.nsf.gov/statistics/infbrief/nsf13300

Citation at a glance | Section in a Web document (APA)

To cite a section in a Web document in APA style, include the following elements:

1 Author(s)
2 Date of publication or most recent update ("n.d." if there is no date)
3 Title of section
4 Title of document
5 URL of section

WEB DOCUMENT CONTENTS PAGE

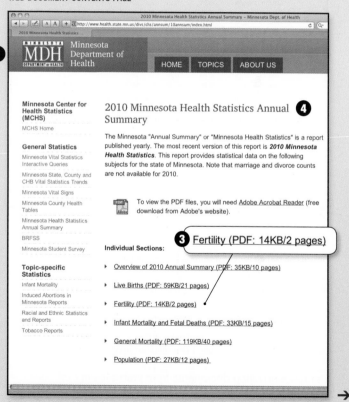

→

(continued)

5 🌐 http://www.health.state.mn.us/divs/chs/annsum/10annsum/Fertility2010.pdf

ON-SCREEN VIEW OF DOCUMENT

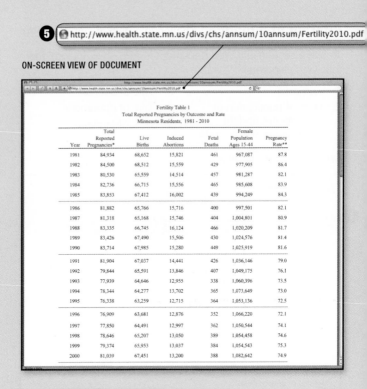

Fertility Table 1
Total Reported Pregnancies by Outcome and Rate
Minnesota Residents, 1981 - 2010

Year	Total Reported Pregnancies*	Live Births	Induced Abortions	Fetal Deaths	Female Population Ages 15-44	Pregnancy Rate**
1981	84,934	68,652	15,821	461	967,087	87.8
1982	84,500	68,512	15,559	429	977,905	86.4
1983	80,530	65,559	14,514	457	981,287	82.1
1984	82,736	66,715	15,556	465	985,608	83.9
1985	83,853	67,412	16,002	439	994,249	84.3
1986	81,882	65,766	15,716	400	997,501	82.1
1987	81,318	65,168	15,746	404	1,004,801	80.9
1988	83,335	66,745	16,124	466	1,020,209	81.7
1989	83,426	67,490	15,506	430	1,024,576	81.4
1990	83,714	67,985	15,280	449	1,025,919	81.6
1991	81,904	67,037	14,441	426	1,036,146	79.0
1992	79,844	65,591	13,846	407	1,049,175	76.1
1993	77,939	64,646	12,955	338	1,060,396	73.5
1994	78,344	64,277	13,702	365	1,073,649	73.0
1995	76,338	63,259	12,715	364	1,053,136	72.5
1996	76,909	63,681	12,876	352	1,066,220	72.1
1997	77,850	64,491	12,997	362	1,050,544	74.1
1998	78,646	65,207	13,050	389	1,054,458	74.6
1999	79,374	65,953	13,037	384	1,054,543	75.3
2000	81,039	67,451	13,200	388	1,082,642	74.9

REFERENCE LIST ENTRY FOR A SECTION IN A WEB DOCUMENT

1 **2** **3** **4**

Minnesota Department of Health. (n.d.). Fertility. In *2010 Minnesota health*

5

statistics annual summary. Retrieved from http://www.health.state

.mn.us/divs/chs/annsum/10annsum/Fertility2010.pdf

For more on citing documents from Web sites in APA style,
see items 45 and 46.

47. Blog post   Begin with the writer's real name or screen name. If both are given, put the real name first, followed by the screen name in brackets. Add the date of the post (or "n.d." if the post is undated). Place the label "Blog post" in brackets following the title of the post. If there is no title, use the bracketed material as the title. End with the URL for the post.

Kerssen, T. (2012, October 5). Hunger is political: Food Sovereignty Prize
    honors social movements [Blog post]. Retrieved from http://www
    .foodfirst.org/en/node/4020

48. Blog comment   Cite as a blog post, but add "Re" and a colon before the title of the original post and the label "Blog comment" following the title.

Studebakerhawk_14611. (2012, December 5). Re: A people's history of MOOCs
    [Blog comment]. Retrieved from http://www.insidehighered.com/blogs
    /library-babel-fish/people's-history-moocs

Audio, visual, and multimedia sources

49. Podcast

Schulz, K. (2011, March). *Kathryn Schulz: On being wrong* [Video podcast].
    Retrieved from TED on http://itunes.apple.com/

Taylor, A., & Parfitt, G. (2011, January 13). *Physical activity and mental
    health: What's the evidence?* [Audio podcast]. Retrieved from Open
    University on http://itunes.apple.com/

50. Video or audio on the Web

Kurzen, B. (2012, April 5). *Going beyond Muslim-Christian conflict in
    Nigeria* [Video file]. Retrieved from http://www.youtube.com
    /watch?v=JD8MIJOA050

Malone, T. W. *Collective intelligence* [Video file]. Retrieved from http://edge
.org/conversation/collective-intelligence

Bever, T., Piattelli-Palmarini, M., Hammond, M., Barss, A., & Bergesen,
A. (2012, February 2). *A basic introduction to Chomsky's linguistics*
[Audio file]. Retrieved from University of Arizona, College of Social
& Behavioral Sciences, Department of Linguistics website: http://
linguistics.arizona.edu/node/711

51. Transcript of an audio or a video file

Malone, T. W. *Collective intelligence* [Transcript of video file]. Retrieved from
http://edge.org/conversation/collective-intelligence

Glass, I. (2012, September 14). *Back to school* [Transcript of audio file No. 474].
In *This American life*. Retrieved from http://www.thisamericanlife.org/

52. Film (DVD, BD, or other format) Give the director, producer, and other relevant contributors, followed by the year of
the film's release and the title. In brackets, add a description
of the medium. Use "Motion picture" if you viewed the film
in a theater; "Video file" if you downloaded the film from the
Web or through a streaming service such as Netflix; "DVD"
or "BD" if you viewed the film on DVD or Blu-ray Disc. For a
motion picture or a DVD or BD, add the location where the
film was made and the studio. If you retrieved the film from
the Web or used a streaming service, give the URL for the
home page.

Affleck, B. (Director). (2012). *Argo* [Motion picture]. Burbank, CA: Warner
Bros.

Ross, G. (Director and Writer), & Collins, S. (Writer). (2012). *The hunger
games* [Video file]. Retrieved from http://netflix.com/

53. Television or radio program

a. Series

Hager, M. (Executive producer), & Schieffer, B. (Moderator). (2012). *Face the nation* [Television series]. Washington, DC: CBS News.

b. Episode on the air

Harleston, R. (Host). (2012, December 1). Federal role in support of autism [Television series episode]. In *Washington journal*. Washington, DC: C-SPAN.

c. Episode on the Web

Morton, D. (Producer). (2012). Fast times at West Philly High [Television series episode]. In M. Hager (Executive producer), *Frontline*. Retrieved from http://www.wgbh.org/

Glass, I. (Host). (2012, November 23). Little war on the prairie (No. 479) [Radio series episode]. In *This American life*. Retrieved from http://www.thisamericanlife.org/

54. Music recording

Chibalonza, A. Jubilee. (2012). On *African voices* [CD]. Merenberg, Germany: ZYX Music.

African voices [CD]. (2012). Merenberg, Germany: ZYX Music.

55. Lecture, speech, or address

Verghese, A. (2012, December 6). *Colonialism and patterns of ethnic conflict in contemporary India*. Address at the Freeman Spogli Institute, Stanford University, Stanford, CA.

Donovan, S. (2012, June 12). *Assisted housing mobility in challenging times* [Video file]. Address at the 5th National Conference on Assisted Housing Mobility, Urban Institute, Washington, DC.

56. Data set or graphic representation of data (graph, chart, table) Give information about the type of source in brackets following the title. If there is no title, give a brief description of the content of the source in brackets in place of the title. If the item is numbered in the source, indicate the number in parentheses after the title. If the graphic appears within a larger document, do not italicize the title of the graphic.

U.S. Department of Agriculture, Economic Research Service. (2011). *Daily intake of nutrients by food source: 2005-08* [Data set]. Retrieved from http://www.ers.usda.gov/data-products/food-consumption-and-nutrient-intakes.aspx

Gallup. (2012, December 5). *In U.S., more cite obesity as most urgent health problem* [Graphs]. Retrieved from http://www.gallup.com/poll/159083/cite-obesity-urgent-health-problem.aspx

57. Mobile application software (app) Begin with the developer of the app, if known (as in the second example). Add the label "Mobile application software" in brackets after the title of the program.

MindNode Touch 2.3 [Mobile application software]. (2012). Retrieved from http://itunes.apple.com/

Source Tree Solutions. mojoPortal [Mobile application software]. (2012). Retrieved from http://www.microsoft.com/web/gallery/

58. Video game Begin with the creator of the video game, if known. Add the label "Video game" in brackets after the title of the program. If the game can be played on the Web or was downloaded from the Web, give the URL instead of publication information.

Firaxis Games. (2010). Sid Meier's Civilization V [Video game]. New York, NY: Take-Two Interactive. Xbox 360.

Atom Entertainment. (2012). Edgeworld [Video game]. Retrieved from http://www.addictinggames.com/

59. Map

Ukraine [Map]. (2008). Retrieved from the University of Texas at Austin
    Perry-Castañeda Library Map Collection website: http://www.lib.utexas
    .edu/maps/cia08/ukraine_sm_2008.gif

Syrian uprising map [Map]. (2012, October). Retrieved from http://www
    .polgeonow.com/2012/10/syria-uprising-map-october-2012-7.html

60. Advertisement

VMware [Advertisement]. (2012, September). *Harvard Business Review, 90*(9), 27.

61. Work of art or photograph

Olson, A. (2011). *Short story* [Painting]. Museum of Contemporary Art,
    Chicago, IL.

Crowner, S. (2012). *Kurtyna fragments* [Painting]. Retrieved from http://
    www.walkerart.org/

Weber, J. (1992). *Toward freedom* [Outdoor mural]. Sherman Oaks, CA.

62. Brochure or fact sheet

National Council of State Boards of Nursing. (2011). *A nurse's guide to
    professional boundaries* [Brochure]. Retrieved from https://www.ncsbn
    .org/

World Health Organization. (2012, September). *Road traffic injuries* (No. 358)
    [Fact sheet]. Retrieved from http://www.who.int/mediacentre
    /factsheets/fs358/en/index.html

63. Press release   Generally, list the organization responsible for the press release. Give the exact date.

Urban Institute. (2012, October 11). Two studies address health policy on campaign trail [Press release]. Retrieved from http://www.urban.org /publications/901537.html

64. Presentation slides

Boeninger, C. F. (2008, August). *Web 2.0 tools for reference and instructional services* [Presentation slides]. Retrieved from http://libraryvoice.com /archives/2008/08/04/opal-20-conference-presentation-slides

65. Lecture notes or other course materials   Cite materials that your instructor has posted on the Web as you would a Web document or a section in a Web document (see item 45 or 46). If the materials are handouts or printouts, cite whatever information is available in the source. Cite the instructor's personal notes or material that is not posted (such as slides) as personal communication in the text of your paper (see items 15 and 16 on p. 182).

Blum, R. (2011). Neurodevelopment in the first decade of life [Lecture notes and audio file]. In R. Blum & L. M. Blum, *Child health and development*. Retrieved from http://ocw.jhsph.edu/index.cfm/go/viewCourse/course /childhealth/coursePage/lectureNotes/

Personal communication and social media

66. E-mail   E-mail messages, letters, and other personal communication are not included in the list of references. (See p. 182 for citing these sources in the text of your paper.)

67. Online posting   If an online posting is not archived, cite it as a personal communication in the text of your paper and do not include it in the list of references. If the posting is archived, give the URL and the name of the discussion list if it is not part of the URL.

McKinney, J. (2006, December 19). Adult education-healthcare partnerships [Electronic mailing list message]. Retrieved from http://www.nifl.gov /pipermail/healthliteracy/2006/000524.html

68. Twitter post (tweet) Use the author's real name, if it is given, and give the screen name in brackets exactly as it appears in the source (including capitalization and punctuation). If only the screen name is known, begin with that name and do not enclose it in brackets. Include the entire text of the tweet as the title, followed by the label "Tweet" in brackets; end with the URL.

CQ Researcher. (2012, December 5). Up to 80 percent of the 600,000 processed foods sold in America have sugar added to their recipes. See http://bit.ly/UmfA4L. [Tweet]. Retrieved from https://twitter.com /cqresearcher/status/276449095521038336

69. Facebook post Use the author's name exactly as it appears in the post. In place of a title, give a few words of the post followed by the label "Facebook post" in brackets. Include the date you retrieved the source and the URL for the poster's Facebook page. If you are citing a personal Facebook page that will not be accessible to your readers, cite it as personal communication in your text, not in the reference list (see item 15 on p. 182).

U.S. Department of Education. (2012, October 9). They are resilient [Facebook post]. Retrieved October 15, 2012, from http://www .facebook.com/ED.gov

The guidelines in this section are consistent with advice given in the *Publication Manual of the American Psychological Association*, 6th ed. (Washington, DC: APA, 2010) and with typical requirements for undergraduate papers.

APA manuscript format

The guidelines on pages 218–21 describe APA's recommendations for formatting the text of your paper. For guidelines on preparing the reference list, see pages 221–23.

Formatting the paper

Font   If your instructor does not require a specific font, choose one that is standard and easy to read (such as Times New Roman).

Title page   Begin at the top left, with the words "Running head," followed by a colon and the title of your paper (shortened to no more than fifty characters) in all capital letters. Put the page number 1 flush with the right margin.

About halfway down the page, on separate lines, center the full title of your paper, your name, and your school's name. At the bottom of the page, you may add the heading "Author Note," centered, followed by a brief paragraph that lists specific information about the course or department or provides acknowledgments or contact information. See page 224 for a sample title page.

Page numbers and running head   Number all pages with arabic numerals (1, 2, 3, and so on) in the upper right corner one-half inch from the top of the page. Flush with the left margin on the same line as the page number, type a running head consisting of the title of the paper (shortened to no more than fifty characters) in all capital letters. On the title page only, include the words "Running head" followed by a colon before the title. See pages 224–32.

Margins, line spacing, and paragraph indents   Use margins of one inch on all sides of the page. Left-align the text.

Double-space throughout the paper. Indent the first line of each paragraph one-half inch.

Capitalization, italics, and quotation marks   In headings and in titles of works that appear in the text of the paper, capitalize all words of four letters or more (and all nouns, pronouns, verbs, adjectives, and adverbs of any length). Capitalize the first word following a colon if the word begins a complete sentence.

In the body of your paper, italicize the titles of books, journals, magazines, and other long works, such as Web sites. Use quotation marks around the titles of articles, short stories, and other short works.

NOTE: APA has different requirements for titles in the reference list. See page 222.

Long quotations   When a quotation is forty or more words, set it off from the text by indenting it one-half inch from the left margin. Double-space the quotation. Do not use quotation marks around it. (See p. 232.)

Footnotes   If you insert a footnote number in the text of your paper, place the number, raised above the line, immediately following any mark of punctuation except a dash. At the bottom of the page, begin the note with a one-half-inch indent and the superscript number corresponding to the number in the text. Insert an extra double-spaced line between the last line of text on the page and the footnote. Double-space the footnote. (See p. 226 for an example.)

Abstract and keywords   An abstract is a 150-to-250-word paragraph that provides readers with a quick overview of your essay. It should express your main idea and your key points; it might also briefly suggest any implications or applications of the research you discuss in the paper.

If your instructor requires one, include an abstract on a new page after the title page. Center the word "Abstract" (in regular font, not boldface) one inch from the top of the page. Double-space the abstract and do not indent the first line.

A list of keywords follows the abstract; the keywords help readers search for a published paper on the Web or in a database. Leave one line of space after the abstract and begin the next line with the word "Keywords," italicized and indented one-half inch, followed by a colon. Then list important words related to your paper. Check with your instructor for requirements in your course. (See p. 225 for an example of an abstract.)

Headings   Although headings are not always necessary, their use is encouraged in the social sciences. For most undergraduate papers, one level of heading is usually sufficient. (See pp. 225–33.)

First-level headings are centered and boldface. In research papers and laboratory reports, the major headings are "Method," "Results," and "Discussion." In other types of papers, the major headings should be informative and concise, conveying the structure of the paper.

Second-level headings are flush left and boldface. Third-level headings are indented and boldface, followed by a period and the text on the same line.

In first- and second-level headings, capitalize the first and last words and all words of four or more letters (and nouns, pronouns, verbs, adjectives, and adverbs of any length). In third-level headings, capitalize only the first word, any proper nouns, and the first word after a colon.

First-Level Heading Centered

Second-Level Heading Flush Left

    Third-level heading indented. Text immediately follows.

Visuals (tables and figures)   APA classifies visuals as tables and figures (figures include graphs, charts, drawings, and photographs).

Label each table with an arabic numeral (Table 1, Table 2, and so on) and provide a clear title. Place the label and title on separate lines above the table, flush left and double-spaced. Type the table number in regular font; italicize the table title.

If you have used data from an outside source or have taken or adapted the table from a source, give the source information in a note below the table. Begin with the word "Note," italicized and followed by a period. If any data in the table require an explanatory footnote, use a superscript lowercase letter in the table and in a footnote following the source note. Double-space source notes and footnotes; do not indent the first line of each note. (See p. 229.)

For each figure, place the figure number and a caption below the figure, flush left and double-spaced. Begin with the word "Figure" and an arabic numeral, both italicized, followed by a period. Place the caption, not italicized, on the same line. If you have taken or adapted the figure from an outside source, give the source information immediately following the caption. Use the term "From" or "Adapted from" before the source information.

In the text of your paper, discuss the most significant features of each visual. Place the visual as close as possible to the sentences that relate to it unless your instructor prefers that visuals appear in an appendix.

Preparing the list of references

Begin your list of references on a new page at the end of the paper. Center the title "References" one inch from the top of the page. Double-space throughout. For a sample reference list, see page 233.

Indenting entries Type the first line of each entry flush left and indent any additional lines one-half inch.

Alphabetizing the list Alphabetize the reference list by the last names of the authors (or editors) or by the first word of an organization name (if the author is an organization). When a work has no author or editor, alphabetize by the first word of the title other than *A, An,* or *The.*

If your list includes two or more works by the same author, arrange the entries by year, the earliest first. If your list includes two or more works by the same author in the same year, arrange the works alphabetically by title. Add the letters "a," "b," and so on within the parentheses after the year. For journal articles, use only the year and the letter: (2012a). For articles in magazines and newspapers, use the full date and the letter in the reference list: (2012a, July 7); use only the year and the letter in the in-text citation.

Authors' names Invert all authors' names and use initials instead of first names. Separate the names with commas. For two to seven authors, use an ampersand (&) before the last author's name. For eight or more authors, give the first six authors, three ellipsis dots, and the last author (see item 3 on p. 186).

Titles of books and articles In the reference list, italicize the titles and subtitles of books. Do not italicize or use quotation marks around the titles of articles. For both books and articles, capitalize only the first word of the title and subtitle (and all proper nouns). Capitalize names of journals, magazines, and newspapers as you would capitalize them normally.

Abbreviations for page numbers Abbreviations for "page" and "pages" ("p." and "pp.") are used before page numbers of newspaper articles and selections in anthologies (see item 15 on p. 197 and item 31 on pp. 203–04). Do not use "p." or "pp."

before page numbers of articles in journals and magazines (see items 13 and 14 on pp. 192 and 196).

Breaking a URL or DOI When a URL or a DOI (digital object identifier) must be divided, break it after a double slash or before any other mark of punctuation. Do not insert a hyphen; do not add a period at the end.

Sample APA research paper

On the following pages is a research paper on the effectiveness of treatments for childhood obesity, written by Luisa Mirano, a student in a psychology class. Mirano's assignment was to write a literature review paper documented with APA-style citations and references.

Running head: CAN MEDICATION CURE OBESITY IN CHILDREN?   1

A running head consists of a title (shortened to no more than fifty characters) in all capital letters. On the title page, it is preceded by the label "Running head." Page numbers appear in the upper right corner.

Can Medication Cure Obesity in Children?

A Review of the Literature

Luisa Mirano

Northwest-Shoals Community College

Full title, writer's name, and school name are centered halfway down the page.

An author's note lists specific information about the course or department and can provide acknowledgments and contact information.

Author Note

This paper was prepared for Psychology 108, Section B, taught by Professor Kang.

Marginal annotations indicate APA-style formatting.

CAN MEDICATION CURE OBESITY IN CHILDREN?   2

                                        Abstract

In recent years, policymakers and medical experts have expressed
alarm about the growing problem of childhood obesity in the United
States. While most agree that the issue deserves attention, consensus
dissolves around how to respond to the problem. This literature review
examines one approach to treating childhood obesity: medication. The
paper compares the effectiveness for adolescents of the only two drugs
approved by the Food and Drug Administration (FDA) for long-term
treatment of obesity, sibutramine and orlistat. This examination of
pharmacological treatments for obesity points out the limitations of
medication and suggests the need for a comprehensive solution that
combines medical, social, behavioral, and political approaches to this
complex problem.

        Keywords: obesity, childhood, adolescence, medication, public
policy

Abstract appears
on a separate
page. Heading is
centered and not
boldface.

Keywords help
readers search
for a paper on
the Web or in a
database.

Can Medication Cure Obesity in Children?

A Review of the Literature

Full title, centered and not boldface.

In March 2004, U.S. Surgeon General Richard Carmona called attention to a health problem in the United States that, until recently, has been overlooked: childhood obesity. Carmona said that the "astounding" 15% child obesity rate constitutes an "epidemic." Since the early 1980s, that rate has "doubled in children and tripled in adolescents." Now more than nine million children are classified as obese.[1] While the traditional response to a medical epidemic is to hunt for a vaccine or a cure-all pill, childhood obesity is more elusive. The lack of success of recent initiatives suggests that medication might not be the answer for the escalating problem. This literature review considers whether the use of medication is a promising approach for solving the childhood obesity problem by responding to the following questions.

1. What are the implications of childhood obesity?

2. Is medication effective at treating childhood obesity?

3. Is medication safe for children?

4. Is medication the best solution?

Understanding the limitations of medical treatments for children highlights the complexity of the childhood obesity problem in the United States and underscores the need for physicians, advocacy groups, and policymakers to search for other solutions.

What Are the Implications of Childhood Obesity?

Headings, centered and boldface, help readers follow the organization.

Obesity can be a devastating problem from both an individual and a societal perspective. Obesity puts children at risk for a number of

---

[1]Obesity is measured in terms of body-mass index (BMI): weight in kilograms divided by square of height in meters. A child or an adolescent with a BMI in the 95th percentile for his or her age and gender is considered obese.

Mirano uses a footnote to define an essential term that would be cumbersome to define within the text.

medical complications, including Type 2 diabetes, hypertension, sleep apnea, and orthopedic problems (Henry J. Kaiser Family Foundation, 2004, p. 1). Researchers Hoppin and Taveras (2004) have noted that obesity is often associated with psychological issues such as anxiety, depression, and binge eating (Complications section, Table 4).

Obesity also poses serious problems for a society struggling to cope with rising health care costs. The cost of treating obesity currently totals $117 billion per year—a price, according to the surgeon general, "second only to the cost of [treating] tobacco use" (Carmona, 2004). And as the number of children who suffer from obesity grows, long-term costs will only increase.

Is Medication Effective at Treating Childhood Obesity?

The widening scope of the obesity problem has prompted medical professionals to rethink old conceptions of the disorder and its causes. As researchers Yanovski and Yanovski (2002) have explained, obesity was once considered "either a moral failing or evidence of underlying psychopathology" (p. 592). But this view has shifted: Many medical professionals now consider obesity a biomedical rather than a moral condition, influenced by both genetic and environmental factors. Yanovski and Yanovski have further noted that the development of weight-loss medications in the early 1990s showed that "obesity should be treated in the same manner as any other chronic disease . . . through the long-term use of medication" (p. 592).

The search for the right long-term medication has been complicated. Many of the drugs authorized by the Food and Drug Administration (FDA) in the early 1990s proved to be a disappointment. Two of the medications—fenfluramine and dexfenfluramine—were withdrawn from the market because of severe side effects (Yanovski & Yanovski, 2002, p. 592), and several others

---

In a signal phrase, the word "and" links the names of two authors; the date is given in parentheses.

Because the author (Carmona) is not named in the signal phrase, his name and the date appear in parentheses.

Ellipsis mark indicates omitted words.

were classified by the Drug Enforcement Administration as having the "potential for abuse" (Hoppin & Taveras, 2004, Weight-Loss Drugs section, para. 6). Currently only two medications have been approved by the FDA for long-term treatment of obesity: sibutramine (marketed as Meridia) and orlistat (marketed as Xenical). This section compares studies on the effectiveness of each.

Sibutramine suppresses appetite by blocking the reuptake of the neurotransmitters serotonin and norepinephrine in the brain (Yanovski & Yanovski, 2002, p. 594). Though the drug won FDA approval in 1998, experiments to test its effectiveness for younger patients came considerably later. In 2003, University of Pennsylvania researchers Berkowitz, Wadden, Tershakovec, and Cronquist released the first double-blind placebo study testing the effect of sibutramine on adolescents, aged 13-17, over a 12-month period. Their findings are summarized in Table 1.

After 6 months, the group receiving medication had lost 4.6 kg (about 10 pounds) more than the control group. But during the second half of the study, when both groups received sibutramine, the results were more ambiguous. In months 6-12, the group that continued to take sibutramine gained an average of 0.8 kg, or roughly 2 pounds; the control group, which switched from placebo to sibutramine, lost 1.3 kg, or roughly 3 pounds (p. 1808). Both groups received behavioral therapy covering diet, exercise, and mental health.

These results paint a murky picture of the effectiveness of the medication: While initial data seemed promising, the results after one year raised questions about whether medication-induced weight loss could be sustained over time. As Berkowitz et al. (2003) advised, "Until more extensive safety and efficacy data are available, . . . weight-loss medications should be used only on an experimental basis for adolescents" (p. 1811).

In a parenthetical citation, an ampersand links the names of two authors.

Table 1

Effectiveness of Sibutramine and Orlistat in Adolescents

Medication	Subjects	Treatment[a]	Side effects	Average weight loss/gain
Sibutramine	Control	0-6 mos.: placebo 6-12 mos.: sibutramine	Mos. 6-12: increased blood pressure; increased pulse rate	After 6 mos.: loss of 3.2 kg (7 lb) After 12 mos.: loss of 4.5 kg (9.9 lb)
	Medicated	0-12 mos.: sibutramine	Increased blood pressure; increased pulse rate	After 6 mos.: loss of 7.8 kg (17.2 lb) After 12 mos.: loss of 7.0 kg (15.4 lb)
Orlistat	Control	0-12 mos.: placebo	None	Gain of 0.67 kg (1.5 lb)
	Medicated	0-12 mos.: orlistat	Oily spotting; flatulence; abdominal discomfort	Loss of 1.3 kg (2.9 lb)

Note. The data on sibutramine are adapted from "Behavior Therapy and Sibutramine for the Treatment of Adolescent Obesity," by R. I. Berkowitz, T. A. Wadden, A. M. Tershakovec, & J. L. Cronquist, 2003, *Journal of the American Medical Association, 289*, pp. 1807-1809. The data on orlistat are adapted from *Xenical (Orlistat) Capsules: Complete Product Information*, by Roche Laboratories, December 2003, retrieved from http://www.rocheusa.com/products/xenical/pi.pdf

[a]The medication and/or placebo were combined with behavioral therapy in all groups over all time periods.

A note gives the source of the data.

A content note explains data common to all subjects.

A study testing the effectiveness of orlistat in adolescents showed similarly ambiguous results. The FDA approved orlistat in 1999 but did not authorize it for adolescents until December 2003. Roche Laboratories (2003), maker of orlistat, released results of a one-year study testing the drug on 539 obese adolescents, aged 12-16. The drug, which promotes weight loss by blocking fat absorption in the large intestine, showed some effectiveness in adolescents: an average loss of 1.3 kg, or roughly 3 pounds, for subjects taking orlistat for one year, as opposed to an average gain of 0.67 kg, or 1.5 pounds, for the control group (pp. 8-9). See Table 1.

Short-term studies of orlistat have shown slightly more dramatic results. Researchers at the National Institute of Child Health and Human Development tested 20 adolescents, aged 12-16, over a three-month period and found that orlistat, combined with behavioral therapy, produced an average weight loss of 4.4 kg, or 9.7 pounds (McDuffie et al., 2002, p. 646). The study was not controlled against a placebo group; therefore, the relative effectiveness of orlistat in this case remains unclear.

For a source with six or more authors, the first author's surname followed by "et al." is used for the first and subsequent references.

Is Medication Safe for Children?

While modest weight loss has been documented for both medications, each carries risks of certain side effects. Sibutramine has been observed to increase blood pressure and pulse rate. In 2002, a consumer group claimed that the medication was related to the deaths of 19 people and filed a petition with the Department of Health and Human Services to ban the medication (Hilts, 2002). The sibutramine study by Berkowitz et al. (2003) noted elevated blood pressure as a side effect, and dosages had to be reduced or the medication discontinued in 19 of the 43 subjects in the first six months (p. 1809).

When this article was first cited, all four authors were named. In subsequent citations of a work with three to five authors, "et al." is used after the first author's name.

The main side effects associated with orlistat were abdominal discomfort, oily spotting, fecal incontinence, and nausea (Roche

Laboratories, 2003, p. 13). More serious for long-term health is the concern that orlistat, being a fat-blocker, would affect absorption of fat-soluble vitamins, such as vitamin D. However, the study found that this side effect can be minimized or eliminated if patients take vitamin supplements two hours before or after administration of orlistat (p. 10). With close monitoring of patients taking the medication, many of the risks can be reduced.

Is Medication the Best Solution?

The data on the safety and efficacy of pharmacological treatments of childhood obesity raise the question of whether medication is the best solution for the problem. The treatments have clear costs for individual patients, including unpleasant side effects, little information about long-term use, and uncertainty that they will yield significant weight loss.

In purely financial terms, the drugs cost more than $3 a day on average (Duenwald, 2004). In each of the clinical trials, use of medication was accompanied by an expensive regime of behavioral therapies, including counseling, nutritional education, fitness advising, and monitoring. As journalist Greg Critser (2003) noted in his book *Fat Land*, use of weight-loss drugs is unlikely to have an effect without the proper "support system"—one that includes doctors, facilities, time, and money (p. 3). For some, this level of care is prohibitively expensive.

A third complication is that the studies focused on adolescents aged 12-16, but obesity can begin at a much younger age. Little data exist to establish the safety or efficacy of medication for treating very young children.

While the scientific data on the concrete effects of these medications in children remain somewhat unclear, medication is not the only avenue for addressing the crisis. Both medical experts and policymakers recognize that solutions might come not only from a laboratory but also from policy, education, and advocacy. A handbook designed to educate doctors on obesity called for "major changes in some aspects of western culture" (Hoppin & Taveras, 2004, Conclusion section, para. 1). Cultural change may not be the typical realm of medical professionals, but the handbook urged doctors to be proactive and "focus [their] energy on public policies and interventions" (Conclusion section, para. 1).

Brackets indicate Mirano's change in the quoted material.

The solutions proposed by a number of advocacy groups underscore this interest in political and cultural change. A report by the Henry J. Kaiser Family Foundation (2004) outlined trends that may have contributed to the childhood obesity crisis, including food advertising for children as well as

> a reduction in physical education classes and after-school athletic programs, an increase in the availability of sodas and snacks in public schools, the growth in the number of fast-food outlets . . . , and the increasing number of highly processed high-calorie and high-fat grocery products. (p. 1)

A quotation longer than forty words is indented without quotation marks.

Addressing each of these areas requires more than a doctor armed with a prescription pad; it requires a broad mobilization not just of doctors and concerned parents but of educators, food industry executives, advertisers, and media representatives.

The barrage of possible approaches to combating childhood obesity—from scientific research to political lobbying—indicates both the severity and the complexity of the problem. While none of the medications currently available is a miracle drug for curing the nation's nine million obese children, research has illuminated some of the underlying factors that affect obesity and has shown the need for a comprehensive approach to the problem that includes behavioral, medical, social, and political change.

CAN MEDICATION CURE OBESITY IN CHILDREN? 10

References

Berkowitz, R. I., Wadden, T. A., Tershakovec, A. M., & Cronquist, J. L. (2003). Behavior therapy and sibutramine for the treatment of adolescent obesity. *Journal of the American Medical Association, 289,* 1805-1812.

Carmona, R. H. (2004, March 2). *The growing epidemic of childhood obesity.* Testimony before the Subcommittee on Competition, Foreign Commerce, and Infrastructure of the U.S. Senate Committee on Commerce, Science, and Transportation. Retrieved from http://www.hhs.gov/asl/testify/t040302.html

Critser, G. (2003). *Fat land.* Boston, MA: Houghton Mifflin.

Duenwald, M. (2004, January 6). Slim pickings: Looking beyond ephedra. *The New York Times,* p. F1. Retrieved from http://nytimes.com/

Henry J. Kaiser Family Foundation. (2004, February). *The role of media in childhood obesity.* Retrieved from http://www.kff.org /entmedia/7030.cfm

Hilts, P. J. (2002, March 20). Petition asks for removal of diet drug from market. *The New York Times,* p. A26. Retrieved from http:// nytimes.com/

Hoppin, A. G., & Taveras, E. M. (2004, June 25). Assessment and management of childhood and adolescent obesity. *Clinical Update.* Retrieved from http://www.medscape.com/viewarticle/481633

McDuffie, J. R., Calis, K. A., Uwaifo, G. I., Sebring, N. G., Fallon, E. M., Hubbard, V. S., & Yanovski, J. A. (2002). Three-month tolerability of orlistat in adolescents with obesity-related comorbid conditions. *Obesity Research, 10,* 642-650.

Roche Laboratories. (2003, December). *Xenical (orlistat) capsules: Complete product information.* Retrieved from http://www .rocheusa.com/products/xenical/pi.pdf

Yanovski, S. Z., & Yanovski, J. A. (2002). Drug therapy: Obesity. *The New England Journal of Medicine, 346,* 591-602.

List of references begins on a new page. Heading is centered and not boldface.

List is alphabetized by authors' last names. All authors' names are inverted.

The first line of an entry is at the left margin; subsequent lines indent ½".

Double-spacing is used throughout.

Part VII: Research and Documentation in the Sciences

Finding sources in the sciences

Scientific research generally involves recognizing a scientific problem to be solved, setting up an experiment designed to yield useful data, and interpreting the data in the context of other scientific knowledge. Researchers use library resources to:

- keep up with current thinking in the field so they can identify questions worth asking

- review what is known about a given phenomenon so they can place new knowledge in context

- locate specific information they need to successfully carry out an experiment or a project

The massive volume of scientific research being published can be daunting. However, a number of resources are available to help you find what is relevant to your research. Successful science researchers choose search terms carefully so that they match those used by the sources; work from the most recent publications to earlier ones, sorting out schools of thought and lines of inquiry; and know when to stop, once they have uncovered a selection of the most important and relevant research for their topic.

The resources listed here will give you an idea of where to start. Consult a librarian to determine which resources are best for your research.

General resources

Databases

Google Scholar. Mountain View: Google, 2004–. <http://scholar .google.com/>. Version of the Google search engine focusing on scholarly sources. It searches the content of publications in many fields, including the social sciences, provides links to the publisher's site where the information is frequently behind a paywall, and links to other versions of the source. Particularly useful is the link to sources that have cited it, giving you a quick view of how influential a source has been. Content available in your library may show up as links; if not, you can configure Google Scholar to find library links. For articles and books unavailable locally, you can request them through interlibrary loan rather than buy them; ask a librarian for details.

Science Citation Index. Philadelphia: Thomson Reuters, 1956–. <http: //science.thomsonreuters.com/cgi-bin/jrnlst/jloptions.cgi?PC=k>. An interdisciplinary database covering more than 8,000 journals in the sciences. Part of the *Web of Knowledge*, this database has a cited work search and a function that finds articles that cite the same source.

Scopus. Amsterdam: Elsevier, 2004–. <http://www.elsevier.com/online-tools/scopus>. The largest database of scientific and technical articles published in over 20,000 journals.

Journal online

PubMed Central (PMC). Bethesda: National Library of Medicine, 2000–. <http://www.ncbi.nlm.nih.gov/pmc>. Free archive of peer-reviewed biomedical and life sciences articles. Included are the backfiles of many journals as well as articles reporting research funded by the National Institutes of Health.

Biology

Databases

Biosis Previews. Philadelphia: Thomson Reuters, 2004–. <http:// thomsonreuters.com/biosis-previews/>. Database covering research in biology from 1926 onward, currently covering over 5,000 journals.

ProQuest Biological Science Collection. Ann Arbor: ProQuest, 2007–. <http: //www.proquest.com/products-services/biological_science.html>. Covers over 2,000 journals in biology with abstracts and some full text.

Data online

Plants Database. <http://plants.usda.gov>. Covers individual plants, invasive species, threatened and endangered plants, checklists by state, fact sheets, and over 40,000 photographs. From the U.S. Department of Agriculture.

Chemistry

For background information

Chemistry: Foundations and Applications. Ed. J. J. Lagowski. New York: Macmillan Reference, 2004. Covers basic information on elements, biochemistry, applied chemistry, biographies of important chemists, and chemistry-related topics in other areas such as medicine, environmental chemistry, and energy.

Databases

Reaxys. Amsterdam: Elsevier, 2009–. <http://www.elsevier.com/online-tools/reaxys>. An extensive database of chemistry research and information about compounds, reactions, and pharmaceutical information.

SciFinder. Columbus: Chemical Abstract Service, 1907–. <https://scifinder.cas.org/>. An impressive database of chemistry research, patents, and information about reactions and chemical compounds, with sophisticated search options.

Computer science

Database

ACM Digital Library. New York: Association for Computing Machinery, 1947–. <http://portal.acm.org>. Contains full-text articles from journals, newsletters, and conference proceedings published by the Association for Computing Machinery. Though full text is limited to subscribing libraries, anyone can access the basic search and browse features to find citations and abstracts for free at <http://portal.acm.org>.

Engineering

For background information

Engineering Handbook. Ed. Richard C. Dorf. 2nd ed. Boca Raton: CRC, 2004. A compendium of technical information and formulas from all areas of engineering. Some libraries may have this work in an online collection of CRC handbooks under the name *CRCnetBase.*

Databases

Compendex. Amsterdam: Elsevier, 1970–. <http://www.elsevier.com /elsevier-products/compendex>. Offers abstracts of millions of articles about engineering, including chemical, civil, electrical, mechanical, mining, and all other engineering disciplines.

Engineering Village. Amsterdam: Elsevier, 2000–. <www.engineeringvillage .com/>. The most comprehensive resource covering all engineering disciplines with millions of abstracts of journal articles, technical reports, conference papers, patents, and books. *Compendex* is included in *Engineering Village*.

IEEE Xplore Digital Library. New York: Institute of Electrical and Electronics Engineers, 1998–. <http://ieeexplore.ieee.org/>. Offers millions of full-text sources in the field of engineering: journal articles, books, conference proceedings, course materials, and technical standards.

Environmental sciences

For background information

Encyclopedia of the Biosphere. Ed. Ramon Folch. Detroit: Gale Group, 2000. Covers world habitats such as tropical rain forests, savannahs, prairies, and lakes, in lavishly illustrated volumes. The work is based on a 1998 publication compiled under the sponsorship of UNESCO.

Encyclopedia of World Environmental History. Ed. Shepard Krech, J. R. McNeill, and Carolyn Merchant. New York: Routledge, 2004. Covers topics, events, people, natural resources, and aspects of human interaction with the environment worldwide. This work provides historical surveys of environmental issues such as deforestation and extinction; it also offers regional and national overviews as well as essays on subfields such as environmental philosophy.

Database

GreenFILE. Ipswich: EBSCO, 2008–. <http://www.greeninfoonline .com>. Offers scholarly and popular articles on environmental issues, as well as government documents and reports. Though free to all, using a link in your library's Web site will make it easier to locate articles found in library subscriptions.

Documents and data online

Environmental Data Explorer. Geneva: United Nations Environment Program, 2006–. <http://geodata.grid.unep.ch/>. Offers a wealth of global environmental data that can be searched for quick statistics or used to create tables and maps.

World Resources Institute. Washington: WRI, 1982–. <http://www.wri.org>. An international organization that examines environmental issues in connection with human and economic development. Its site offers reports and data sets on topics such as population, energy, water resources, biodiversity, and economic issues affecting the environment.

Geology

Database

GeoRef. Alexandria: American Geosciences Institute, 1966–. <http://www.americangeosciences.org/georef/about-georef-database>. A comprehensive database of more than 3.4 million references to articles, books, maps, papers, reports, and theses covering the geosciences internationally.

Documents and data online

U.S. Geological Survey. <http://www.usgs.gov>. Offers a vast amount of current and historical geologic information and mapping services. Its Web site catalogs information about earthquakes, environmental and biological material, geospatial data and mapping projects, and other geologic resources.

Mathematics

Database

MathSciNet. Ann Arbor: American Mathematical Society, 1940–. <http://www.ams.org/mathscinet/>. The most comprehensive database for mathematics research, covering all types of publications with annotations written by mathematicians.

Physics and astronomy

Databases

arXiv. Ithaca: Cornell University Library, 1991–. <http://arxiv.org/>. A repository of open-access research papers in physics and other fields first established at the Los Alamos National Laboratory, now hosted at Cornell University.

Physical Review Online Archive (PROLA). College Park: American Physical Society, 1997–. <http://journals.aps.org/archive/>. Indexes and provides full-text access to articles published in the most prominent series of physics research journals from 1893 to the most recent five years. The database includes abstracts of current articles; full text is available only with a library subscription.

SAO NASA Astrophysics Data System (ADS). Cambridge: Harvard-Smithsonian Center for Astrophysics, 1997–. <http://www.adsabs .harvard.edu>. A database containing millions of references to publications in astronomy, physics, and astrophysics.

Citing sources in the sciences: CSE style

In many science classes, you may be asked to use one of three systems of documentation recommended by the Council of Science Editors (CSE) in *Scientific Style and Format: The CSE Manual for Authors, Editors, and Publishers*, 8th ed. (Chicago: Council of Science Editors, 2014).

CSE documentation systems

The three CSE documentation systems specify the ways that sources are cited in the text of the paper and in the reference list at the end of the paper.

In the citation-sequence system, each source is given a superscript number the first time it appears in the paper. Any subsequent references to that source are marked with the same number. At the end of the paper, a list of references provides full publication information for each numbered source. Entries in the reference list are numbered in the order in which they are mentioned in the paper.

In the citation-name system, the list of references is created first, with entries alphabetized by authors' last names. The entries are numbered according to their alphabetical order, and the numbers are used in the text to cite the sources from the list.

In the name-year system, the author of the source is named in the text or in parentheses, and the date is given in parentheses. The reference list at the end of the paper is arranged alphabetically by authors' last names.

Pages 240–54 describe formatting of in-text citations and the reference list, respectively, in all three systems.

CSE in-text citations

In-text citations in all three CSE systems refer readers to the reference list at the end of the paper. The reference list is organized differently in the three systems (see pp. 244–54).

1. Basic format

Citation-sequence or citation-name

Scientists are beginning to question the validity of linking genes to a number of human traits and disorders.[1]

Name-year

Scientists are beginning to question the validity of linking genes to a number of human traits and disorders (Allen 2009).

2. Author named in the text

Citation-sequence or citation-name

Smith,[2] studying three species of tree frogs, identified variations in coloring over a small geographic area.

Name-year

Smith (2010), studying three species of tree frogs, identified variations in coloring over a small geographic area.

3. Specific part of source

Citation-sequence or citation-name

Our data differed markedly from Markam's study[3(Figs. 2,7)] on the same species in North Dakota.

Researchers observed an immune response in "19 of 20 people who ate a potato vaccine aimed at the Norwalk virus," according to Langridge.[4(p. 68)]

Name-year

Our data differed markedly from Markam's study (2010, Figs. 2, 7) on the same species in North Dakota.

Researchers observed an immune response in "19 of 20 people who ate a potato vaccine aimed at the Norwalk virus," according to Langridge (2009, p. 68).

4. Work by two authors See item 2 on page 244 for a work with multiple authors in the reference list.

Citation-sequence or citation-name

Follow item 1, 2, or 3, depending on how you use the source in your paper. Use "and" between the two authors' names in parentheses or in the text.

Name-year

Use "and" between the two authors' names in parentheses or in the text.

Self-organization plays a complex role in the evolution of biological systems (Johnson and Lam 2010).

Johnson and Lam (2010) explored the complex role of self-organization in evolution.

5. Work by three or more authors   See item 2 on page 244 for a work with multiple authors in the reference list.

Citation-sequence or citation-name
Follow item 1, 2, or 3 on page 241, depending on how you use the source in your paper.

Name-year
Give the first author's name followed by "et al." in parentheses or in the text.

Orchid seed banking is a promising method of conservation to preserve species in situ (Seaton et al. 2010).

Seaton et al. (2010) provided a range of in situ techniques for orchid seed banking as a method of conservation of species.

6. Multiple works by one author

Citation-sequence or citation-name
Gawande's work[4,5,6] deals not just with the practice of modern medicine but more broadly with the way we rely on human expertise in every aspect of society.

Name-year: works in different years
Gawande's work (2003, 2007, 2009) deals not just with the practice of modern medicine but more broadly with the way we rely on human expertise in every aspect of society.

Name-year: works in the same year
The works are arranged in the reference list in chronological order, the earliest first. The letters "a," "b," and so on are added after the year, in both the reference list and the in-text citation.

Scientists have investigated the role of follicle stimulating hormone (FSH) in the growth of cancer cells beyond the ovaries and testes (Seppa 2010a).

7. Organization as author

Citation-sequence or citation-name

Follow item 1, 2, or 3 on pages 240–41, depending on how you use the source in your paper.

Name-year

Developing standards for handling and processing biospecimens is essential to ensure the validity of cancer research and, ultimately, treatment (OBBR 2010).

The reference list entry gives the abbreviation for the organization's name, followed by the full name of the organization

(Office of Biorepositories and Biospecimen Research); only the abbreviation is used in the in-text citation. (See item 3 on p. 245.)

CSE reference list

In the citation-sequence system, entries in the reference list are numbered in the order in which they appear in the text of the paper. In the citation-name system, entries in the reference list are put into alphabetical order and then numbered in that order. In the name-year system, entries are listed alphabetically in the reference list; they are not numbered. See pages 240–44 for examples of in-text citations using all three systems. See pages 255–57 for details about formatting the reference list.

Basic guidelines

1. Single author

Citation-sequence or citation-name

1. Bliss M. The making of modern medicine: turning points in the treatment of disease. Chicago (IL): University of Chicago Press; 2011.

Name-year

Bliss M. 2011. The making of modern medicine: turning points in the treatment of disease. Chicago (IL): University of Chicago Press.

2. Two or more authors For a source with two to ten authors, list all authors' names; for a source with more than ten authors, list the first ten authors followed by a comma and "et al." (for "and others").

Citation-sequence or citation-name

2. Seaton PT, Hong H, Perner H, Pritchard HW. Ex situ conservation of orchids in a warming world. Bot Rev. 2010;76(2):193-203.

Name-year

Seaton PT, Hong H, Perner H, Pritchard HW. 2010. Ex situ conservation of
   orchids in a warming world. Bot Rev. 76(2):193-203.

3. Organization as author

Citation-sequence or citation-name

3. American Cancer Society. Cancer facts and figures for African Americans
   2005-2006. Atlanta (GA): The Society; 2005.

Name-year

Give the abbreviation of the organization name in brackets at
the beginning of the entry; alphabetize the entry by the first
word of the full name. (For an in-text citation, see the name-
year model in item 7 on p. 243.)

[ACS] American Cancer Society. 2005. Cancer facts and figures for African
   Americans 2005-2006. Atlanta (GA): The Society.

4. Two or more works by the same author

Citation-sequence or citation-name

In the citation-sequence system, list the works in the order in
which they appear in the paper. In the citation-name system,
order the works alphabetically by title. (The following examples are presented in the citation-name system.)

4. Gawande A. Better: a surgeon's notes on performance. New York (NY):
   Metropolitan; 2007.

5. Gawande A. The checklist manifesto: how to get things right. New York
   (NY): Metropolitan; 2009.

6. Gawande A. Complications: a surgeon's notes on an imperfect science. New
   York (NY): Picador; 2003.

Name-year

List the works chronologically, the earliest first.

Gawande A. 2003. Complications: a surgeon's notes on an imperfect
science. New York (NY): Picador.

Gawande A. 2007. Better: a surgeon's notes on performance. New York
(NY): Metropolitan.

Gawande A. 2009. The checklist manifesto: how to get things right. New
York (NY): Metropolitan.

5. Two or more works by the same author in the same year

Citation-sequence or citation-name

In the citation-sequence system, list the works in the order in
which they appear in the paper. In the citation-name system,
order the works alphabetically by title. (The following examples are presented in the citation-sequence system.)

5. Seppa N. Protein implicated in many cancers. Sci News. 2010 Oct 20
[accessed 2011 Jan 22]. http://www.sciencenews.org/view/generic
/id/64426.

5. Seppa N. Anticancer protein might combat HIV. Sci News. 2010 Nov 20:9.

Name-year

List the works in chronological order, the earliest first, and add
the letters "a," "b," and so on after the year. If the works have
only a year but not exact dates, arrange the entries alphabetically by title.

Seppa N. 2010a Jul 31. Fish oil may fend off breast cancer: other
supplements studied show no signs of protection. Sci News. 13.

Seppa N. 2010b. Ovary removal boosts survival: procedure shown to benefit
women with BRCA mutations. Sci News. 12.

Articles and other short works

Use the basic format for an article in print publications when citing articles or other short works in most other media. See also "Online sources" on page 250.

6. Article in a print journal

Citation-sequence or citation-name

6. Wasserman EA, Blumberg MS. Designing minds: how should we explain the origins of novel behaviors. Am Sci. 2010;98(3):183-185.

Name-year

Wasserman EA, Blumberg MS. 2010. Designing minds: how should we explain the origins of novel behaviors. Am Sci. 98(3):183-185.

7. Article in a print magazine

Citation-sequence or citation-name

7. Quammen D. Great migrations. Natl Geogr. 2010 Nov:31-51.

Name-year

Quammen D. 2010 Nov. Great migrations. Natl Geogr. 31-51.

8. Article in a print newspaper

Citation-sequence or citation-name

8. Wald M. Scientists call for new sources of critical elements. New York Times (New York Ed.). 2011 Feb 19;B5 (col. 1).

Name-year

Wald M. 2011 Feb 19. Scientists call for new sources of critical elements. New York Times (New York Ed.). B5 (col. 1).

9. Selection or chapter in an edited book

Citation-sequence or citation-name

9. Underwood AJ, Chapman MG. Intertidal ecosystems. In: Levin SA, editor.
   Encyclopedia of biodiversity. Vol. 3. San Diego (CA): Academic Press;
   2000. p. 485-499.

Name-year

Underwood AJ, Chapman MG. 2000. Intertidal ecosystems. In: Levin SA,
   editor. Encyclopedia of biodiversity. Vol. 3. San Diego (CA): Academic
   Press; p. 485-499.

Books and other long works

Use the basic format for a print book when citing books
and other long works in most other media. See also "Online
sources" on page 250.

10. Print book

Citation-sequence or citation-name

10. Tobin M. Endangered: biodiversity on the brink. Golden (CO):
    Fulcrum; 2010.

Name-year

Tobin M. 2010. Endangered: biodiversity on the brink. Golden
   (CO): Fulcrum.

11. Book with an editor

Citation-sequence or citation-name

11. Kurimoto N, Fielding D, Musani A, editors. Endobronchial
    ultrasonography. New York (NY): Wiley-Blackwell; 2011.

Name-year

Kurimoto N, Fielding D, Musani A, editors. 2011. Endobronchial
   ultrasonography. New York (NY): Wiley-Blackwell.

12. Edition other than the first

Citation-sequence or citation-name

12. Mai J, Paxinos G, Assheuer J. Atlas of the human brain. 2nd ed.
    Burlington (MA): Elsevier; 2004.

Name-year

Mai J, Paxinos G, Assheuer J. 2004. Atlas of the human brain. 2nd ed.
  Burlington (MA): Elsevier.

13. Report from an organization or a government agency

Citation-sequence or citation-name

13. National Institute on Drug Abuse (US). Inhalant abuse. Bethesda (MD):
    National Institutes of Health (US); 2010 Jul. NIH Pub. No.: 10-3818.
    National Clearinghouse on Alcohol and Drug Information, Rockville,
    MD 20852.

13. National Institute on Drug Abuse (US). Inhalant abuse. Bethesda (MD):
    National Institutes of Health (US); [accessed 2011 Jan 23]. NIH Pub.
    No.: 10-3818. http://www.drugabuse.gov/ResearchReports/Inhalants/
    inhalants.html.

Name-year

[NIDA] National Institute on Drug Abuse (US). 2010 Jul. Inhalant abuse.
  Bethesda (MD): National Institutes of Health (US).
  NIH Pub. No.: 10-3818. National Clearinghouse on Alcohol and Drug
  Information, Rockville, MD 20852.

[NIDA] National Institute on Drug Abuse (US). 2010 Jul. Inhalant
  abuse. Bethesda (MD): National Institutes of Health (US); [accessed
  2011 Jan 23]. NIH Pub. No.: 10-3818. http://www.drugabuse.gov/
  ResearchReports/Inhalants/inhalants.html.

14. Conference proceedings

Cite a paper or presentation from the conference proceedings as you would a selection in an edited book (see item 9).

Citation-sequence or citation-name

14. Proceedings of the 2004 National Beaches Conference; 2004 Oct 13-15; San Diego, CA. Washington (DC): Environmental Protection Agency (US); 2005 Mar. Document No.: EPA-823-R-05-001.

Name-year

Proceedings of the 2004 National Beaches Conference. 2005 Mar. 2004 Oct 13-15; San Diego, CA. Washington (DC): Environmental Protection Agency (US). Document No.: EPA-823-R-05-001.

Online sources

15. Entire Web site

Citation-sequence or citation-name

15. American Society of Gene and Cell Therapy. Milwaukee (WI): The Society; c2000-2011 [cited 2011 Jan 16]. http://www.asgt.org/.

Name-year

[ASGCT] American Society of Gene and Cell Therapy. c2000-2011. Milwaukee (WI): The Society; [accessed 2011 Jan 16]. http://www .asgt.org/.

16. Short work from a Web site

Begin with the author of the short work, if there is one, and include the date of the short work in brackets as an "updated" or "modified" date. Include the title of the Web site and publishing information for the Web site.

Citation-sequence or citation-name

16. Butler R. The year in review for rain forests. Mongabay.com. Menlo Park (CA): Mongabay; c2011 [updated 2011 Dec 28; accessed 2012 Jan 11]. http://news.mongabay.com/2011/1228-year_in_ rainforests_2011.html.

Name-year

Butler R. c2011. The year in review for rain forests. Mongabay.com. Menlo
  Park (CA): Mongabay. [updated 2011 Dec 28; accessed 2012 Jan 11].
  http://news.mongabay.com/2011/1228-year_in_rainforests_2011.html.

17. Online book

Citation-sequence or citation-name

17. Wilson DE, Reeder DM, editors. Mammal species of the world. Washington
      (DC): Smithsonian Institution; c2011 [accessed 2012 Oct 14]. http://
      www.vertebrates.si.edu/msw/mswcfapp/msw/index.cfm.

Name-year

Wilson DE, Reeder DM, editors. c2011. Mammal species of the world.
  Washington (DC): Smithsonian Institution; 3rd ed. Baltimore (MD):
  Johns Hopkins University Press; [accessed 2012 Oct 14]. http://www
  .vertebrates.si.edu/msw/mswcfapp/msw/index.cfm.

18. Article in an online journal or magazine

Give whatever publication information is available as for a
print source. End with the URL and DOI (if any).

Citation-sequence or citation-name

18. Leslie M. The power of one. Science. [accessed 2011 Feb 3];331(6013):
      24-26. http://www.sciencemag.org/content/331/6013/24.1.summary.
      doi:10.1126/science.331.6013.24-a.

18. Matson J. Twisted light could enable black hole detection. Sci Am.
      2011 Feb 14 [accessed 2011 Feb 28]. http://www.scientificamerican
      .com/article.cfm?id=twisting-light-oam.

Name-year

Leslie M. 2011. The power of one. Science. [accessed 2011 Feb 3];331(6013):
  24-26. http://www.sciencemag.org/content/331/6013/24.1.summary.
  doi:10.1126/science.331.6013.24-a.

Matson J. 2011 Feb 14. Twisted light could enable black hole detection.
  Sci Am. [accessed 2011 Feb 28]. http://www.scientificamerican.com
  /article.cfm?id=twisting-light-oam.

19. Article from a database

Citation-sequence or citation-name

19. Logan CA. A review of ocean acidification and America's response. BioScience. 2010 [accessed 2011 Jun 17];60(10):819-828. General OneFile. http://find.galegroup.com.ezproxy.bpl.org/. Document No.: A241952492.

Name-year

Logan CA. 2010. A review of ocean acidification and America's response. BioScience. [accessed 2011 Jun 17];60(10):819-828. General OneFile. http://find.galegroup.com.ezproxy.bpl.org/. Document No.: A241952492.

20. Blog post

Citation-sequence or citation-name

20. Salopek P. The river door [blog post]. Out of Eden walk: dispatches from the field from Paul Salopek. 2014 Apr 17 [accessed 2014 May 19]. http://outofedenwalk.nationalgeographic.com/.

Name-year

Salopek P. 2014 Apr 17. The river door [blog post]. Out of Eden walk: dispatches from the field from Paul Salopek. [accessed 2014 May 19]. http://outofedenwalk.nationalgeographic.com/.

21. Social media

National Science Foundation. Facebook [organization page]. 2013 Jan 21, 10:31 a.m. [accessed 2013 Jan 22]. https://www.facebook.com/US.NSF.

22. E-mail or other personal communication   CSE recommends not including personal communications such as e-mail and personal letters in the reference list. A parenthetical note in the text usually suffices: (2010 e-mail to me; unreferenced).

Audio, visual, and multimedia sources

23. CD, DVD, or Blu-ray disc

Citation-sequence or citation-name

23. NOVA: secrets beneath the ice [DVD]. Seifferlein B, editor; Hochman
        G, producer. Boston (MA): WGBH Educational Foundation; 2010. 1
        DVD: 52 min.

Name-year

NOVA: secrets beneath the ice [DVD]. 2010. Seifferlein B, editor;
    Hochman G, producer. Boston (MA): WGBH Educational Foundation.
    1 DVD: 52 min.

24. Online video

Citation-sequence or citation-name

24. Life: creatures of the deep: nemertean worms and sea stars [video].
        Gunton M, executive producer; Holmes M, series producer. 2010 Mar 21,
        2:55 min. [accessed 2011 Feb 4]. http://dsc.discovery.com/videos
        /life-the-series-videos/?bcid=73073289001.

Name-year

Life: creatures of the deep: nemertean worms and sea stars [video]. 2010
    Mar 21, 2:55 min. Gunton M, executive producer; Holmes M, series
    producer. [accessed 2011 Feb 4]. http://dsc.discovery.com/videos
    /life-the-series-videos/?bcid=73073289001.

25. Podcast

Citation-sequence or citation-name

25. Mirsky S, host; Conrad N, interviewee. The spirit of innovation: from
        high school to the moon [podcast]. Scientific American. 2011 Feb 17,
        19:26 min. [accessed 2011 Feb 27]. http://www.scientificamerican.com
        /podcast/episode.cfm?id=from-high-school-innovation-to-the-11-02-17.

Name-year

Mirsky S, host; Conrad N, interviewee. 2011 Feb 17, 19:26
    min. The spirit of innovation: from high school to the moon

[podcast]. Scientific American. [accessed 2011 Feb 27]. http://www.scientificamerican.com/podcast/episode .cfm?id=from-high-school-innovation-to-the-11-02-17.

CSE manuscript format

The guidelines in this section are adapted from advice given in *Scientific Style and Format: The CSE Manual for Authors, Editors, and Publishers*, 8th ed. (Chicago: Council of Science Editors, 2014). When in doubt about the formatting required in your course, check with your instructor.

Formatting the paper

Font If your instructor does not require a specific font, choose one that is standard and easy to read (such as Times New Roman).

Title page Center all information on the title page: the title of your paper, your name, the course name, and the date.

Pagination The title page is counted as page 1, although a number does not appear. Number the first page of the text of the paper as page 2. Type a shortened form of the title followed by the page number in the top right corner of each page.

Margins, spacing, and indentation Leave margins of at least one inch on all sides of the page. Double-space throughout the paper. Indent the first line of each paragraph one-half inch. When a quotation is set off from the text, indent the entire quotation one-half inch from the left margin.

Abstract An abstract is a single paragraph at the beginning of the paper that summarizes the paper and might include your research methods, findings, and conclusions. Do not include citations in the abstract.

Headings CSE encourages the use of headings to help readers follow the organization of a paper. Common headings for papers reporting research are Introduction, Methods, Results, and Discussion.

Visuals A visual, such as a table, figure, or chart, should be placed as close as possible to the text that discusses it. In general, try to place visuals at the top of a page.

Appendixes Appendixes may be used for relevant information that is too long to include in the body of the paper. Label each appendix and give it a title (for example, Appendix 1: Methodologies of Previous Researchers).

Acknowledgments An acknowledgments section is common in scientific writing because research is often conducted with help from others. Place the acknowledgments at the end of the paper before the reference list.

Formatting the reference list

Basic format Begin on a new page. Center the title "References" and then list the works you have cited in the paper. Double-space throughout.

Organization of the list In the citation-sequence system, number the entries in the order in which they appear in the text.

In the citation-name system, first alphabetize all the entries by authors' last names (or by organization name or by title for works with no author, ignoring any initial *A*, *An*, or *The*); for two or more works by the same author, arrange the entries alphabetically by title.

In both systems, number the entries in the order in which they appear in the list. Make the first line flush with the left margin and indent subsequent lines one-quarter inch. In both systems, use the number from the reference list whenever you refer to the source in the text of the paper.

In the name-year system, alphabetize the entries by authors' last names (or by organization name or by title for works with no author, ignoring any initial *A*, *An*, or *The*). Place the year after the last author's name, followed by a period. For two or more works by the same author, arrange the entries by year, the earliest first. For two or more works by the same author in the same year, see item 5 on page 246. Type the first line of each entry flush left, and indent any additional lines one-quarter inch.

Authors' names   Give the last name first; use initials for first and middle names, with no periods after the initials and no space between them. Do not use a comma between the last name and the initials. For a work with up to ten authors, use all authors' names; for a work with eleven or more authors, list the first ten names followed by a comma and "et al." (for "and others").

Titles of books and articles   Capitalize only the first word and all proper nouns in the title and subtitle of a book or an article. Do not underline or italicize titles of books; do not place titles of articles in quotation marks.

Titles of journals   Abbreviate titles of journals that consist of more than one word. Omit the words *the* and *of* and apostrophes. Capitalize all the words or abbreviated words in the title; do not underline or italicize the title: Science, Sci Am, N Engl J Med, Womens Health.

Page ranges   Do not abbreviate page ranges for articles in journals or periodicals or for chapters in edited works. When an article appears on discontinuous pages, list all pages or page ranges, separated by commas: 145-149, 162-174. For chapters in edited volumes, use the abbreviation "p." before the numbers (p. 63-90).

Breaking a URL or DOI   When a URL or a DOI (digital object identifier) must be divided, break it before or after a double slash, a slash, or any other mark of punctuation. Do not insert a hyphen.

Sample pages from a CSE research paper

The following sample pages are from a review of the literature written by student Briana Martin for a biology class. Martin follows the style of the Council of Science Editors (CSE) in the text of her paper and uses the CSE citation-sequence system for citing her sources.

Hypothermia, the Diving Reflex,
and Survival

Briana Martin

Biology 281
Professor McMillan
April 17, 2002

ABSTRACT

This paper reviews the contributions of hypothermia and the mammalian diving reflex (MDR) to human survival of cold-water immersion incidents. It also examines the relationship between the victim's age and MDR and considers the protective role played by hypothermia. Hypothermia is the result of a reduced metabolic rate and lowered oxygen consumption by body tissues. Although hypothermia may produce fatal cardiac arrhythmias such as ventricular fibrillation, it is also associated with bradycardia and peripheral vasoconstriction, both of which enhance oxygen supply to the heart and brain. The MDR also causes bradycardia and reduced peripheral blood flow as well as laryngospasm, which protects victims against rapid inhalation of water. Studies of drowning and near drowning of children and adults suggest that victim survival depends on the presence of both hypothermia and the MDR, as neither alone can provide adequate cerebral protection during long periods of hypoxia. Future research is suggested to improve patient care.

INTRODUCTION

Drowning and near-drowning incidents are leading causes of mortality and morbidity in both children[1] and adults.[2] Over the past 30 years, there has been considerable interest in cold-water immersion incidents, particularly the reasons for the survival of some victims under seemingly fatal conditions. Research suggests that both hypothermia and a "mammalian diving reflex" (MDR) may account for survival in many near-drowning episodes.[3] However, the extent to which these two processes interact is not fully understood. Controversy also exists regarding the effect of the victim's age on the physiological responses to cold-water immersion. In this paper, I provide an overview of recent research on the protective value of hypothermia and the MDR in cold-water immersions. I also examine hypotheses concerning the effects of age on these processes and conclude with suggestions about future lines of research that may lead to improved patient care.

Hypoxia during drowning and near-drowning incidents

The major physiological problem facing drowning victims is hypoxia, or lack of adequate oxygen perfusion to body cells.[1,4] Hypoxia results in damage to many organs, including the heart, lungs, kidneys, liver, and intestines.[4] Generally, the length of time the body has been deprived of oxygen is closely related to patient prognosis. Only 6-7 s of hypoxia may cause unconsciousness; if hypoxia lasts longer than 5 min at relatively warm temperatures, death or irreversible brain damage may result.[5] However, some victims of cold-water immersion have survived after periods of oxygen deprivation lasting up to 2 h. . . .[4]

CONCLUSIONS

Recent research on cold-water immersion incidents has provided a better understanding of the physiological processes occurring during drowning and near-drowning accidents. Current findings suggest that the cooperative effect of the MDR and hypothermia plays a critical role in patient survival during a cold-water immersion incident.[3] However, the relationship between the two processes is still unclear. Because it is impossible to provide an exact reproduction of a particular drowning incident within the laboratory, research is hampered by the lack of

The student goes on to highlight the major controversies and to add interpretation and analysis.

complete details. Consequently, it is difficult to draw comparisons among published case studies.

More complete and accurate documentation of cold-water immersion incidents — including time of submersion; time of recovery; and a profile of the victim including age, sex, and physical condition — will facilitate easier comparison of individual situations and lead to a more complete knowledge of the processes affecting long-term survival rates for drowning victims. Once we have a clearer understanding of the relationship between hypothermia and the MDR — and of the effect of such factors as the age of the victim — physicians and rescue personnel can take steps to improve patient care at the scene and in the hospital.

ACKNOWLEDGMENTS

I would like to thank V. McMillan and D. Huerta for their support and suggestions throughout the research and writing of this paper. I am also grateful to my classmates in Biology 281 for their thoughtful comments during writing workshops. Finally, I thank Colgate University's interlibrary loan staff for help securing the sources I needed for this review.

CITED REFERENCES

1. Kallas HJ, O'Rourke PP. Drowning and immersion injuries in children. Curr Opin Pediatr. 1993;5(3):295-302.

2. Keatinge WR. Accidental immersion hypothermia and drowning. Practitioner 1997;219(1310):183-187.

3. Gooden BA. Why some people do not drown — hypothermia versus the diving response. Med J Aust. 1992;157(9):629-632.

4. Biggart MJ, Bohn DJ. Effect of hypothermia and cardiac arrest on outcome of near-drowning accidents in children. J Pediatr. 1999;117(2 Pt 1):179-183.

5. Gooden BA. Drowning and the diving reflex in man. Med J Aust. 1972;2(11):583-587.

6. Bierens JJ, van der Velde EA. Submersion in the Netherlands: prognostic indicators and the results of resuscitation. Ann Emerg Med. 1999;19(12):1390-1395.

7. Ramey CA, Ramey DN, Hayward JS. Dive response of children in relation to cold-water near drowning. J Appl Physiol. 1987;62(2):665-688.

List of Style Manuals

Research and Documentation in the Digital Age describes four commonly used systems of documentation: MLA, used in English and the humanities (see pp. 32–120); APA, used in psychology and the social sciences (see pp. 162–233); *Chicago,* used in history and some humanities (see pp. 121–61); and CSE, used in biology and other sciences (see pp. 234–62). Following is a list of style manuals used in a variety of disciplines.

BIOLOGY (See pp. 234–62.)

Council of Science Editors. *Scientific Style and Format: The CSE Manual for Authors, Editors, and Publishers.* 8th ed. Reston: Council of Science Eds., 2014. Print.

BUSINESS

American Management Association. *The AMA Style Guide for Business Writing.* New York: AMACOM, 1996. Print.

CHEMISTRY

Coghill, Anne M., and Lorrin R. Garson, eds. *The ACS Style Guide: Effective Communication of Scientific Information.* 3rd ed. Washington: Amer. Chemical Soc., 2006. Print.

ENGINEERING

Institute of Electrical and Electronics Engineers. *IEEE Editorial Style Manual.* IEEE, n.d. Web. 9 Sept. 2009.

ENGLISH AND OTHER HUMANITIES (See pp. 32–120.)

MLA Handbook for Writers of Research Papers. 7th ed. New York: Mod. Lang. Assn., 2009. Print.

GEOLOGY

Bates, Robert L., Rex Buchanan, and Marla Adkins-Heljeson, eds. *Geowriting: A Guide to Writing, Editing, and Printing in Earth Science.* 5th ed. rev. Alexandria: Amer. Geological Inst., 2004. Print.

GOVERNMENT DOCUMENTS

Garner, Diane L. *The Complete Guide to Citing Government Information Resources: A Manual for Social Science and Business Research.* 3rd ed. Bethesda: Congressional Information Service, 2002. Print.

United States Government Printing Office. *Style Manual.* 30th ed. GPO, 2008. Web. 9 Sept. 2009.

HISTORY (See pp. 122–61.)

The Chicago Manual of Style. 16th ed. Chicago: U of Chicago P, 2010. Print.

JOURNALISM

Goldstein, Norm, ed. *Associated Press Stylebook and Briefing on Media Law.* Rev. ed. New York: Associated Press, 2013. Print.

LAW

Harvard Law Review et al. *The Bluebook: A Uniform System of Citation.* 19th ed. Cambridge: Harvard Law Rev. Assn., 2010. Print.

LINGUISTICS

Linguistic Society of America. *Language Style Sheet.* LSA, n.d. Web. 9 Sept. 2009.

MATHEMATICS

American Mathematical Society. *AMS Author Handbook.* AMS, Updated 2012. Web. 17 Jan. 2014.

MEDICINE

American Medical Association. *AMA Manual of Style: A Guide for Authors and Editors.* 10th ed. New York: Oxford UP, 2007. Print.

MUSIC

Holoman, D. Kern, ed. *Writing about Music: A Style Sheet from the Editors of* 19th-Century Music. Berkeley: U of California P, 2nd ed. 2008. Print.

PHYSICS

American Institute of Physics. *Style Manual: Instructions to Authors and Volume Editors for the Preparation of AIP Book Manuscripts.* 5th ed. New York: AIP, 1995. Print.

POLITICAL SCIENCE

American Political Science Association. *APSA Style Manual for Political Science.* Rev. ed. Washington: APSA, 2006. Print.

PSYCHOLOGY AND OTHER SOCIAL SCIENCES (See pp. 162–233.)

American Psychological Association. *Publication Manual of the American Psychological Association.* 6th ed. Washington: APA, 2010. Print.

SCIENCE AND TECHNICAL WRITING

American National Standards Institute. *American National Standard for the Preparation of Scientific Papers for Written or Oral Presentation.* ANSI, 2005. Web. 9 Sept. 2009.

Microsoft Corporation. *Microsoft Manual of Style for Technical Publications.* 4th ed. Redmond: Microsoft, 2012. Print.

Rubens, Philip, ed. *Science and Technical Writing: A Manual of Style.* 2nd ed. New York: Routledge, 2001. Print.

SOCIAL WORK

National Association of Social Workers Press. *NASW Press Author Guidelines.* NASW P, 2012. Web. 17 Jan. 2014.

Part VIII. Glossary of Research Terms

abstract A summary of a work's contents. An abstract usually appears at the beginning of a scholarly or technical article. Databases and indexes often contain abstracts that can help you decide whether an article is relevant for your purposes.

annotated bibliography A list of sources that gives the publication information and a short description—or annotation—for each source. Each annotation is generally three to seven sentences long. In some bibliographies, the annotation merely describes the content and scope of the source; in others, the annotation also evaluates the source's reliability, currency, and relevance to a researcher's purpose.

anthology A collection of writings compiled into a book. The selections in anthologies are usually connected by a common topic, time period, or group of authors.

archives A collection of documents and artifacts, usually unpublished, that constitute the organized historical record of an organization or of an individual's life. Many academic libraries house their institution's archives and may have other archival materials as well. *See also* **special collections**.

argument Unlike the common use of the word to mean dispute or disagreement, scholars use the word "argument" to mean the main idea an author proposes and supports with evidence or examples.

authentication An online verification process that allows users to access library resources such as databases from off campus. Authentication generally requires logging in with a campus ID.

bias Though writers approach ideas with a point of view and make arguments that support a particular position, "bias" generally refers to a position a writer takes without taking alternative positions into account, representing only one side.

bibliography (1) A list of sources, usually appearing at the end of a research paper, an article, a book, or a chapter in a book. The list documents sources used in the work and points out sources that might be useful for further research. Entries provide publication information so that interested readers can track down and examine sources for themselves. (2) A list of recommended readings on a given topic, usually sorted into subcategories. *See also* **annotated bibliography**.

blog A blog (short for *Weblog*) is a frequently updated Web site that often invites readers to post comments. Though some blogs are personal diaries and others are devoted to partisan politics, many journalists and academics maintain blogs that cover topics of interest to researchers.

Boolean operators The words *and, or,* and *not* used in search queries to relate the contents of two or more sets of data in different ways. When search terms are combined with *and*, the search results contain only those items that include all the terms. When *or* is used, the results include items that contain anyone of the terms. *Not* is used to exclude items containing a term.

call number The letter and number combination that indicates where a book is kept on a library's shelves. Call numbers are assigned using a system that locates books on the same subject next to one another for easy browsing. Most academic libraries use the Library of Congress (LC) system; public libraries typically use the Dewey decimal system.

catalog A set of records for the location information and other details about materials owned by a library. Most catalogs are online, though a library may have all or part of its catalog on printed cards. Online catalogs usually can be searched by author, title, subject heading, or keyword; search results provide a basic description of the item (book, journal title, video, or other) and a call number. *See also* **call number**; **subject heading**.

citation A reference to a book, an article, a Web page, or another source that provides enough information about the source to allow a reader to retrieve it. Citations in a paper must be given in a standard format (such as MLA, APA, *Chicago*, or CSE), depending on the discipline in which the paper is written.

citation management software Program that stores bibliographic references and notes in a personal database and that can automatically format bibliographies, reference lists, or lists of works cited based on a particular documentation style (MLA, APA, *Chicago*, CSE, for example). Such programs may generate inaccurate or incomplete citations, so writers should proofread all results.

citation network (or trail) The network of citations formed when a reference work refers to sources that in turn refer to other sources. The process used by researchers to track down additional sources on a topic is sometimes referred to as following the path of a "citation trail" or "citation network."

cite (1) As a verb, to provide a reference to a source. (2) As a noun, a shortened form of *citation*. (*Note:* This term is frequently confused with *site*, as in *Web site*.)

corporate author An organization, an agency, an institution, or a corporation identified as the author of a work.

database A collection of information organized for retrieval. In libraries, databases usually contain references to sources retrievable by a variety of means. Databases may contain bibliographic citations, descriptive abstracts, full-text documents, or a combination.

descriptors Terms assigned by compilers of a database to describe the subject content of a document. Descriptors are chosen so that all of the work on a particular topic can be found with a single word or phrase, even though there may be many different ways of expressing the same idea. For example, the *PsycINFO* database uses *academic achievement* as a descriptor to help researchers locate texts on the subject of scholastic achievement or grade-point average. *See also* **database**; **subject heading**; **tags**.

digital object identifier (DOI) A string of characters, such as 10.1000/182, assigned by a publisher to a particular article or other document that is unique to that document and can be used to search for that document on the Web or in library databases. Because many publishers in the sciences and social sciences participate in this system, some citation styles, such as APA, include it when available.

discipline An academic field of study such as history, psychology, or biology. Disciplines develop their own writing conventions, scholarly societies, theories, and research methodologies. Often books and articles published by members of a discipline and intended for other scholars are called *the literature of the discipline*—referring not to literary expression but to research publications in the field. Interdisciplinary fields are ones that bridge disciplines, such as biochemistry or neuroscience. Often scholars take an interdisciplinary approach to a subject—studying medicine from a sociological perspective or researching the economics of alternative energy. Area studies, such as African studies, often draw on ideas from multiple disciplines.

discovery service Many library Web sites have software that unifies searching across databases, providing researchers with a single search box that will search dozens of databases and the library catalog simultaneously. This search box is usually found on the home screen of the library's Web site.

field (1) An area of study within an academic discipline. (2) A particular area in a database in which the same type of information is regularly recorded. One field in an article database may contain the titles of articles, for example, while another field may contain the names of journals the articles are in. Many search engines allow a user to limit a search to one or more specific fields.

full text A complete document contained in a database or on a Web site. Some databases search all of the contents of full-text documents; others search only the citation or abstract. In some cases, researchers can set their own search preferences to include or exclude words in the full text of documents.

holdings Librarians use this term to refer to items a library owns, such as the specific issues of a magazine or journal or the volumes in a book series.

index (1) In a book, an alphabetical listing of topics and the pages on which information about them can be found. The index is located at the back of the book. (2) An ongoing publication that lists new articles or other publications by author and topic. Though databases have replaced many printed indexes, researchers occasionally still use print indexes, especially for historical research.

journal A publication that appears regularly and contains articles written for specialized or scholarly audiences. *See also* **scholarly journal**.

keyword A word used to search the Web or a library database. Keyword searches locate results by simply matching the search word to an item in the resource being searched. For example, a search using the keyword *third world* will find items containing that term but may not include related items using the term *developing countries*. This variability requires researchers to pay attention to the words they encounter during their search and reformulate their search terms as needed. *See also* **descriptors**; **subject heading**; **tags**.

library catalog *See* **catalog**.

licensed database *See* **subscription database**.

literature review 1) A section of an article that summarizes previous related research to put new findings in context, particularly common in writing for the sciences and social sciences. 2) An article that systematically organizes and describes published research on a particular topic (sometimes called a *review article*), summarizing the state of research on a particular topic. "Systematic reviews" in medicine synthesize research findings about a medical issue to recommend evidence-based practice.

magazine A type of periodical containing articles that are usually written for general and popular audiences. Magazines, once primarily sold on newsstands or by subscription, are increasingly being distributed through Web sites, often with some content available only to paying subscribers. Library databases often include the content of magazines so that students don't have to pay for access.

microform Before the Internet, microform was a technology libraries used to store a large amount of material in a small space by reproducing texts in reduced size on plastic. When stored on reels, it is called *microfilm*. Flat sheets are called *microfiche*. Both forms must be read on special machines that magnify the text.

online catalog *See* **catalog**.

OPAC (online public access catalog) *See* **catalog**.

open access Material that can be accessed by anyone with an Internet connection, not requiring purchase or a subscription. Many journals and some scholarly books are being published online and are available to readers at no charge. In some cases, an author makes a copy or a version of an article available for free online. *See also* **paywall**.

PAC (Public Access Catalog) *See* **catalog**.

paywall When material is only available for purchase or to subscribers (whether an individual or a library), it is considered "behind a paywall," sometimes called "toll access." Much of the material found in library databases is in this category; it is paid for on behalf of the students and faculty at a particular institution and requires a login when off campus. *See* **authentication**.

peer review Part of the publication process for scholarly publications in which selected experts read the draft of an article or book to determine whether it should be published, published with revisions, or rejected. Though not foolproof, it's a way for external authorities to control for quality. *See also* **refereed publication**.

periodical A publication issued at regular intervals. Periodicals may be magazines, journals, newspapers, or newsletters. *See also* **serial**.

periodical index A list of all the articles that have been published in magazines, journals, newspapers, or newsletters, or in a set of periodicals. Many periodical indexes have been converted to online databases.

plagiarism The unattributed use of a source of information that is not considered common knowledge. In general, the following acts are considered plagiarism: (1) failing to cite quotations or borrowed ideas, (2) failing to enclose borrowed language in quotation marks, (3) failing to put summaries or paraphrases in your own words, and (4) submitting someone else's work as your own.

popular Often used to refer to sources written for a general audience; often contrasted with **scholarly**.

primary source An original source, such as a speech, a diary, a novel, a legislative bill, a laboratory study, a field research report, or an eyewitness account. While not necessarily more reliable than a secondary source, a primary source has the advantage of being closely related to the information it conveys and as such is often considered essential for research, particularly in history. In the sciences, reports of new research written by the scientists who conducted it are considered primary sources.

professional journal A journal containing scholarly articles addressed to a particular professional audience such as doctors, lawyers, teachers, engineers, or accountants. Professional journals differ from trade publications, which usually do not include in-depth research articles. *See also* **scholarly journal**; **trade publications**.

record An entry in a database or a library catalog. Records contain the details about the books, articles, or other sources that users will find in a database.

refereed publication A publication in which articles have been put through a peer review process. Refereed publications are considered relatively authoritative because experts have evaluated the material in advance of publication. *See also* **peer review**.

reference (1) A source used in research and mentioned by a researcher in a paper or an article. (2) In libraries, a part of the library's collection that includes encyclopedias, handbooks, directories, and other publications that provide useful overviews, common practices, and facts. (3) An advisory service provided by librarians to researchers.

review article *See* **literature review**.

scholarly Often used to describe books, periodicals, or articles that are written for a specialized audience of academics or researchers. These sources are generally formal in style and include references to other published sources. *See also* **popular**.

scholarly journal A journal that is primarily addressed to scholars, often focusing on a particular discipline. Scholarly journals are often refereed publications and for some purposes may be considered more authoritative than magazines. Articles in scholarly journals usually are substantial in length, use specialized language, contain footnotes or endnotes, and are written by academic researchers rather than by journalists. *See also* **refereed publication; magazine**.

search engine A computer program, such as Google, that searches for information across the Internet or within a database, usually by matching words found in sources and ranking results according to relevance.

secondary source A source that comments on, analyzes, or otherwise relies on primary sources. An article in a newspaper that reports on a scientific discovery or a book that analyzes a writer's work is a secondary source. *See also* **primary source**.

serial A term used in libraries to encompass all publications that appear in a series: magazines, journals, newspapers, and books that are published regularly (such as annual reviews). *See also* **periodical**.

special collections A section of a library devoted to unusual or valuable materials that cannot be checked out, including rare books, artwork, photographs, posters, and pamphlets. Researchers are generally required to use these rare materials in a reading room with special assistance. Many rare materials are being scanned for easier access through digital archives or repositories. *See also* **archives**.

subject heading A word or phrase assigned to an item in a database to describe the item's content. This content information can help a researcher evaluate whether a book or an article is worth further examination. Subject headings also suggest alternative terms or phrases to use in a search. Most academic library catalogs use the

Library of Congress Subject Headings to describe the subjects of books in the catalog. Other databases create their own list, or thesaurus, of accepted descriptive terms. In some databases, subject headings are called *descriptors*. See also **descriptors**; **tags**; **thesaurus**.

subscription database A database that can be accessed only by paying a fee. Most of the online materials that libraries provide free to their patrons are paid for by the library through a subscription. Often the material provided in a subscription database is more selective and quality-controlled than sources that are freely available on the Web. Because these databases are often provided through a license agreement, they are sometimes referred to as *licensed databases*.

systematic review See **literature review**.

tags User-supplied words or phrases describing the subject of a document, image, or video. Tags are frequently used in social media forums such as *Flickr*. Unlike subject headings or descriptors used in databases, the wording of tags is often determined by individual users. See also **descriptors**; **subject heading**; **thesaurus**.

theory In common usage, the word theory means "speculation" or "an educated guess." Scholars use the word differently. When scholars talk about a theory, they generally mean a way of thinking about a body of knowledge that has been found valid and useful for explaining a wide variety of things. In the humanities, a theory may be a critical approach to culture that may have started with one intellectual or a group of thinkers and has been expanded on and applied by others in new situations. It is an interpretive framework. In the sciences, a theory is an explanation of phenomena that has been confirmed experimentally to the point that it has become a foundation for a wide range of scientific knowledge and a basis for further hypotheses and experimentation.

thesaurus (1) A collection of synonyms; a tool commonly found in word processing programs. (2) In a database, a list of the subject headings or descriptors that are used in a particular catalog or database to describe the subject matter of each item. A thesaurus is useful to researchers because it identifies which term among available synonyms has been used by the database compilers to describe a topic. Some databases provide a searchable thesaurus that helps researchers choose the most effective search terms before they start searching.

toll access *See* **paywall**.

trade publications Magazines or newsletters covering specialized news and information for members of a particular profession or industry. Unlike scholarly journals, trade publications do not include in-depth research articles.

truncation In search engine or database queries, a shortened version of a search term. In some search engines and databases, the truncated term plus a wildcard symbol (such as an asterisk or a question mark) can be used to search all possible variations of the word. *See also* **wildcard**.

URL (uniform resource locator) An Internet address. Most URLs consist of a protocol type (such as *http*), a domain name and extension (such as *hackerhandbooks.com*), and a series of letters and/or numbers to identify an exact resource or page within the domain. Articles found in many electronic databases have long URLs that are generated in the course of a search and vary each time a search is conducted. In some cases, a database record may contain a "persistent URL" that can be used to locate the item again.

wiki A collaborative Web platform for user-contributed content. *Wikipedia* uses a wiki platform.

wildcard A symbol used to substitute any letter or combination of letters in a search word or phrase. A wildcard may replace a single letter (as in *wom*n*, to search for *women* or *woman* in one search) or any number of letters (as in *psycholog** to search for *psychology, psychologist,* and *psychological*). Typical wildcard symbols are asterisks, question marks, and exclamation points. *See also* **truncation**.